The Social Inheritance of the Holocaust

The Social Inheritance of the Holocaust

Gender, Culture and Memory

Anna Reading

First published 2002 by
PALGRAVE MACMILLAN
Houndmills, Basingstoke, Hampshire RG21 6XS and
175 Fifth Avenue, New York, N.Y. 10010
Companies and representatives throughout the world

PALGRAVE MACMILLAN is the global academic imprint of the Palgrave
Macmillan division of St. Martin's Press, LLC and of Palgrave Macmillan Ltd.
Macmillan® is a registered trademark in the United States, United Kingdom
and other countries. Palgrave is a registered trademark in the European
Union and other countries.

ISBN 0–333–76147–2 hardback

This book is printed on paper suitable for recycling and made from fully
managed and sustained forest sources.

A catalogue record for this book is available from the British Library.

Library of Congress Cataloging-in-Publication Data

Reading, Anna.
    The social inheritance of the Holocaust: gender, culture, and memory
    Anna Reading.
        p. cm.
    Includes bibliographical references and index.
    ISBN 0–333–76147–2
    1. Holocaust, Jewish (1939–1945) – Influence. 2. Memory – Social
    aspects. 3. Memory – Psychological aspects. 4. Women. I. Title

    D804.3 R42 2002
    940.53'18--dc21

                                                                2002070638

10   9   8   7   6   5   4   3   2   1
11   10   09   08   07   06   05   04   03   02

Printed and bound in Great Britain by
Antony Rowe Ltd, Chippenham and Eastbourne

This book is dedicated to people who practice true friendship
by opening their homes to the 'foreigner' alone
in a strange land, especially,
Kim and Cliff.

Contents

Preface

O, tu kalo ciriklo, lidza mage mro lidoro
Lidza, lidza mra romnake
Hoi som phandlo Auschwitzate

[O, you black bird, take this letter for me
take it to my wife
say that I am imprisoned in Auschwitz]
(Anonymous Romany song, cited in
Kenrick and Puxon, 1995:130)

This book is about gender, cultural identities and social memories of the past, in particular our socially inherited memories of the Nazi Holocaust. My aim as a media academic and writer is to explore the complex relationships and heterogeneous processes by which the Holocaust is being handed down through different media texts and cultural mediations in ways that are gendered. In this book, I analyse the articulations and rearticulations of gender and genocide in historical texts, in people's autobiographies, in documentary and feature films, in memorial landscapes and museums, and in the life stories of young people recalling their socially inherited memories of the Holocaust.

The book is based on original empirical research that includes analyses of a range of media texts and cultural mediations, as well as analyses of life histories expressed in writing, interviews and focus groups conducted in the USA, Britain and Poland with young people of various religious, ethnic and cultural backgrounds. The life history and memory work was carried out between 1998 and 2001 as part of a modest research project funded by South Bank University, London, UK. Research at and analyses of a number of Holocaust memorial sites and Holocaust museums in the USA, Britain and Poland were conducted during the same period.

In this book, I have sought to do several things. First, I wanted to bring some of the insights developed within feminist media and cultural studies to an analysis of how socially inherited memories of the Holocaust are being constituted and handed down to the post-Holocaust generation in ways that are not only connected with *seen it as a neglected area.*

individuals various cultural backgrounds and environments but in ways that are also articulated and configured through and by discourses and practices of gender. Second, this book seeks to raise public debate in this relatively neglected area and to provide a touchstone for engendering further thinking about the significance of gender in teaching and learning about cultural mediations of history, and the Holocaust in particular. Third, in exploring relationships which, so far, have been relatively ignored, I have sought to rethink established paradigms and to extend our theoretical understanding of how people in societies, through different mediations, inherit the past.

In the process of researching and writing this book I have been asked many times where, as a media scholar, my interest in the Holocaust stems from. The truth is that there is no single or simple explanation: my intellectual trajectory, in part, arises from particular lived experiences in Israel and Poland, as well as the UK. Mostly, though, my interest has been generated from the feeling of being imbricated with a complicated past and from a strong desire to understand it. We are all, it seems to me, men and women, struggling to articulate in some form social and historical legacies much greater than ourselves.

Anna Reading,
London, UK
December, 2001

Acknowledgements

The research and writing of this book would not have been possible without a matrix of support from friends, colleagues, and co-thinkers, as well as a number of public institutions. First, I would like to acknowledge the support provided by South Bank University's Faculty of Humanities and Social Science Research Committee, especially Professor Jeffrey Weeks. His positive encouragement has been invaluable. People at a number of institutions provided substantial assistance in terms of advice, archival help, materials and intellectual input, including the Anti-Defamation League, Annenberg School of Communication, Auschwitz and Birkenau State Museum, The British Council in Gdansk and Cracow, The Museum of Jewish Heritage, The Imperial War Museum, Stutthof State Museum, Gdansk University, The Jagiellonian University, Lodz University English Department, Murray Bergtraum High School, New York University, The US Holocaust Museum and the University of Maryland. I am especially grateful to those people at museums and institutions in the USA, Britain and Poland who gave me their time to talk to me about their involvement in the construction of memories of the Holocaust, especially, Suzanne Bardgett (MBE) at the Imperial War Museum; Ivy Barsky and David Liebmann at the Museum of Jewish Heritage; and Joan Ringelheim at the US Holocaust Museum. I am very thankful to Toby Haggith and Mathew Waites at the Imperial War Museum Film Archive for their help and expertise in locating films and associated materials, as well as Stephen Walton, Document Archivist at the Imperial War Museum for his expertise and help in locating original documents relating to the liberation of Belsen. I am also very thankful to Aaron Kornblum at the US Holocaust Museum Archive for his assistance and expertise in locating a range of materials I could not find elsewhere.

I would like to thank the Editorial Board members of *Media, Culture and Society*, Raymond Boyle, John Corner, Nicholas Garnham, Paddy Scannell, Philip Schlesinger and Colin Sparks for their friendship and guidance over the years and for allowing me to publish in the journal nascent ideas related to this project. Without Colin Sparks's positive comments, intellectual intervention, contacts and encouragement while I was his Phd student and a researcher at the University of Westminster in the 1990s, the idea for this project would not have developed in the way that it subsequently did. I also greatly value the feedback and comments received from colleagues at various conferences where I gave papers related to this subject. Those conversations helped build much of the thinking in this book. I would like to thank Jo Campling, my managing editor, for mentoring me with encouragement, support and faith in this project. Thanks go also to Heather Gibson, my editor, and Kate Schofield, editorial assistant, at Palgrave Macmillan and Linda Auld, Editorial Services Consultant, for their patience and work in overseeing the process of the book's production. Terhi Rantanen at London School of Economics and Jenny Owen at South Bank University deserve special thanks for their comments on earlier drafts of the manuscript.

I owe special thanks to the following friends and colleagues for their intellectual support, practical help and friendship. They shared ideas with me, passed on interesting books, articles and references, gave me their contacts, read earlier drafts, helped set up focus groups and interviews, opened their homes to me, and let me know that the project was worthwhile: Amanda Carr, Richard Drain, Rolando Gaete, Colin Harvey, Philip Hammond, Michael Gurevitch, Hannah Kliger, Yvonne Kyriakides, Emilia Leskowicz, Mark Crispin Miller, Michael Peplar, Anna Stasiewicz, Hillegonda Rietveld, Barbara Robotycka, Richard Rooke, Tadeusz Wolaqski and Barbie Zelizer.

Heartfelt thanks go to friends, colleagues and neighbours, who over the years have helped me on my journey with a rich network of love, integrity, joy, soul-food and intellectual sparks, without which this book could not have been written: Kimberley Bonheim and Clifford Birbrower, Elizabeth Bonheim-Bodek and Haim Bodek, Emma Brooker and Edward Chell, Joanne Baker and Richard Huscroft, Simon Clackson, Louise Dawson, Paige Daniel, Andrew and Catherine Dewdney, Martin Gabriel, Charlotte Jones and David Starr with their children, Evie Starr, Florence Starr and Xavier Starr; Erika and Arata Okihara, Michael Gleeson and Gabriel Toyos, Stephanie Mckeon, Vincent O'Connell, Jill and Jim Howard, Jenny Owen and Mike Philips, Elaine Shepherd and Richard Bolt, Rosa Tsaragousianou, Nigel Parkinson and Daniel Barrow, Terhi Rantanen and Richard Collins, Fiona and John Sawyer, Peter Speck, James Woolf and Philippa Carr. Thanks to Sarah Pritchard for keeping my Chi flowing, Janka Bielska for keeping the dust at bay and Dandelion for reminding me to play while keeping my feet warm. Many thanks go also to Jane Baker, Dave Edye, Arial Khan, Tim Osborn, and Anne Knox for their friendship and sharing their passion and faith in the power of the word; thanks to those members of Forest Hill Society of Friends (Quakers) especially Hock Lim, John Holroyd, Sally Kent, Joanna Scott and Kerri Wright for sharing their visions, doubts and beliefs; and many thanks to Val and the Goldsmiths artists for sharing their trust and giving me a special place to paint and sculpt.

I would also like to thank my family, particularly my brother Barry Reading and sister-in-law Patricia for their love over the years, and my grandmother, Edith May Caiger, for her wisdom and her special way of being. My thanks also to my late grandparents Edward Reading and Winifred Reading, both of whom, sadly, died during the writing of this book and whose memories I inherit. Very special thanks are for my father, Keith Reading and mother, Ellen Reading, for their friendship and enduring love. Their letters, cards, e-mails, telephone calls, and our walks and meals together have provided an anchor and renewed me with hope in challenging times.

Finally, this book would not have been written without the young people in three countries who talked to me and wrote to me about their socially inherited memories of the Holocaust. Fifty-four young people from London, Gdansk, Lodz, Cracow, New York and Washington, DC gave me their time and their trust, and thoughtfully took a role in focus groups and interviews. This book is also dedicated to them: Dorota Adamska, Shannan Bowen, Tamara Bryan, Tak Cheun Chan, John Coides, Ryan J. Donahue, Alicja Fandrejewska, Tyrone Green, David Miguel Ferreira, Gabriel Fraas, Nate Hein, Joanna Hewett, Debra Hoffman, Marcin Kwiatkowski, Eliza Kasztelan, Julie Ana Klausner, Malgorzata Kowalczyk, Anita Kolaczek, Agnieszka Kusmierz, Rebecca Levi, Katarzyna Lomancyk, Cindy Lorenz, Mariela S. Marinez, Piotr Pezik, Florian Pertynski, Anna Pietrzak, Sarah Rosenburg, Donequa Sougrin, Shana Sokol, Suzanne Stamile, Anna Stasiewicz, Agnieszka Swida, Richard M Todaro, Peter Vasquez, Kira Kandice Woods, Antwan Williams, Anna Wilson, Mikulaj Ryehto Yok, Xing Xiu Yu and Izabela Zebrowska – as well as the others included in the project who did not wish to be named.

1
Introduction

'Escape for thy life; look not behind thee ... but his wife looked back from behind him, and she became a pillar of salt.'
(Genesis 20:15) 23–4

Salt. A white powder or colourless crystalline solid; consisting mainly of sodium chloride and used for seasoning and preserving food. (*Collins English Dictionary*, 1990:1029)

Remembering men, petrifying women

The meaning of 'looking back', embedded in the story of Lot and his wife and handed down in Genesis in the Bible's Old Testament, is one that has been explored by several authors and poets. Janice Haaken (1998) describes the sadness that remained with her as a young girl from 'the woman with no name' (p. 1). The Russian poet Anna Akhmatova vows in her poem 'Lot's Wife' 'in my heart she will not be forgot/who, for a single glance, gave up her life.' (Cosman, Keefe and Weaver, 1984:191). To me as a girl the story was petrifying: it was a warning. Lot's wife looks back, disobeying God's commandment not to do so while he destroys the cities and people of Sodom and Gomorrah. In looking back – in witnessing his act of mass destruction, she is literally petrified – transformed from living flesh to granules of sodium chloride; she becomes nothing but a voiceless, colourless pillar left amid the burning landscape to erode. Abraham, in contrast, watching from a distant hill, we are later told, is the right person, in the right place, at the right time. He is able to witness the destruction and he is later remembered by God.

One reading of this culturally specific story, handed down within Christianity and Judaism, is that women should be wary of disobeying patriarchal authority: if they attempt to witness the destruction caused by it they may themselves be destroyed and forgotten. The story in this respect *is* petrifying. Yet, at the same time, Lot's wife is not entirely forgotten – the story of her looking back is embedded in the memories of some. And, she is here, the puzzle of her story told again. But why do we not know her name? Why, when she looked back, was she petrified? Is this particular story indicative of what happens in societies and cultures more broadly when it comes to women and men looking back at atrocities?

How memory works – who looks back, who has the authority to look back, who is believed when they look back, who is remembered as witnesses by those with authority, who is threatened with being forgotten – is complex. It is also, I argue in this book and as the story of Lot and his wife suggests, gendered.

all about gender

Hanging on to the past

This book examines the relationships between gender, culture and memory, to consider how we inherit 'collective', or what I term socially inherited, memories of the past through a variety of cultural mediations in ways that are gendered. It explores the role of and different relationships between media in relation to gendered discourses and structures. It considers why certain aspects of the past are forgotten and others remembered and how this is connected with gender. It explores the relationships between cultural mediation and individual and collective memories, and how these are linked with identities.

The reason, I would argue, for investigating memory at this moment in time, as an academic in the field of media and cultural studies, is that mediations of history and the past are at a key interstices to understanding late capitalist social and cultural forms and their reproduction. Memory, on many different levels, is a major obsession of the epoch. People do therapeutic memory work to uncover past feelings, thoughts and events in their personal lives in order to make their present and future happier or better or more fulfilling of their potential. People use a range of media, such as photographs and videos, to record not just celebrations and collective events, but also the ordinary, prosaic and spontaneous moments of their lives. These have come to include the most intimate and private, from a marriage proposal to giving birth, to even imaging and including in a baby album the process of human embryonic growth in a mother's womb. While revolutions in digital prosthetic memory are enabling us to record more and more of our leisure times, the microchip and the expanded possibilities of the memory storage capacities of computers also lie at the heart of much surveillance, control and commercial intelligence gathering. Digital cameras and recording devices retain in electronic form memories of street crimes, speeding offences or call centre customer service interactions for future training or litigation purposes. Our weekly shopping preferences are recorded and remembered through the electronic till, our plastic credit cards and supermarket 'loyalty' cards. The sym chips in our mobile telephones recall our family's numbers and digital switchboards keep a record of our 'best friends'. Computer servers have records of individuals online internet journeys and people keep bookmarks of favorite spaces and places in cyperspace. At the same time, older and more established forms of prosthetic memory and mediations of the past persist: memorials are built to the victims of war and genocide; museums make artifacts out of everything from a scrap of Roman mosaic to a Victorian toilet; states and cities seek to preserve the past in the retention of buildings and industrial landscapes; tourist packages offer a plethora of possibilities for following the trails of ancestors and historical events; as people travel they buy up packaged pieces of the past and souvenirs of their trips to show friends and remind them in the future. As Andreas Huyssen suggests, as time and space have been transformed and as global capitalism continually seeks to make profit through the destruction of the old and the invention of the new, it is as if we must hang on to the remnants of the past to remind ourselves that we continue to exist beyond the present (Huyssen, 1995:3–6).

Memory, though, is not purely an obsession of the current epoch . As James McConkey's collection on the subject, *The Anatomy of Memory*, suggests, it is something that is central to human existence: it configures and reconfigures peoples identities, it enables us to understand the world we live in, and, it underpins creativity (Mcconkey, 1996:1). As the biblical story of Lot and his wife also indicates, memory and looking back have long since been an important element of stories and practices at different times in history and in a variety of cultures. Studies of Britain's neolithic monuments and geographies show how ritual paths linked particular places in the landscape with tombs, which in turn marked the places where ancestors bones were kept, and where people would gather to listen to stories and genealogies (Edmonds, 1999:157). Memory and narratives of the past were an essential part of Ancient Greek thought (Shrimpton, 1997:67). The Romans considered the artificial development of memory using highly complex memory systems as one of the main arts of rhetoric (Yates, 1999:28). In the Middle Ages stained glass, murals and paintings of vices and virtues were created with a view to assisting lay people's memory of them (Carruthers, 1992). Protestants, who disapproved of the arousal of fantasies in the art of memory, developed alternative memory systems based on 'image free summary' and 'ordered classification' (Yates, 1999:231–42).[1]

Memory within many cultures and certainly within western cultures has also been intertwined with shared ideas of life and death, religion and spirituality, or some form of inherited, or 'collective', memory. Within Plato's (427–347 BC) thinking, he believed that within individual memories, there were residual traces of memories of collective ideas that came from a time before the soul entered this life (Yates, 1999:51). The individual was thought to be a combination of his or her present experience as well as, through memory, part of a larger collective whole. This idea became syncretised within early Christian thought in which individual memory was understood to be something deeply spiritual, and larger than the individual's personal experience. St Augustine in his *Confessions*, for example, describes how he is lost in wonder at the power of memory.

> All this goes on inside me, in the vast cloisters of my memory. In it are the sky, the earth, and the sea, ready at my summons ... in it I meet myself as well. I remember myself and what I have done, when and where I did it, and the state of my mind at the same time. In my memory, too, are all the events that I remember, whether they are things that have happened to me or things that I have heard from others ... The power of the memory is prodigious ... it is a faculty of my soul. (St Augustine, *Confessions*, 1996:7)

Recent ideas about memory vary enormously from more essentialist conceptualizations that draw primarily on the traditions of brain studies, psychology and psychoanalytical perspectives to social constructivist conceptualizations that recognise that memory in itself, the value given to remembering or forgetting, the ideas about and practices around memory and the way in which human beings learn to use their memories, to recollect and give meaning to memories is socially situated. There is also the recognition that memory is not something limited to the individual, but that it has a constructed collective dimension. In Stephen Rose's *The Making of Memory*, for example, he argues that memories are best understood within a nexus of social behaviours, practices and contexts.

> Think about Britain in the last half-century, and you may recall images ranging from the camaraderie of London under the Blitz to the piles of rubbish in the street during the 'winter of discontent' in 1979. For very few of us are these images and their interpretation our own; each has been in some measure manufactured in the effort to create a certain type of social cohesion and viewpoint about the world and how we could and should live in it. (Rose, 1996:57–8)

Indeed, the concept of some form of 'collective' or socially inherited memory has become increasingly important within the social sciences and the humanities, providing an interdisciplinary framework for exploring the broader workings of individuals, communities and societies (Connerton, 1989; Lakoff and Johnson, 1980; Mead, 1964). Concepts of 'collective' memory in various forms – public memory, national memory, cultural memory, historical memory – in different ways have been developed and explored to suggest how memories are developed and configured to create social cohesion through a broader consensus about the past (Lipitz, 1990; Halbwach, 1980; Le Goff, 1992; Samuels, 1994; Nora, 1984;). Scholars working within the fields of media and cultural studies now use various conceptualisations of collective memory to understand the role of the media in handing on the past (Wallace, 1996; Wood, 1999; Zelizer, 1992).

The gender memory gap

What I noticed, however, is that there is an important gap: what remains relatively unexplored within all these investigations of memory, especially those within media and cultural studies, are the ways in which gender is a factor in the collective construction, mediation and articulation of memories of historical events. Few studies in relation to broader questions of media and culture specifically investigate social memory from an interdisciplinary gendered perspective.

Raphael Samuel's seminal work *Theatres of Memory* (1994), examines memory in relation to questions of expanding historical culture in Britain. He addresses the claim that the emphasis on heritage is indicative of a form of national dereliction or decay. He argues that, in contrast, the growth in culture that seeks to remember the past is providing for a more pluralist historical vision. Yet, while Samuel's does mention issues related to femininity and feminism, these constitute just 14 lines out of 379 pages: gender is marginal to Samuel's empirical analysis and theoretical perspective. Other memory classics, such as Maurice Halbwachs's *The Collective Memory* (1980), that examine what is meant by collective memory and how American society has collective memories embedded within aspects of popular culture, while discussing the broader conceptualization of collective memory and how collective memory works in relation to society and the individual does not explore issues relating to gender. Similarly, Jacques Le Goff's *History and Memory* (1992) questions the relationships between what is meant by history and how we remember it, but does not ask whether these processes maybe articulated by relationships that are gendered or whether how we remember history may be different for men and women. Other major classics including Pierre Nora's monumental *Les Lieux de Memoire* (1984; 1986; 1992) which examines the memorial matrices of France since 1945, though considering a variety of social identities, does not include gender in his analysis. This is also the case for a range of other key works that consider a variety of cultural mediations of the past, including, George Lipsitz (1990) *Time Passages: Collective Memory and American Popular Culture* and Christine Boyars's (1994) *The City of Collective Memory: Its Historical Imagery and Architectural Entertainments*. Even collections such as Jonathan Boyarin's (ed) (1994), *Remapping Memory: The Politics of Timespace* which consider aspects of memory from a whole number of perspectives and consider the ways in which modern societies are changing our concept of memory over time and space, do not include the question of how gender may be configured in this process.

Within the field of oral history, however, there has been a growing interest in gender and memory for some time. Selma Leydesdorff, Luisa Passerini and Paul Thompson (1996) seminal edition of the *International Yearbook of Oral History and Life Stories* was entirely devoted to oral history research that considered gender differences. Where these touch on aspects of cultural mediation, I draw on the insights this field provides. In addition, a few studies do consider gender within the context of other issues or other aspects of social identities. Celia Lury's (1998) fascinating *Prosthetic Memory: Photography, Memory and Identity* takes a specific medium – photography – and examines its role in modern societies in shaping memory and identity. Lury does draw on established feminist literature at certain points to raise the question of gender and spectatorship within consumer culture but, overall, this is part of a broader thesis concerned with a range of identity issues. It is also only in relation to the specific medium of photography and Lury's analyses of photographs as texts. Similarly, Lynne Hanley's (1991), *Writing War: Fiction, Gender and Memory* while considering gender, does so only in relation to how the past is articulated within the genre of war fiction. Its perspective is literary and addresses through an analysis of a number of texts the question of how writers remember war. Likewise, Faith Beasley's (1990) *Revising Memory: Women's Fiction and Memoirs in 17th century France* while considering women and question's of individual and collective memory making, only does so within the narrower focus of historical French memoirs. The closest study, some of the insights of which I refer to later in this book, is Janice Haaken's (1998), *Pillar of Salt: Gender, Memory and Looking Back* which reframes from a gendered perspective how we think about memory and fantasy by using the concept of transformative remembering to consider how women's stories of sexual abuse reveal layers of gendered and ambiguous meanings.

Old Lady Meng's Soup

Despite the dearth of academic research, particularly within media and cultural studies, looking specifically at gender in relation to socially inherited memory, its significance is embedded not only in the culturally specific story of Lot and his wife but is also suggested by the iconography of memory in different cultures. In the Ancient Greeks' world, memory was understood to be the precursor to all human thinking and was represented in the form of the goddess, Mnemosyne. She was the mother of all nine muses and was, in the last analysis, 'the progenitor of all the arts and sciences, among them history' (Samuels, 1994:vii). History, in turn, was represented by another female figure, Clio, who was memory's daughter, and would not sing unless homage was first paid to her mother. Thus both memory and history were envisaged as female figures – not as gods, but as related goddesses. These views of memory, subsequently, became socially inherited and syncretized within Europe by the Romans, who, drawing on the beliefs of the Ancient Greeks, conceived of memory as the fountain of thought and the mother of all other pedagogies (Yates, 1999).

In elements of Hindu culture memory is also feminine. The tenth chapter of the Hindu *Bhagavadgita*, for example, describes the divine glories fit for meditation, including the feminine form of memory.

I am death, the all-devouring and the origins of things that are yet to be; and of feminine beings, fame, prosperity, speech, memory, intelligence, firmness and patience. (Cited in *Bhandare*, 1993:3)

Likewise, in Indian and Tibetan Buddhism, an important element in memorisation and mindfulness are the female matikas. The word, from the original Sanskrit for 'mother', is understood to be the seed from which the building blocks of Buddhist texts are remembered and recalled.

In sum, the matikas seem to combine, in a distinctly Buddhist fashion, elements of memorisation, mindfulness and meditation: from the womb of the matikas these emerge as one. (Gethin, 1993:167)

In contrast, within Chinese lore, it was and is forgetting rather than remembering that was represented by a female icon: a person who would not forget the past was someone who was said to have not drunk Old Lady Meng's soup. The soup is believed to cast people into oblivion. The figure of Old Lady Meng in turn was syncretised originally from Buddhism in which the soup of oblivion was thought to be given to souls departing this world: after drinking the soup, the soul goes over the bridge of Pain and demons hurl the soul into waters for new life (Schwarcz, 1998:40).

These icons of memory, though, are not necessarily indicative of the value of women and men or the authority given to their articulations of the past within these societies. Within Ancient Greek society a goddess did not denote the same qualities as those attributed to human females. Women in Athenian society were treated as minors, segregated from men, treated as the property of men, and largely denied educational and intellectual experience. Silence was seen as a woman's best virtue and being talked about as one of her sins (Okin, 1980:18–20). In Chinese culture, girl babies are still less valued than boy babies, to the extent that each year thousands are of girl babies abandoned, neglected, given away or sent away to children's homes or made permanent residents at boarding schools (Yen Mah, 1997). Even in Chinese communities abroad the lesser value given to girls permeates their lives, with memory itself a key element in the social construction of femininity and masculinity.

> In China your father had a sister who killed herself. She jumped into the family well. We say that your father has all brothers because it is as if she had never been born ... Don't humiliate us. You wouldn't like to be forgotten as if you had never been born. (Hong Kingston, 1981:11, 13)

What this suggests, as with the earlier example of the story of Lot and his Wife, is the manner in which cultural mediations involving memory and forgetting are used to articulate, disarticulate and rearticulate aspects of gender relations and sexuality to create and maintain social cohesion. This particular cultural mediation – the handed-down story, related by Maxine Hong Kingston in *The Woman Warrior,* about an aunt who became pregnant by another man while her husband was away – was often recollected by family members. The threat was that if the girl child went against the norm then family history would be rewritten and the girl symbolically annihilated and her selfhood forgotten – like Lot's wife, who was disobedient and looked back on the mass destruction of men, women and children in the cities of sin.

Not only are tales of the past important in gaining social consensus concerning aspects of gender, but studies of the role and construction of collective memory in earlier societies also suggest that the recording and recollection of the past is itself articulated in complex ways by different media in relation to gendered discourses and structures. Research on collective memory practices in Ancient Mesopotamia, has shown that when memory was locally organised through offerings and ritual practice around statues at local temples, women and men participated equally, but with the shift to writing in Babylonian society, the names retained in cultural memory were decided by male scribes (Yonkers, 1995:89). Increasing centralisation led to the gradual erasure of the memory of women and their role in the family and society (Yonkers, 1995:237). Women were rarely used as witnesses in medieval Europe, so much so that male historiographers of the time usually felt it necessary to explain and justify why they had used a woman's testimony in a document (Van Hoots, 1999:51). To some, the witch hunts in Europe, in which as many as nine million people were tortured and burnt as witches between the fourteenth and seventeenth centuries, as well as being virulently antisemitic, were also part of a process of discrediting the word of women as witnesses: only if they failed to burn at the stake was their word deemed truthful. (Kramarae and Treichler, 1985). This distrust of a woman's word could be seen to have continued with the withdrawal of Sigmund's Freud's thesis of 1896 that his female patients hysteria could be explained by abuse by fathers or male relatives (Schur, 1972:104). Later, patients' stories of abuse were described as fantasies rather than actual memories (Masson, 1984).

Yet today, are women's testimonies still less accepted than men's? In cultural mediations of the past are women's accounts included equally in voice and image alongside men? Are gender-specific experiences articulated or silenced? Do men and women remember or forget different aspects of the past? This book aims to raise public debate concerning these questions by addressing the current gap in the research on memory and culture. I combine some of the critical insights provided by media and cultural studies with other approaches from the fields of literature, history, psychoanalysis, museum studies, film studies, gender and women's studies to explore a range of cultural mediations of the past. The book places the question of gender at the heart of its enquiry to consider how memories of historical events are handed down through a range of cultural forms, including the written word, the moving image and museums. It also looks at how men and women in different countries and within different cultures develop socially inherited memories of historical events and the ways in which different media (the written and spoken word, visual media, memorial sites and museums) configure personal and social memories of events.

Which memories, whose past?

One way of exploring gender, culture and memory would be to look at gender and the articulation of the past at different moments and through a variety of media. However, this would not allow for the careful and thorough discernment of patterns, changes and linkages between different cultural forms and genres. Therefore, some clear boundaries to these reflections are needed with a central focus. One key area of looking back suggested by the story of Lot and his wife is how atrocities and memories of mass killing are remembered. In this respect one could focus on a number of experiences: the Armenian genocide, the mass killings in Rwanda, the death of millions in Cambodia. Looking further back one could analyse gender and the socially inherited memory of the torture and deaths of millions of Africans that resulted from the slave trade, or the social memory of the post-Colombian holocaust resulting in the deaths of millions of indigenous peoples in the Americas. However, the particular historical events and social memories that this book takes as its central focus are what Edith Wyschogrod (1998:xiii) has called the 'nadir point of recent history' – the Nazi Holocaust.

The Holocaust lies at the dark heart of twentieth-century European societies; it informs not only what has followed since but also casts a shadow on what went before. It irrevocably altered the peoples and cultures of not only modern Europe but all the places where Holocaust memories and populations have been scattered as a result of its diasporic effects around the world (Hartmann, 1994). As Zygmunt Bauman in probably his most influential book, *Modernity and the Holocaust*, suggests:

> The Holocaust was born and executed in our modern rational society, at the high stage of our civilisation and at the peak of human cultural achievement, and for this reason it is a problem of that society, civilisation and culture. (Bauman, 1989a: x)

It is arguable that aspects of the Nazi Holocaust are unique – the method of 'industrialised' mass killing for example – and therefore cannot be compared with other events in history. Yet the attempt to annihilate populations because of their 'race', nationality or religion is not – as Article II of the Genocide Convention of 1948 recognises. In this respect reflecting on this aspect of the past, while recognising and being mindful of particularities, provides a touchstone for understanding the social inheritance and cultural mediations of other atrocities.

How people and societies remember the Nazi Holocaust has certainly, since the late 1970s onwards, become the subject of much scholarly enquiry (Friedlander, 1993; Hartmann, 1994; Huyssen, 1995; Krondorfer, 1995; Langer, 1991; Novick, 1999; Zelizer, 1998). As James Young (1988) argues, this is because it is not only what happened that remains important but understanding how this is intertwined with cultural forms and structures.

> It was not 'the facts' in and of themselves that determined action taken by the victims of the Holocaust – or by the killers themselves; but it was the structural, mythological, and figurative apprehension of these facts that led to action on their behalf'. (14)

The issue of memory and its obliteration is also central to the events of the Holocaust historically and to its aftermath. At each stage

towards the Final 'Solution' the media, culture and their role in relation to memory were part of the process of civic exclusion and annihilation. What was attempted was the total erasure of Jewish people, as
well as their history and culture throughout Europe (Young, 1988:
189).[2] The Nazis ordered and carried out the destruction of synagogues,
Jewish cemetaries, libraries and theatres. In some places – as in
Warsaw – this involved the systematic reduction of the Nazi-created
Jewish ghetto and its 450,000 inhabitants to a 'stone desert'. Jewish
gravestones were used for walls and roads, with the Nazi's also
specifically designing buildings to mock Jewish culture and the
memory of Jewish lives: the ghetto wall in Cracow, for example, was
ordered to be built to resemble Jewish gravestones (Cracow Ghetto
Museum exhibition, 1998). In concentration, work and death camps
people were denied not only links with the outside world but also anything which provided memories of their previous lives, such as photographs of loved ones.[3] In these and in many other ways the
Holocaust was what survivor Primo Levi subsequently called a 'war
against memory' (Levi, 1998:18). This war against memory involved
the attempted erasure of the key medium of memory – language: Levi
remarks on the fact that on entering the concentration camp the only
language that had any currency among the Nazis was German (Levi,
1988:71). Studies of survivors have shown since that those who could
speak German or some German had a much better chance of survival
since the non-understanding of an instruction could result in death
(Laski, 1983). Anne Frank (1997), in drawing up 'The Rules of the
Annexe' in a satirical reversal of genocidal doctrine, states in her
diaries: 'It is absolutely forbidden to listen to German news bulletins'
and 'Only the language of civilised people may be spoken, thus no
German' (Frank and Presster, 1997:70). In the camps, the German language was used to tell the opposite of truth with euphemisms and
slogans. With more than twenty languages spoken by prisoners, language was a Babel, with even German itself not 'real German' but a
dehumanised version of it, with people's names stripped to a number.
As Bober (1998) explores, Yiddish, the language of central European
Jews, with all the memories it conveyed, was virtually eradicated in
Europe by the end of the Second World War, along with its speakers.

Towards the end of the War, as the Soviet Army entered the occupied territories from the East and the Allies approached from the West,
the war on memory was accelerated in the attempt to eradicate all
traces of the memories of the atrocities themselves. The places where
atrocities took place were often destroyed;[4] records of deaths had been

kept with meticulous inaccuracies with causes of death for murdered victims put down as medical disorders; throughout the processes of genocide, many witnesses were murdered to ensure that no living memory of atrocities remained. This included, as Primo Levi describes, the 'Crematoria Ravens', the Jewish men who were forced to cremate the bodies of the victims of mass gassings, who were themselves killed every two weeks so that they could not tell others what was happening (Levi, 1998:38). The Nazi's objective, in Himmler's famous words, was that the Holocaust would be 'a never-to-be-written page in history' (cited in Young, 1988:17). Hitler then planned, having obliterated both Jewish memory and history, to replace them with his own version of the past in the form of a museum in Prague to the extinct Jewish 'race' (Altshuler and Cohn, 1983:24–38).

Sadly the war on memory did not cease with the end of the war and the liberation of the camps. Rather, in the aftermath, many survivors met with personal denial in various forms. State policies, particularly those in Eastern Europe until the 1980s, although they did not deny the existence of the camps, did choose to forget the centrality of Jewish genocide (Young, 1988). The denial movement, particularly in the 1980s and 1990s gained increasing prominence, as Deborah Lipstadt documents in *Denying the Holocaust* (1994). This denial in many ways is a re-enactment of the Nazi's drive to eradicate the memory of atrocity and genocide. At the same time, though, in recent decades there has been the emphasis on the need to remember while survivors and witnesses are still alive. Survivors' autobiographies provide testimonies of the past; novels and films, such as Stephen Spielberg's *Schindler's List*, have sought to mediate and hand down to us aspects of the events. Museums, not only in Europe but also in the US and as far as field as Australia and Japan, seek to provide state-sanctioned or com-munity versions of the past; memorials at the sites of atrocity provide topographical memories of events. In more recent years, as the Holocaust recedes from living memory, the realisation of its meaning and impact for second and third generations is also being documented (Grant, 1998; Hass, 1990; Marcus and Rosenberg, 1989; Pines, 1993), and explored in recent autobiographies by the children of survivors (Bober, 1998; Karpf, 1997) and in literary fiction (Michaels, 1997; Powers, 1997; Schlink, 1999) .

The Holocaust provides a significant and complex focal point for understanding the relationships between socially inherited memory, cultural mediations and history. Part of the structural, mythological and figurative comprehension of those lessons, this book suggests, concerns gender. Yet, I would anticipate that raising this debate could be contentious: for while it is evident that memory is central to the events of the Holocaust and its aftermath, it may seem that questions and concerns relating to gender are, amid the experience and memory of ethnic slaughter and genocide, irrelevant. Certainly an approach that reflects on gender, as Joan Ringelheim (1998) discusses, is controversial to some Holocaust survivors and scholars. The fear is that an analysis that takes a gendered perspective may provide the guise for another form of revisionism by marginalising the issue of antisemitism. Yet, an approach that does take gender into account is not denying the fact that central to the Holocaust were antisemitic Nazi policies and practices that defined Jews as non-persons to be eliminated. As Ofer and Weitzman stress in *Women and the Holocaust,* 'Nazi policy targeted all Jews as Jews, and the primary status of Jews was their "race" not their gender' (p. 2). To raise the issue of gender is also not in denial of the fact that other ethnic, social and cultural groups were subject in different ways to racist Nazi policies, imprisonment and murder, including Romany and Sinti ('gypsies'), the mentally and physically ill or disabled, Slavs (particularly Poles), Afro-Germans, and gay men and lesbians, as well as Communists and Socialists, Jehovah's Witnesses and Freemasons (see Berenbaum, 1990; Friedman, 1990). However, as Hilberg (1992) suggests in relation to Jews, the Nazi's victims were all marked for annihilation, but their experiences of events often specifically 'affected men as men and women as women.' (p. 126). A distinguishing feature of Nazi genocide was the slaughter of women and children, rather than the treatment of them as spoils of war (Ringelheim, 1998:344).

An approach that brings to our attention how gender is articulated in social memories of the events is not meant to detract but to deepen and enrich our understanding. As James Young (1988) argues in relation to his analysis of the national dimensions of Holocaust memory in Holocaust testimony and autobiography, critical literary historiography – or in this case critical cultural historiography – is not about denying the facts or producing 'clever readings' but is about considering the 'possible consequences of interpretation' to understand how historical actuality has since been represented (pp. 4–5). My intention is to consider aspects of the terrible events in Nazi Germany and its occupied territories and some of the mediations that endeavour to recall and remind people of those events in a way that may modestly supplement ongoing efforts to make sense of what happened and to indicate from this possible requisite implications for an understanding of how people remember events in history and particularly atrocities in societies.

The Holocaust, gender and memory

The book speaks for a relative silence in the literature on the social and cultural memory of the Holocaust since most work in the area does not recognise gender issues. Andreas Huyssen's erudite analysis in *Twilight Memories* (1995) of the historical inheritance of the Holocaust in a range of media, including museums, monuments, art and literature, raises important questions in relation to time, memory and the Holocaust, but does not acknowledge the importance of gender. James Young's (1988) excellent scholarly work considers how history, memory and state policy have intersected in different cultural contexts in relation to the Holocaust. He looks at how state policy in Poland, for example, silenced the Jewish identity of victims in the memorialisation of the Holocaust by the post-war communist regimes. There is, however, no mention of the ways in which part of the matrix also included state cultural policies relating to gender. Nancy Wood's (1999) fascinating study of memory vectors of the Holocaust, including, historiography, war crimes trials, novels and films in Germany and France explores the identity politics expressed through these, but not gender as part of those politics. Other significant work on the memorialisation of the holocaust does not address gender issues either (Friedlander, 1993; Krondorfer, 1995; Hartmann, 1994; Herf, 1997; Hirsch, 1995; Huyssen, 1995 Lang, 1999; Langer, 1991; Novick, 1999; Young, 2000; Zelizer, 1998).

There is, however, a small but growing interest in the aspect of gender within the field of historical studies in relation to the Holocaust. Individual memoirs and collections of memoirs by women especially are testament to this (Eibeshitz and Eilenberg-Eibeshitz, 1994; De Silva, 1996; Laska, 1983; Gurewitsch, 1998; Rittner and Roth, 1993). These provide us with an important legacy of primary source details and personal testimonies, and I examine some of them in more detail in Chapter 2. In addition, there is now a small but growing body of historical research within Holocaust studies that does concern itself with different aspects of women and gender (Bridenthal et al., 1984; Ofer and Weitzman, 1998), as well as specific studies that focus on a variety of aspects of the Nazis and the Nazi regime from a gendered perspective (Bock, 1993; Martin, 1993); or that include throughout the particular experiences of women as well as men (Kaplan, 1998), as well s of women's resistance and experience (Oldfield, 1987; 995). These studies provide crucial historical and factual anchorage for the discussions in this book concerning how different cultural forms are articulating the events for subsequent generations. Likewise, work on genocide and gender more generally provides the analysis of memory with important context.

These are also in part supplemented by a limited number of studies that focus on gender and the representation of the Holocaust in specific media, such as the written word (Goldenberg, 1996; Heinemann, 1986). The work of Sarah Horowitz, in particular, provides us with some extraordinary insights into the way in which gender is embedded in Holocaust fiction and testimony (Horowitz, 1994, 1997, 1998). Judith Doneson's (1978) essay, ' The Jew as female figure in Holocaust Film' and Barbie Zelizer's essay (2001) 'Gender and Atrocity: Women in Holocaust Photographs' both aid our discussion of gender and images. I also make some links to pioneering studies on gender, Judaism and the memory of the Holocaust in the State of Israel (Dworkin, 2000; Lentin, 2000). Overall, though, there is relatively little cross-cultural work that examines the relationships between the ways in which the Holocaust has been remembered and the extent to which gender is a factor in the cultural and historical inheritance of handed down stories and mediated versions of events.

Scope and aims of the book

This study necessarily includes some recasting of theoretical frameworks and concepts, as well as the gathering and analysis of a substantial range of empirical material from different cultural environments. The book aims to provide an intervention into current reflections on 'collec- tive' memory through its interdisciplinary gendered perspective. The book also aims to provide some new and original analysis of a variety of media texts (written testimonies, moving images, memorial spaces and museums)[5] that have engendered social and cultural memories in rela- tion to the Holocaust, as well as original empirical qualitative data on young people's inherited stories about the Holocaust in the US, Britain and Poland.

The reasons underpinning the scope of the research for the book are severalfold. The choice of countries – the US, Britain, and Poland – stem from both personal experience and my academic background. I witnessed some aspects of the collapse of the Communist regimes in Eastern Europe in 1989 while living in Lodz, Poland and did field research in four Eastern European countries in the 1990s. At the same time, as an academic working in the latter half of the 1990s within the arts and media department at a British university, this is also the culture and mediascape with which I am now most familiar. My established research and publications are on aspects of culture, gender and the media in Eastern Europe and Britain (Reading 1992, 1996; Sparks and Reading, 1998; Stokes and Reading, 1999) as well as some earlier essays on the Holocaust and memory (Reading, 1999, 2001). The choice of countries also reflects a research framework that seeks to be intercultural, comparing the articulation of gender within countries that may have different cultural mediations of the events as well as important links between their communities and mediations. Poland under Nazi occupation, as the site for key death camps, experienced some of the greatest devastation in the Second World War (Piotrowski, 1998). After the War, under its communist government, particular memories of the events that marginalised the Jewish dimension of the events were established by the state (Young, 1988). As Michael Steinlauf (1997) explores, Poland has experienced a reconfiguration of its collective memories of the past in relation to communist and post-communist governments: this makes it particularly interesting for any study concerning aspects of identity such as gender. Britain's social memory, because of its involvement in the Second World War and with its armed forces playing a key role as part of the liberating forces of some of the Western camps in 1945, makes for an interesting comparison. The US has much written about it in terms of the changing politics and dominance of its Holocaust memory (see, for example, Nowick, 1999; Shandler, 1999) but has little work that analyses the gendered dimensions of these memories. Its also worth remembering that both the Jewish and Polish diaspora during and after the Holocaust links communities in the US, Poland and Britain very strongly.

The scope of cultural mediations chosen for analysis includes primarily historical texts, survivors' life-writings, the moving image (propaganda, documentary and feature film), memorial sites and museums, and people themselves. Within media studies, some of these – historiography, life-writing and museums for example, are not usually included within this field of study and might be seen as more appropriate to historical, literary, cultural or museum studies. However, along with Jane Stokes (Stokes and Reading, 1999), I have previously tried to establish a broader sense of what constitutes media in people's everyday lives: in *Media in Britain* we included essays on publishing, literary texts, museums and theatre, as well as the more 'traditional' mass media of newspapers, film, music and television. People's understanding of the Holocaust, I argue, is not something exclusively handed down in the mass media of newspapers, television and film: I wanted to explore the links in a communicative chain of mediations that build people's socially inherited memories of events, including how families and interpretative communities hand on stories as well as different mass media. However, particular cultural mediations – the written word, films and museums and memorial sites – are given precedence in this book over other possible mediations for a number of reasons. The written word is an important dimension of Jewish culture, history and memory (Hoffman, 1998:90). Research shows that the moving image is now a key medium for communicating history to many people (Rosenwieg and Thelen, 1999:15–16). Whereas autobiographies provide us with an example of how individual stories may enter the collective memory, film provides us with examples of collectively produced representations generally circumscribed by more dominant commercial imperatives. Memorial sites provide us with an example of how gender relations of atrocity are viscerally embedded in actual places, while museums offer the opportunity to consider interactive multimedia versions of the Holocaust within institutional and State-sanctioned public settings. Exploring the sense people make of these through interviews and focus groups demonstrates how men and women construct and articulate different kinds of memories.

The core emphasis in the book concerns exploring gender primarily in relation to the Jewish experience of the Holocaust, giving focus mostly to the perspectives of victims and survivors. I could have chosen other groups and other perspectives and examined, for example, the different memories of perpetrators, rescuers or bystanders or looked at gender in relation to the memory of other Nazi-targeted groups, including Roma and Sinti, Afro-Germans, Jehovahs Witnesses, the disabled, gay men and lesbians and political prisoners.[6] However, as I show in Chapter 2, partially this is because the majority of historical research on the Holocaust that considers gender focuses on the Jewish experience and this provides a necessary epistemological foundation for the exploration of memory within other popular cultural forms. It is also the case that antisemitism was central to Nazi genocide. The Jewish experience has in more recent years become central to the socially inherited memory in the countries under study. This is thus an important starting point to enrich our understanding of this aspect of our social memory but with a view to being mindful of other groups that were victimized by the Nazis and bearing in mind that there are other perspectives within the dynamics of genocide. There are also, of course, important links and overlaps between differing groups and perspectives which the book does at times explore.

Methods of research

In the research for this book, I use a variety of methodologies established within media studies and the social sciences and humanities more broadly. I draw on archival materials; textual analyses of memoirs and moving images, as well as spatial/textual readings of museums and urban memorial sites to examine the topography of memory. In the analysis of the written word – historical accounts and men' and women's written autobiographies about their experiences of the Holocaust, I use forms of feminist post-structuralist textual analysis. For the analysis of moving images, which includes Nazi propaganda films, 'liberation' films, post-war documentaries as well as dramatised versions of events, I combine work on the historical context of the production of the films under examination with readings drawing on documentary analyses and film studies. The analyses of memorial sites and museums in the US, Britain and Poland are based on research visits to these memorial sites and museums during 1998–2001. Visits and intertextual analyses of the memorialisation of the Holocaust were conducted at Stutthof Concentration Camp and Museum and Auschwitz Death Camp and Museum in April 1998. This was followed by analyses of the memorialisation of the Holocaust at the Museum of Jewish Heritage, New York and the US Holocaust Museum, Washington DC in March 1999, with final visits to and analyses of the Imperial War Museum's Holocaust Exhibition in January 2001. In all cases, my own analyses were supplemented with informal discussions with visitors and educators as well as formal interviews with key museum staff. In Poland, my method emulated Martin Gilbert's (1997) intertextual 'Holocaust journey' in which the researcher/visitor connects sites of Jewish communities with sites of atrocity through relating/reading historical sources while travelling what Stuart Hall (1995) has referred to as 'research routes/roots'. The journey to a place and its locality, as Karen Elizabeth Till (1996) notes, in her ethnography of museums and memorials in Berlin, is an important part of the context (p. 219) . In this way, I made journey links between significant places in Poland by train and by foot making notes over days and weeks. For this, I also drew on the idea of walking as method – but, rather than Michele de Certeau's 'flanneur in the city' encountering the past in an unpremeditated state of distraction (Urry, 1996:51), I walked with the particular intent of making historical links – 'chronalking' the past. In my readings of the museums in all three countries, I draw on the approach suggested by Gaby Porter (1996) in which she suggests an attentiveness to gender through a consideration of the interrelationships of exhibition, curator(s) and visitor, the interartefactuality of objects and the interplay of presence and absence to reveal gendered codes, assumptions and omissions. I also refer to work on narrrative, as the US Holocaust Museum, Museum of Jewish Heritage and the Permanent Exhibition at the Imperial War Museum in London are narrative museums, with a set route that visitors follow, rather than the traditional collectors museums in which visitors are free to wander at will. Over several days, in each case, I noted the environment, the design, the structure of the narrative, the inclusion and arrangement of visual, material and aural culture and my own responses to them, as well as the responses and interactions of other visitors in ways that made additional connections.

For the aspect of the book that addresses how socially inherited memories come to be configured in and re-articulated by individuals' memories in ways that are gendered I draw on some of the methods and theories established within audience studies and reception theory in the field of media studies. I use the results of empirical research conducted with young people between 1998 and 2001 in the US, Britain and Poland. The sample of respondents was by no means 'representative': the enquiry – as is usual with much qualitative audience research – was a modest study, seeking to explore some of the complexities and depth of gendered historical inscription and involvement, rather than providing broad statistical data. The research consisted of life-history work with young people with varied cultural legacies and religious upbringings ánd beliefs, including people who identified themselves as Jewish (non-believers, Liberal and Orthodox), Buddhist, Hindu, Muslim, Christian and atheist. The research was conducted in the cities of London, New York City, Washington DC, Gdansk, Crakow and Lodz. A total of 54 people, mostly aged between 16 and 35, were included in the study. The aim was to give voice to and explore the meanings and constructions of socially inherited memories for the generation of people who would not have experienced the events of the holocaust themselves, although they may have family or older friends who did. I look at how young women and men have integrated and identified with and recall different cultural mediations and family memories of the Holocaust. Their voices provide important connecting links for different chapters in this book, as well as informing a substantial element of the book's penultimate chapter. The prime methodology for this aspect of the study was the 'life history', pioneered by Herbert Blumer (1933) and used more recently by Kevin Barnhurst (1998) in his study of young people's development of citizenship, and Annette Kuhn (1999) in her study of recollections of cinema going in 1930s Britain. I asked predominantly high school and college students to write down and then talk about their social 'memories' of the Holocaust, beginning with the first moment in their childhood when they became aware of it. I then asked them to trace the genesis of their understanding, feelings and thoughts on the Holocaust, including stories and images that stayed in their minds. Since methods research shows that focus groups can exclude less powerful members, these group verbalised accounts were preceded by individual written life-histories based around the same questions and followed up in some cases with depth interviews. The respondents were acquainted with each other through school or college, which can have positive results in enabling an initial atmosphere of trust for difficult or painful subjects. The interviews and focus groups were taped, transcribed and then coded to identify linked tropes and forms of discourse. Rather than focusing on objective measurements, the analysis considers the respondents subjective experience and the ways in which young people of different cultural backgrounds are in contemporary societies making sense of and remembering the Holocaust across three national contexts. I resist analysing people's memories of the Holocaust based on the storehouse model of memory – in which discrete images or packets of information are understood to accumulate over time to be accessed subject to decay or erosion – and take instead an approach that is an extension of the storyteller model outlined by Janice Haaken (1998). This recognises that personal memory processes take place within the context of broader personal and social narratives and social relationships. Focus is given to 'constellations of preserved knowledge' and 'how things "hook together"' rather than purely on constituent elements of memory (Haaken, 1998:43). The convention used to describe respondents is with a first-name pseudonym, combined with self-defined aspects of their identity that they have indicated are important to them, such as their nationality, 'race', sexuality, religious upbringing and beliefs.

It should be stressed that the qualitative research involving human subjects does not in any way purport to be all-encompassing or in any way conclusive, but it was considered important to add another much needed dimension to how we might consider the workings and structures of social memory. Their voices tell us a little about the gendered processes of identification and non-identification among young people in relation to the mediations of the Holocaust.

Establishing terms

Following Helen Fein's suggestion (1987:ix), I use the term 'antisemitism', rather than 'anti-semitism', throughout the book to suggest the necessity to take antisemitism seriously as a thesis without an antithesis. As Ronit Lentin (2000:25) points out, there is no 'Semitism'. Although I recognise that some critics reject the English term 'Holocaust' (Young, 1990:87) which literally means 'whole burnt', I use this throughout the book, rather than the Hebrew term, Shoah, meaning catastrophe or catacyclsm, or other terms of value originating from other groups subject to genocide, such as the Romany term, 'Porrajmos' or 'Parrajmos', meaning 'the devouring'. I do not use the term 'gendercide', as suggested by Mary Anne Warren (1985) in her work on gender selective mass killing in history or as used by other scholars who stress the gender selective nature of mass killing (see www.gendercide.org 14.7.01). Rather, I use throughout the more widely recognised and established term 'genocide', meaning acts committed with the intent to destroy, in whole or in part, a 'racial', religious or national group as defined by the Genocide Convention of 1948 (see Stein, 1996). I use the term with the aim of exploring how gendered policies and experiences are embedded as part of the genocidal process.

Following feedback from colleagues at the Imperial War Museum's conference on Holocaust Film and Television (2001), I favour the term cultural mediations and/or cultural constellations of memory, rather 'vectors' of memory as preferred by media scholar, Nancy Wood 1999:3). The term 'vector', first used by Henry Rousso (1991) in *The Vichy Syndrome: History and Memory in France Since 1945* appears useful since it suggests memory as dynamically constituted in time. But the term is also problematic: it suggests a specific, singular direction for the conveyancing of memory rather than the more complex polylogical process suggested by the cultural analyst Jesus Martin Barbaro's term 'mediations' or what Janice Haaken has described as 'constellations of preserved knowledge' underpinning my term – constellations of memory, intended to include the broader feelings and thoughts associated with memory as well as 'knowledge'. The terms are used as indicative of an approach in this book that considers how memories may dynamically link together through a communicative chain, rather than a focus on memory in terms of constituent fixed elements (Haaken, 1998:43).

Another concept I use throughout as a way of theorising the complex relationships between mediations, memory and gender is Laclau and Mouffe's (1985) concept of articulation developed in *Hegemony and Socialist Strategy* (p. 105). The concept refers to the process by which relationships between different elements are established in ways that modify identity through articulatory practice. I extend this, using the concepts of articulation, disarticulation and re-articulation to explain how representations of the past in various cultural mediations interlock in specific situations with subjectivities so that socially inherited memories and memory practices acquire meanings that are within particular contexts gender specific.

Central to the arguments of each chapter is also the concept of some form of 'collective' memory as distinct from history. I take my starting-point from Jacques Le Goff (1992) in *History and Memory* in which he defines 'history' as a modern form of recording the past dependent on literacy and the written and printed word (p. 171). From this, however, I include historical texts for analysis as in part constituting people's 'collective' memories, with this 'formal' writing of the past configuring shared cultures. Yet, how we then describe or conceptualise some form of 'collective' memory and what is meant by it is not without contention or difficulty. There are many terms for socially shared memory in circulation, including historical memory, public memory, popular memory, family memory and national memory. The term I favour throughout is 'social memory' or '*socially inherited memory*' which I define as in some way also inclusive of these other forms of 'collective' or shared memory (see Reading, 1996). The term socially inherited memory I use to signal that 'some tangible presence of the past can be discerned beyond the level of the individual and in specific social milieux' (Wood, 1999:1). I use it in preference to other terms to indicate that it is not necessarily bounded by divides between public and private; or by the individual and the nation state. Neither is it necessarily complicit with history or an articulation of the 'popular'. Socially inherited memories may be constituted through a variety of cultural forms: they may be at times both public and private, their boundaries may shift and change. I use the term socially inherited memory not as something distinct and separate from our individual memories, but as polylogically interconnected. As Maurice Halbwachs (1980) suggests, collective memories provide the nexus for individual memories, while elements of personal recollections come to constitute the collective versions of our pasts. Throughout the book, I suggest that individuals are inscribed into and through the shared versions of the past that people in different ways inherit; personal articulations of the past, in turn, may then come to be articulated socially through publicly disseminated mediations. Such an historical and intercultural analysis reveals the ways in which the concept and practice of memory in itself is a social construct in which are embedded important technologies of gender and sexuality, especially in socially inherited memories of genocide. This in turn may suggest the need for a more extensive theoretical critique of the established bivalent logic of Western conceptualisations of memory, since mechanisms of gender and sexuality interconnect in multivalent ways in terms of the constellations of memory, memory practices and mediations in different cultural and national contexts.

About the book

Chapter 2, 'The "Wrong" Question: Historiographies' begins by exploring conceptualisations of history in relation to memory. It argues that although social memories of the Holocaust are handed down through a variety of more 'popular' media, historical texts and the teaching of history was still shown to be important in young people's development and understanding of the events. At the same time, before examining gender, memory and more popular cultural mediations of the Holocaust, we first need a firm grasp of the historical events themselves and a clear sense of how, in the stages towards the 'Final Solution' gender was enmeshed with ethnicity. The chapter then discusses how in most mainstream or well-known Holocaust research gender is absent or marginalised. In recent years, however, gender issues are being explored by feminist Holocaust scholars. These feminist historiographical sources provide an important record of Jewish gender relations prior to the War and show the kinds of gendered effects Nazi policies had at each stage towards the 'Final Solution' as well as its gendered articulation in its aftermath. At different stages and places prior to the outbreak of war, Nazi policies and ideology articulated, disarticulated and rearticulated aspects of gender in a variety of ways. In the process, the cultural scaffolding of femininity and masculinity in articulation with Jewish identity was initially exaggerated and then gradually stripped in a process of dehumanization. A brief overview is provided of gendered experiences before the War, in the ghettos, in the resistance, in the camps, at liberation and in the aftermath. Finally, along with what is remembered, I consider some of the enduring silences within feminist historiographical research: how the predominant emphasis in this literature is primarily on Jewish women's experiences, with some emphasis on German 'Aryan' women's experiences, but with little work, as yet, on men's particular experiences or on other groups, such as Romany and Sinti and Afro-Germans.

Chapter 3, 'The Demolition of a Man: Autobiographies' focuses on some autobiographies by Jewish men and women Holocaust survivors to explore the articulations and disarticulations of gender and memory in the medium of the written individual account. The chapter examines what it is about the medium of the written word that is important to the processes of men and women's individual and social memories. It draws on broader feminist work on autobiography as a genre to explore what particular texts reveal about the ways in which individual and social memory and forgetting are constructed in ways that are gendered. The focus, mostly, is on published written testimonies because their availability means that they are more central to peoples' collective memory of the events. Jewish men and women's experiences of going into hiding are examined, experiences of the lesser-known camp of Stutthof (near what was known as Danzig – now Gdansk), and the death and work camps at Auschwitz-Birkenau in what was German-occupied Poland during the War. This is not to deny the validity of accounts by people in other camps, or accounts by non-Jewish survivors, but it is rather to provide a focal point that allows for an in-depth analysis, as well as a cogent framework for comparison. The main texts I consider are primarily those that were remembered by young people in the US, Britain and Poland as important to them and which, culturally, tend to be well known and easily available: *The Diary of a Young Girl*, by Anne Frank (Frank and Pressler, 1997), Elie Wiesel's *Night* (1982) and Primo Levi's *If This is a Man* (2000). To ensure the inclusion of at least some subaltern memories of the Holocaust, though, I have included analyses of less well-known published accounts by women survivors, including Fanya Gottesfeld Heller's (1993) *Strange and Unexpected Love: A Teenage Girl's Holocaust Memoirs*, Rena Kornreich Gelissen's (1997) *A Story of Two Sisters in Auschwitz: Rena's Promise* as well as unpublished testimonies such as Charlotte Arpadi's life-story which is lodged with the US Holocaust Archives, Washington DC.

Chapter 4, 'Moving Memories: Propaganda, Documentary and Holocaust Feature Films' explores the role of the medium of film in relation to gender and the memory of the Holocaust. It argues that films form a major part of young people's socially inherited memories of events: many feature films take the Holocaust as their central theme, such as *Sophie's Choice* (Dir: Pakula, 1982) and *Schindler's List* (Dir: Spielberg, 1994). This chapter examines the ways in which different film genres articulate and disarticulate gender in relation to the Holocaust. Since Nazi propaganda films and films shot by the liberating armies have been reused in many documentaries and feature films since 1945, as well as forming a part of many museum narratives, I begin by discussing Nazi propaganda films and filming as part of gendered atrocities. I then reflect on the capacities of film as witness to render gender and atrocities – focusing on the film made by the British army, *Memory of the Camps* (1946*)*. In the third section of the chapter, I address how documentary films after 1945 have constructed our memories of the events in gender terms, by examining Claude Lanzmann's *Shoah* and Alain Renais *Nuit et Brouillard* (*Night and Fog*). Finally I look at how popular feature films have depicted the Holocaust, using the example of Stephen Spielberg's *Schindler's List*. As with the choice of autobiographies, the films I look at are, on the whole, ones that were described as in some way significant to the memories of young people I interviewed. They are also films that are, generally, easily available to enable readers, educators and scholars to develop their own analyses and comparisons.

Chapter 5, 'The Absence of Women's Hair' explores the configuration of gender and Holocaust memories within the media of memorial sites and museums in the US, Britain and the UK. Statistical evidence and qualitative research shows that museums and memorial sites are now just as much part of young people's polylogical development of Holocaust social memory as history books, life-stories and films. The chapter looks at the memorialisation of the Holocaust by the Polish State in the Nazi death camps at Auschwitz and Birkenau; and the reconstruction and narrativization of the events in the Museum of Jewish Heritage in New York and in the US Holocaust Museum in Washington DC. Finally, I analyse the Holocaust annex to the Imperial War Museum in London. I base the analysis on research visits to these memorial sites and museums during 1998 to 2001.

The chapter explores how, embedded within differing national memories, gender is articulated in a variety of ways in different museum and memorial environments. At Auschwitz-Birkenau, the site of mass murder and genocidal atrocities, it suggested that gender is emptied and buried, its memory visible only in the physical line on a map and in the empty remains of the women's camp. The consequence is that the usual dialogical process involved in remembering breaks down for the visitor in a memorial reenactment of genocidal trauma. At post-Holocaust museums more distant from the place of suffering and murder, gender is articulated in other ways. At the US Holocaust Museum the roles of women are more passive, shallow and underdeveloped in relation to the more active voice given to men's roles and experiences which tend to be more fully pronounced and open. Gender resonances are in places of the narrative left mystified or incomplete. Both the Museum of Jewish Heritage and the Imperial War Museum's Holocaust Exhibition, through a careful balancing of accounts, give a more equal voice to men and women as Jewish victims but the Imperial War Museum also goes a step further in articulating the memory of the Nazi's other victims, as well as women's roles in history as perpetrators and liberators.

Chapter 6, 'Grandmas Tales: Young Men and Women's Configurations of Holocaust Memory' explores the making and generation of memories of the Holocaust among young people sixty years on from the events themselves in the US, Britain and Poland. In particular, the chapter considers how people's gendered identities resonate with the reception of history and handed-down stories in different cultural and national contexts. The importance of the cultural communities in which people are raised is explored and the significance of family members, especially grandmothers, in handing down stories and helping young people negotiate between different versions of events. Also addressed are the ways in which men and women who have no direct experience of the Holocaust themselves, develop historical memories from different media. The extent to which women's understanding is gained from written genres and forms and men's from visual forms is analysed, and consideration is given to the ways in which our gender in different cultural contexts and religious backgrounds is important in terms of the ways in which men and women narrativize and articulate an understanding of the Holocaust.

Chapter 7, '(Dis) Articulations of Gender, Culture and Memory' links together the book's reflections on the different configurations of memory within different media and by people themselves to suggest broader patterns that can be discerned from the enquiry. It suggests how those in the fields of media and cultural studies, gender studies and Holocaust studies might begin to think about the process of learning and teaching about the memory of the Holocaust while being attentive to the gendered dimensions of that process. The chapter explores the silences of the book itself – those areas which are not addressed but which could form part of further research and thinking within media studies as well as other fields. It suggests that a reconciliation to the significance that gender has within the socially inherited memory of the Holocaust provides key lessons as to how we might begin to frame our thinking about gender, culture and memory more broadly and in relation to the memories and mediations of more recent atrocities. The chapter argues that being mindful of the gendering processes in the handing down of history, reflecting critically on how memories are made and identified with makes us more fully aware of who we are, providing individuals and societies with additional generative tools to create a more inclusive future.

Although this book has been an individual project, it is ultimately part of a much bigger social endeavour. There are many people who are involved in thinking about the lessons of the Holocaust and related issues and who have worked professionally throughout their lives to research the history of the events and who think critically about how, in what ways and why the memory of the events should be communicated to future generations. This book, from someone who teaches about atrocity and the past situated within the subjects of media and cultural studies, is meant in its own way to contribute to that ongoing process. It is intended to endorse the veracity of what happened while advocating the importance of including an acknowledgement of the significance of gender in how people and societies hand down what happened. The book is dependent on the work and lives of many other people: those Holocaust survivors who have had the courage to write down and record their experiences; those scholars and experts doing research in the field; those arts and media practitioners – television workers, film-makers, photographers, writers and artists – involved in mediating the events; those working in public institutions to maintain archives and construct memorials and museums to educate the public; as well as those young people whose socially inherited memories and stories are included here. Finally, I do not purport to offer a definitive account of gender, culture and memory or the engendering of our social inheritance of the Holocaust. Any gaps and flaws in this book are my own responsibility. During the time of research and at the time of writing, I have done my best and in good spirit, and offer this so that others may use it to do better.

2
The 'Wrong' Question: Historiographies

.

> 'When I met the American liberators ... in 1945 near my last
> concentration camp in Germany, they were surprised that
> women had also been in the concentration camps ... I vowed
> then that one day I shall bring the role of women in the
> cataclysm of World War Two to the attention of the public.'
>
> (Laska, 1983:3).

Why history?

When Holocaust survivor Vera Laska was liberated at the end of the
Second World War, she had a concern that women were already
perceived as marginal to the Holocaust: she subsequently decided that
it would be up to survivors like her to ensure women's experiences
were included within the historical record (Laska, 1983). This chapter
explores the role and medium of the written word in the form of
published historiographies in relation to gender and memories of the
Holocaust. It discusses the ways in which experiences of women, and
gender issues specific to men, have been ignored or left forgotten
within historiographical sources about the Holocaust. It considers how
these silences evolved since 1945, with broader changes in society and
changes within history as an academic field of teaching and enquiry,
into a small but growing body of literature on gender and the
Holocaust. It then examines what it is that is articulated within this
body of work that does give emphasis to women and gender in the
Holocaust.

The reasons for beginning with memory and historiographical
sources are severalfold. First, before examining in subsequent chapters
the constellations of gender and memory within other cultural

mediations, it provides us with a firm grasp of the events themselves and gives us a sense of how gender was intertwined with ethnicity in the different stages of Nazi genocide. Second, although, other aspects of culture, particularly popular cultural forms, play a significant role in the construction and reconstruction of people's socially inherited memories of the Holocaust, historiographical sources remain crucial. The interviews and focus groups I conducted in the US, Britain and Poland between 1998 and 2001 showed that for the young people who have no direct experience of the Holocaust, history books and historical knowledge through schooling continued to form a key element in the construction of their socially inherited memories of events. For some, who decided to study the events more deeply, historiographical discourse formed the core of their understanding and social memory of the Holocaust and the Second World War. Although young people in the focus groups in the US, Britain and Poland stressed the importance of a variety of social and cultural mediations, including family, children's games, literature, films, television, plays, music, museums, memorials and the actual sites of atrocities, for transmitting and passing on memories of the Holocaust, there was a general acknowledgement of the importance of historical accounts and taught history (focus groups, Gdansk, Lodz, Cracow,1998; New York, Washington, 1999; London, 1998, 2000). For young people in Poland, after 1989 and the collapse of Communism, they often looked to history books to explore in more depth the emergence of previously repressed versions of events,

> My own grandfather died in Auschwitz. I still have the telegram saying that he died there. … Thus my own family was also touched. From my own personal memory, I, I also knew Jews in concentration camps. Then in the late 1980s people suddenly started discussing the history of the Jews and the Holocaust. I became very interested and bought a lot of books. (Elzbieta, aged 32, Gdansk, depth interview, April 1998)

The same interviewee said that it was through history books, particularly those that began to be published in the late 1980s, that also gave her a sense of Jewish life in Poland prior to the atrocities:

> I think that also my interest in the 80s and th-that I I was able to find out so many publications about Holocaust, about Jews, and also, you know, I wasn't aware that, for example, Jews um – not

only existed but they, er, were so influential in in Polish history ... I became very interested in our Jewish history in Poland, and I think that this history is really magnificent. (Elzbieta, aged 32, Gdansk, depth interview, April 1998)

Among respondents in the US, history books were particularly important to the construction of Jewish–American memory. One Jewish–American woman described how, from a young child, the Holocaust was part of her and part of her life, with books a key part of this process:

I used to read about it [the Holocaust] all the time. I have a mini library back home on my bookshelf. All these different books about the Holocaust and little children's books and some of them were adult books (Zara, Washington DC, depth interview, April 1999)

A British woman said that, for her, remembered images of the Holocaust after seeing a short documentary at school remained for a long time in a separate part of her mind; it was as if the events took place in another time and another Europe. It was only later, through reading historical accounts, that the reality of the Holocaust became more fully integrated into the narratives of her broader knowledge, understanding and feelings – her social memory – of the events (Suzannah, aged 32, London, depth interview, December 1998)

History and memory

Before exploring further the gender dynamics of the historiography of the Holocaust, its necessary to clarify what constitutes history and how this may differ from memory. The relationship between memory and history is a highly contested one. To Erica Carter and Ken Hirschkop history 'typically refers to a formalised recording of the past' (1997:v) and is seen to be more objective than memory. This is in contrast to memory which refers to the ways in which 'the past emerges, or is invoked, in many different forms' (1997:v). The idea, though, that history is more objective than memory is a relatively new one: Hayden White, for example, locates the development of formal, objective history in the rise of scientific objectivity in the nineteenth century (White, 1978:123). In Europe, the Enlightenment, with its broader shifts in philosophical thought, signalled the beginning of the most significant shift in the conceptualisations of memory and history

(Shrimpton, 1997; Casey, 1987). The ancients' holistic approach to reality, in which memory rather than history was predominant, became superseded by a new 'enlightened' approach. To the Ancient Greeks, in stories about the past, rationality and irrationality could co-exist, with stories about the past allowing for the randomness of chance or disorder (Shrimpton, 1997:30). In contrast, in the seventeenth century, René Descartes's work signalled a change in views of the world that split reality between the spiritual and the material. His ideas were part of the beginning of a restructuring of social values and thinking into hierarchical dichotomies of rationality and irrationality, male and female, sanity and madness, order and disorder (Shrimpton, 1997:30). Memory, which was thought to lack reason, became gradually abandoned in favour of history, which was thought to be based on logic, order and the rational ordering and prioritising of the past. Memory, in comparison, was believed to be unable to provide a guarantee of veracity and was therefore deemed doubtful (Casey, 1987). These shifts are also evidenced by particular forms of remembering becoming pathologised in the seventeenth and eighteenth centuries. Nostalgia, for example, came to be seen as a physical and mental disease. The word, which first appeared in print in 1688, from 'nosos' meaning return to one's ancient land, and 'algos', meaning suffering or grief from the desire to return, was recognised as a potentially terminal illness particularly prevalent in soldiers sent abroad (Colley, 1998:3)[1].

At the same time, some have argued that the distinction in Western culture between memory and history was established to some extent before the Enlightenment: as Jacques Le Goff notes, although interconnected, the ancient Greeks saw history and memory as quite distinct, with philosophers such as Aristotle and Plato 'never succeeding in reconciling the two' (1992:65). This is also the case within early Jewish historiographic thought: James Young points out that in sixteenth-century Jewish writings there was a distinction made between what happened described as 'what was' and 'how-what was' was told (Young, 1989:2).

Memory and history, though, also share a number of obvious features. The dictionary defines history as 'a record or account of past events and developments; all that is preserved of the past, especially in written form' (Hanks, 1989; my emphasis). Memory is defined as 'the ability of the mind to store and recall past sensations, thoughts and knowledge' (Hanks, 1989). Both, in this sense, share a concern with the past. They are also concerned in some way with narrativising the past. However, what distinguishes them in different epochs and in different cultures is the degree to which they are vested with authenticity and authority. In different epochs this has shifted and changed. In its nineteenth-century version, history – purporting to be an objective record – made claims for being the authoritative version of the past. In contrast, in the latter few decades, 'history' has been taken to task by oral historians, feminists and post-modernists who have challenged the idea that it was possible to describe human endeavours in terms of grand narratives, resulting in Francis Fukujama's (1992) argument that what we were witnessing was in a sense the 'end of history'. Yet, this has not meant that discussions and tales of the past no longer count. Rather, how we consider the past is no longer in terms of a singular authoritative historical record by scholars, but it is recognised as an historical record created in conjunction with personal memories which then as a whole form our collective or social memories. As Jacques Le Goff (1992) succinctly puts it:

Memory is the raw material of history. Whether mental, oral, or written, it is the living source from which historians draw. Because its workings are usually unconscious, it is in reality more dangerously subject to manipulation by time and by societies given to reflection than the discipline of history itself. Moreover, the discipline of history nourishes memory in turn, and enters into the great dialectical process of memory and forgetting experienced by individuals and societies. (p. xi).

To some, such as Michel Foucault (1980) history in and of itself, even archival work, is purely a representation constructed, as are other representations, within discursive power relations. However, rather than an approach that totally collapses history and memory together, I tend towards James Young's epistemology in which 'the study of commemorative forms' is included but defined within 'the study of history, making historical inquiry the combined study of both *what happened and how this is passed down to us*'. (Young, 2000:11)

What I would suggest, as did the stories told by respondents in focus groups and interviews, is that our memories of the past are constructed dialectically; they develop in part through history and from historical accounts which in turn are fed back into collective and popular memories of events. History, though connected with memory, can be conceptualised as including the 'search for verifiable fact' as well as 'the search for verifiable, yet highly contingent representations of these facts as they unfolded' (Young, 2000:11). An understanding of how gender and issues particular to men and women have been dealt with in historical accounts of the Holocaust provides a crucial starting-point for our later considerations of the construction and reception of the Holocaust in cultural memory.

In what follows, history in relation to the Holocaust is defined as material that presents itself as being a record and interpretation of those events: in other words, I examine works that declare themselves to be 'history', which are sold as history, which are read as history (rather than, for example, written accounts that present themselves as autobiography, memoirs, diaries or fiction). Under this definition one could possibly include so called 'revisionist history', more accurately described as 'Holocaust denial literature', which purports to offer an alternative of the events. However, in this regard it is important to bear in mind Deborah Lipstadt's (1994) point that Holocaust denial literature can no more offer an 'alternative' to the history of the Holocaust than historians could write an alternative version of the French Revolution in which there was no revolution. In this respect, the discussion of denial literature is kept to a minimum.

Silences in Holocaust historiography

Many thousands of historical books on the Holocaust have been published since 1945. These have explored different facets of the events and their different stages, beginning with the denial of civil rights to Jewish people and ending with mass annihilation (Barkai, 1989). They cover the policies, effects and ideology of the introduction in Germany and then the occupied territories of a series of nearly 2000 legal prohibitions and restrictions, including the rights to trade and work, the rights to vote, own property and travel, and the imprisonment of those that protested (Goldhagen, 1997:130). Historical literature has examined the removal to ghettos, the killing squads, the transport to concentration camps and forced labour and death camps, as well as what later became known as the death marches. It has also looked at the range of social and ethnic groups, in addition to Jewish people, who were targeted by Nazi policies and practices. It has looked at the effects of Nazi policies on those defined as 'half-caste', 'gypsy' (Roma and Sinti), those defined as undesirable elements or a-socials by virtue of working with opposition groups, as well as homosexuals, the disabled, the mentally ill and those defined as subhuman because they were 'Slavs'. However, there is very little in this literature that addresses the issue of gender or issues particular to women, despite the fact that gender was an important factor in the way in which policies impacted on all of these different groups (Reading, 1999). Even the most well-known overviews of the Holocaust do not consider the issue of gender or issues particular to women and men (Roth and Berenbaum, 1989; Gilbert, 1987; Goldhagen, 1997). Neither do overviews by women include any substantial research on women or gender (see Davidowicz, 1975; Levin 1973; Yahil, 1990). In historiographies of the resistance, as Poznanski points out, the role of women has been persistently over-looked. Although many Jewish women were active in organised resistance, they did not necessarily make their presence felt in Jewish political society after the end of the war (Poznanski, 1998:247). As recently as the late 1990s, Joan Ringelheim, historian and Head of Oral History at the US Holocaust Museum wrote: 'One would think that the importance of the study of gender during the Holocaust would be widely accepted today. Unfortunately, however, that is not true' (Ringelheim, 1998:346). Gender has largely been ignored, or seen as a possible distraction from the central features of the history of the Holocaust itself. The eminent Holocaust scholar Lawrence Langer, for example, questioned whether gender should really be an issue that is mentioned at all and suggests that shifting our focus in this way could serve to hide the truth (Langer, 1998:362). The issue of gender has been treated at times with a degree of hostility, as the following letter in response to the suggestion for a conference on women and the Holocaust suggests:

> I think you are asking the wrong question. Not simply the wrong question in the sense of not having found the right one; I think you are asking a morally wrong question, a question that leads us still further down the road of eradicating Jews from history. You are – I hope inadvertently – joining up with the likes of [the Revisionists] who [say] that if it happened to Jews it never happened. (Ozick, cited by Ringelheim, 1998:348)

Here the attempt to include some analysis of gender is perceived as denial, or erasure of the events, and the specificity of the Jewish dimension of the Holocaust in particular. Ringelheim suggests that denial and minimalisation of particular aspects of the Holocaust, such as rape and sexual assault, have resulted in a line dividing 'what is considered peculiar or specific to women from what has been designated as the proper collective memory of, or narrative about, the Holocaust' (Ringelheim, 1998:344).

Gender issues, on the whole, have been dismissed as less memorable than other approaches to the history of the events. In the opening conference of the US Holocaust Memorial Museum, for example, which had 18 panels and 80 participants, including 16 women, there was no specific lecture on women or gender, although there were specific lectures on the disabled, homosexual men and Afro-Germans (Ringelheim, 1998:346). 'When this omission was questioned, the answer sheepishly offered was, "we forgot." This answer was given even though panels on the issue of gender were proposed to the planning committee' (Ringelheim, 1998:346). For survivors themselves, one effect of such 'silence' is a split in Holocaust memory between gender and the Holocaust. One survivor in trying to describe her experience of rape during the Holocaust found difficulty in understanding where her experience fitted in: 'Although Pauline recognized her experiences as different from men's, she did not know how or where to locate them in the history of the Holocaust. Her memory was split between traditional versions of Holocaust history and her own experience' (Ringelheim, 1998:344).

Claudia Koontz has shown how this split also applies, although in a different way, to the writing of the broader history of Nazism and the role of German women within it. She argues that, in many accounts of Germany's Nazi past, German women's participation in the process is missing: the Nazi perpetrators are depicted as predominantly male and their victims an undifferentiated 'race'. Koontz uncovers how a key book by Gertrud Scholtz-Klink, the chief of the Women's Bureau under Hitler, entitled *The Woman in the Third Reich*, despite its evident advocacy of Nazi ideology, is not classified under German law as Nazi literature and is consequently openly sold in feminist book stores in Germany as simply a women's book. The equivalent would be to sell a book advocating homophobic policies in a gay bookstore. Koontz points out that German women's history during the Third Reich 'lacks the extravagant insanity of Hitler's megalomania; often it is ordinary. But there, at the grassroots of daily life, in a social world populated by women, we begin to discover how war and genocide happened by asking who made it happen' (Koonz, 1987:xxxv). Although the details of daily life are not preserved in government archives in the same way as the more public exploits of male Nazis, many of these archives were ordered for destruction by the Nazis towards the end of the war, anyway. In contrast, what were preserved are documents considered unimportant by the Nazis, such as church records and women's association minutes and letters. These provide invaluable insights into the details of everyday life in which German women were involved (Koonz, 1987:9).

These contradictions and splits in historical accounts raise the question of how we should approach silences regarding gender issues in historiographical material. It brings to mind Michel Foucault's treatise on the meaning and function of silence, in *A History of Sexuality* in which he suggests that silence, or 'the things that one declines to say', are not separated off from the things that are said, but that they function alongside the things said, 'with them and in relation to them, within an overall strategy.' Consequently: 'we must try to determine the different ways of not saying such things, how those who can and those who cannot speak of them are distributed, which type of discourse is authorized or which form of discretion is required in either case' (Foucault, 1979:27).

What Foucault highlights is that silence has a function. There is no strict dividing line between the said and unsaid. There are different ways of not speaking. And there are not one, but many silences. In examining gender gaps in the historiography and memory of the Holocaust, it is worth considering what has been written about and what has not; what are the reasons for and functions of these silences? What whispers do we detect between silence and total speech? What happens when women's voices are heard?

Gendering holocaust history

Although mainstream historical literature on the Holocaust has neglected gender, there is now a small but growing body of historical research that does address gender and women's issues. How and why this came about, what it articulates and what so far it fails to articulate, provide an important anchor for any analysis of the way in which gender is treated within other popular discourses that form part of our socially inherited memories of the Holocaust addressed in later chapters.

The earliest gendered historical account dates from a study conducted during the Holocaust itself, although, sadly, much of it was destroyed. Gathering data, diaries and written accounts in the Warsaw Ghetto between 1941 and 1942, Dr Emmanuel Ringelblum, with the staff of his underground archives – the *Oneg Shabbat* – began studying and creating a specific record of women's lives. Cecilya Slepak, a former journalist, was commissioned to undertake and oversee the research project on women, interviewing a range of ghetto women for the historical record (Ringelblum, 1992). Mostly, though, during the War, documentation was highly controlled by the Nazis, including all written records in the Nazi-created ghettos. The written accounts of the Lodz Ghetto – *The Lodz Chronicles* – were predominantly produced by men and there is little mention of specific difficulties that relate to gender (see Dobroszycki, 1984).

Directly after the end of the Second World War, accounts in the form of memoirs and autobiographies by survivors included a significant proportion by women. In fact Judith Baumel (1998:56–7) argues that, at that time, women's accounts substantially outnumbered those by men, but it was not until the 1980s that historical accounts using these as sources and addressing gender issues began to appear (Baumel, 1998:59). One of the earliest studies was in the late 1970s with Marion Kaplan's (1979) research on the Jewish feminist movement in pre-war Germany. This was soon followed by Vera Laska's (1983) *Women in the Resistance and in the Holocaust; The Voices of Eyewitnesses*, Sybil Milton's (1984) study of women and the Holocaust in Bridenthal et al.'s *When Biology Became Destiny: Women in Weimar and Nazi Germany'* and a chapter on the women's camps at Ravensbruck in Konnilyn G. Feig's (1983) study *Hitler's Death Camps: the Sanity of Madness* (1983:133–90). There was also Claudia Koontz's (1987) *Mothers in the Fatherland* which includes a penultimate chapter on Jewish women as victims and survivors. The next key historical text is Carol Rittner and Jon K. Roth's *Different Voices: Women and the Holocaust* first published in 1993 which was generated from Carol Rittner's question 'Where are the women?' to Michael Berenbaum's and John Roth's reprint of classic Holocaust reflections in *Holocaust: Religious and Philosophical Reflections* (1989). More recently, we have seen the publication in 1998 of both Dalia Ofer and Lenore Weitzman's *Women in the Holocaust* and Judith Tydor Baumel's *Double Jeopardy: Gender and the Holocaust*.

This growth of historiographical research on women and the Holocaust can be seen as emerging as a result of broader shifts within academia in historical studies and with the development of women's studies, connected with popular social movements in the late 1960s and their concern with equality in relation to sexuality and gender, particularly the Women's Liberation Movement. Although earlier works had considered women's history, as Deidre Beddoe notes, it was essays such as Anna Davin's (1972) 'Women and History' and Sheila Rowbotham's (1975) *Hidden from History* that signalled the beginnings of monographs, then books on women's history and the founding of journals dealing specifically with feminist scholarship in the 1970s such as *Feminist Review* and *Women's Studies International Quarterly*. This in tandem with the questioning of top-down views of history that concentrated on elites, generated by journals such as *History Workshop*, and a growing interest in oral history began to broaden the territory, focus and established methods of historical studies (Samuels, 1994). Thus, the beginnings of research within Holocaust studies that began to look at women and the Holocaust through focussing on earlier memoirs by women survivors can be viewed as part of these broader changes in the academy. Thus the medium of historiography, the history and subsequent memory of the Holocaust in gender terms is subject to shifts and changes over time. In turn, one could interpret the earlier marginalisation or gendered silences in mainstream Holocaust history as part of the general represssion of women's experiences and roles in the past, rather than something specific to Holocaust studies.

The studies have highlighted the key role that German women played in acting as a communicative channel for Nazism. Claudia Koontz, for example examines the ways in which German women were active in ostracizing and marginalising people defined by the Nazis as non-Aryan in their day-to-day dealings with people, and how the idea of a separate women's space was a key part of Nazi ideology that underpinned its daily processes and development (Koontz, 1987). In relation to Jewish women, historiographical sources provide us with an important record of Jewish gender relations prior to the War and the kinds of gendered effects Nazi policies had at each stage towards the 'Final Solution' as well as its gendered articulation in its aftermath. At different stages and places prior to the outbreak of War Nazi policies and ideology articulated, disarticulated and re-articulated aspects of gender in a variety of ways. In the process, the cultural scaffolding of femininity and masculinity in articulation with Jewish identity was initially exaggerated and then gradually stripped in a process of dehumanization. In the rest of this chapter, these historiographical sources are synthesised with some archival documents to give an indication of some of the key aspects of gendered experiences before the War, in the ghettos, of women and men in the resistance, in the camps, at liberation and in the aftermath of the War.

Experiences before the War

One of the features of atrocity is that it shatters established norms and values: Shail Mayaram's study of genocide and the Meo community in

Mewat, India, in which 82,000 Meo people were killed in 1947, with families dispersed and women raped, shows how part of the trauma involves long-standing gendered categories, roles and values being destroyed (Mayaram, 1997:191). In order to understand the gendered dimensions of the Holocaust historically it is thus important to have some understanding of what constituted established norms and values prior to the denial of civil rights and Nazi atrocities. Having said this, it is also important to stress that there was no such entity as 'the ordinary family' in Germany or *the* Jewish experience in Europe prior to the Second World War. The situation, histories and circumstances of European Jews, for example, were extremely varied, and Jewish men and women's gendered experiences were refracted and constructed through their different cultural, economic and social backgrounds (Hyman, 1998). In bourgeois Jewish families the ideal of women as providers of spiritual and domestic welfare, in contrast to men working outside the home, had begun to break down in the middle of the nineteenth century, with women beginning to limit family size and working outside the home, although in lower-paid and lower-status jobs than men. In traditional Jewish families of Eastern Europe, however, the ideal for women was the 'strong, capable working woman' anyway (Hyman, 1998:33). In Germany and Western Europe, Jewish women were, generally, less assimilated than Jewish men (Ofer and Weitzman, 1998); in Eastern European countries, such as Poland, the opposite was generally true (Hoffman, 1998; Weitzman, 1998). In Poland, in the inter-war period, while boys tended to be educated in Yiddish and Hebrew at Jewish schools, girls were much more likely to attend Polish schools and consequently be more familiar with the Polish language and culture (Stampfer, 1993; Bacon, 1998). The higher levels of pre-war assimilation among Jewish women in parts of Poland meant that women were better equipped to 'pass' as Aryans because they had a better understanding of Polish language and culture and also had Polish contacts and friends (Weitzman, 1998).

In the early stages of Nazism, one assault on Jewish people was through antisemitic propaganda, developed and controlled by the Ministry for Propaganda and Enlightenment and fed to the German population through film, newspapers, magazines, and public displays and rallies. Much of this material was imbricated with particular ideas about gender, especially what subsequently became known as the *Greuelmarchen* (horror fables) in which, pregnant German women would be shown being attacked or harmed by genderless 'subhumans' (Bielenberg, 1984:36). In parallel, German men and women in propaganda were represented in ways that stressed the power of Aryan masculinity and comradeship (Rupp, 1978; Taylor, 1979). In Germany, as Nazi policies after 1933 gradually denied Jewish people their public and cultural voice, the right to own property and the right to earn a living in various professions, it was, initially, Jewish men who bore the brunt of this, experiencing a degree of economic emasculation in being unable to support their families (Reading, 1999:494). In the cultural industries, for example, when in 1933 *Volksfremde Elemente* (elements foreign to the nation) were removed from top jobs, this disproportionately effected Jewish men at the time as there were far fewer women in managerial positions (Lacey, 1996:84). Similarly, in Poland, Gershon Bacon has argued that resolutions brought in prior to the War restricting the number of Jewish students at Polish universities, disproportionately affected Jewish men studying the law and medicine, since women tended to study humanities at the time (Bacon, 1998:61). As Jewish people were excluded from the public sphere, many Jewish women in Germany became active culturally and, in terms of social work, began to help children and families in the *Judischer Kulturbund* (Felstiner, 1997:71).

As the Nazis restricted Jewish people's lives more and more, many sought to escape abroad. Yet even in this, women and men had different attitudes to emigration: initially men often wanted to stand their ground, because they had more invested economically and in terms of their careers, while women wanted to flee to protect their families. However, after *Kristallnacht* in 1938 when many Jewish men were forced to flee, sons tended to be the first to emigrate, while daughters were often left to care for elderly relatives (Kaplan, 2000). Those who were left behind were to find themselves subject to transportation, forced work, ghettoization, imprisonment, and murder in labour and death camps.

Experiences in the Ghettos

As the spectre of Nazism spread into German occupied territories in 1939, those who could not flee or go into hiding were subject to resettlement and ghettoization. Documentary sources from the time, show that in Lodz in Poland, when the territory became part of the Third Reich on 7 November 1939, Jewish people were suddenly put under a host of directives that included the freezing of bank accounts, a curfew, banning of religious ceremonies, forced labour and a prohibition from using public transport (Dobroszycski, 1984:xxxiii). This was quickly followed by the forced resettlement of Jewish people to the East and the creation of a sealed ghetto on 30 April 1940 (Eisenbach, 1957:35–50). Documentary records show that the numbers of women who entered the ghettos far outnumbered men. Between October and November 1941, for example, there were 2467 women transported to the Lodz ghetto from Berlin in comparison with 1587 men (Dobroszycski, 1984, Table Iii). In *The Lodz Chronicles*, written by historians in the ghetto at the time, one writer notes 'there is a constant, increase in the number of women' (Dobroszycski, 1984:66). Historians have suggested that the reason for the gender imbalance stems from the fact that people thought that the Nazis would respect traditional gender rules and would not harm women and children. Certainly, prior to the War and the occupation of Poland, those in greatest danger from Nazi policies were Jewish men and they were the first to flee to safety (Ofer and Weitzman, 1998) In contrast, many women were left with small children or elderly relatives to care for and were unable to travel easily because of this. Once inside the ghetto, though, men were less able to withstand the appalling living conditions, which in turn resulted in a higher male mortality rate (Unger, 1998:124). Within the ghettos, despite the higher numbers of women, the *Judenrat* – the ruling structure imposed by the Nazis to replace the disbanded all-male *Kehillah* – reproduced the male gender bias of the outside world. In Theresienstadt, the Judenrat consisted of men only, and all the heads of the various departments except one were men. This was despite the fact that women comprised 60 per cent of the inhabitants (Bondy, 1998:312–13). Michael Unger argues that in the first two years in the Lodz ghetto women performed mainly domestic duties, struggling to keep their families alive by bartering for scarce food. Later, though, women became part of the ghetto workforce, combining long hours doing menial work with their domestic tasks. In many families at this stage women became the main breadwinners (Unger, 1998:133–4). As Ofer (1998) notes, in the ghettos women 'were not policy-makers' but their roles increased as the War progressed and they became essential to running the public soup kitchens which for many kept starvation at bay (p. 158).

Women and men in the Resistance

Both women and men were involved in underground organisations and resistance activities both in the ghettos and outside. In the resistance groups in the forests, Nechama Tec has found that the fate of women and men differed: most of the connecting links – the couriers who went between resistance groups – were women, as it was easier for women to disguise themselves and pass themselves off as non-Jews. Circumcision made Jewish men immediately suspect, while in Poland women's knowledge of Polish was of great benefit to them in permitting their survival as couriers (Klibanski, 1998:181). Yet, in the groups themselves, the image of the partisan as a strong fighter devalued women's roles and, usually, women were only accepted into the groups if they were young and beautiful or if they had medical training. In some instances male resistance fighters used women as prostitutes, as in the case of the Warsaw Ghetto Uprising, where in the height of their defiance against the Nazis three Jewish women were rounded up and used as prostitutes (Dworkin, 2000). Women who were sent away from resistance groups sometimes formed their own separate family camps. Within mixed groups, a woman usually did not carry arms and her fate tended to depend on whether she was attached to a man and to whom. Single women were given just basic food to survive (Tec, 1999). In the French–Jewish resistance women were primarily active in tasks associated with maintaining its infrastructure: providing food, places to sleep, means of communication and so on (Poznanski, 1998). In addition to those who escaped the ghettos and camps by working for organised resistance groups, there were also Jewish people who resisted Nazi policies by passing as Aryans, taking on Gentile identities and papers and living by their wits. The overwhelming majority of these, because of their greater ease at assimilating, were women (Weitzman, 1998:187).

Experiences in the camps

In most work, concentration and extermination camps, men and women were generally separated. In extermination camps, a number of studies have shown how Nazi ideology and the policies that were developed towards the mass murder and genocide that took place were underpinned by ideas relating to 'race' and biology that were gendered (Bock, 1993; Ofer and Weitzman, 1998). Jewish women came to be seen as a direct threat to the development of a pure Aryan State because they could reproduce the next generation. Thus SS Sturmbannfuhrer Rolf Heinz Hoppner, in a memorandum to Adolf Eichman dated 16 July 1941, proposed that 'all Jewish women capable of bearing children be sterilized in that camp so that the Jewish problem would be fully solved to all intents and purposes with this generation' (Hoppner, 1971:88). Nazi state policies resulted in the territorialization of non-'Aryan' women's bodies through enforced sterilisation (Bock, 1993). The specific development of using Zyklon B gas as a method of mass murder can be seen as emerging from the contradictions of Nazi racism imbricated with a gendered world view in which women were still seen as more vulnerable than men. Initial methods of mass killing involved shooting by Nazi mobile killing squads, but evidence suggests that this was creating 'a psychological burden' on the men who had been ordered to kill Jewish women and children as well as Jewish men: as Auschwitz-Birkenau Commandant Rudolf Hoess stated:

> It would soon be necessary to start the mass extermination of the Jews, and until that moment neither I nor [Adolf] Eichmann had known how to conduct a mass killing... now we had the gas and the way of using it. I had always been concerned at the thought of the mass shootings, *particularly women and children*. I was already sick of executions. Now my mind was at ease. (Proces Hossa; xx.34. My emphasis)

At extermination camps, such as Auschwitz- Birkenau, when people disembarked from the transport trains, families were torn apart, and those selected for work were separated from those selected for immediate death.

> First the men and the women are divided ... Husbands and wives are separated, mothers wave to their sons for the last time ... Now the SS Doctor begins to segregate those who are fit for work, in his opinion, from those who are not. *As a rule, mothers with little children are classed as not fit for work.* (Broad, cited in Swiebocka, 1995:142, Auschwitz, my emphasis).

Women made up the majority of those not deemed fit for work as they were usually the prime carers for the children with them (Felstiner, 1997:206; Swiebocka, 1995:140). When women in the family camp at Birkenau were given the choice of leaving their babies to be murdered or going with their babies and children to the gas chambers, the majority chose the latter (Bondy, 1998). At Auschwitz-Birkenau 67.5 percent of men were selected for labour but only 32.5 per cent of women; the rest of the women and men were sent immediately to their deaths. Of the Jewish prisoners who survived until liberation 83 per cent were men and 17 per cent were women. The Soviet army found 836,525 dresses in contrast to 324,820 men's suits (Felstiner, 1997:206). As Mary Lowenthal Felstiner puts it, 'genocide is the act of putting women and children first. Of all the deceptions a death camp settled on, this one went down deepest. This was the core of the Holocaust' (Felstiner, 1997:208).

In rare cases, men and women stayed together – in the 'gypsy ' camp in Birkenau II and in the Jewish family camp B/2/B in Birkenau, families were kept together. In other work and death camps men and women shared the common experience of being stripped of their own clothes and belongings, with those women and men selected to live separated, subjected to a starvation diet, in cramped, dirty living conditions with hard labour and hour upon hour of standing roll-calls in all weathers. Many were reduced to walking skeletons, the men derisively called *Musselmanner* (Moslems) and the women *Schmuckstuke* (pretty pieces) by the Nazis (Koontz, 1987:380). Women often found it more difficult than men to adjust to the harsh working conditions (Karay, 1998:290). Although women developed strong mutual assistance networks, in camps in German-occupied Poland, for example, they were also more divided by language and culture, whereas Jewish men were more often united by their traditional education (Karay, 1998:294). Both men and women died from overwork, starvation, disease, hangings and shootings in work camps.

Despite women selected for labour having separate barracks from men, this did not prevent them from being vulnerable to sexual exploitation and rape, as well as the attendant dangers of pregnancy and abortion. 'Their stories demonstrate shared fears about and experiences of sexual vulnerability as women, not only about mortal danger as Jews' (Ringelheim, 1993:376). Women in the work camps often experienced sexual harrassment and assault and individual and mass rape (Karay, 1998:290). Further, although both men and women were equally de-humanized, these experiences were sometimes articulated differently. For example, women's experience of being shaved and stripped by men made them feel sexually as well as physically vulnerable. Shaving for orthodox Jewish women also had particular resonance, since in the 'normal' pre-war world shaving one's head as a woman took place only after marriage: As Auschwitz survivor Rena Kornreich Gelissen describes:

> I try to prevent tears from falling down my disinfected cheeks. Only married women shave their heads. Our traditions, our beliefs, are scorned and ridiculed by the acts they commit. (1997:63)

In contrast, the shaving of ear-locks and beards of Orthodox Jewish men had the effect of symbolically emasculating them and turning them symbolically from men into boys (Kornreich Gelissen, 1997:24). Women experienced the loss of menstruation in the camps. Those women who had managed to hide the fact that they were pregnant usually had to abort their babies or other women helped them kill their baby at birth to save the mother's life.

Liberation and aftermath

Women's rates of survival, experiences of liberation and the aftermath of the Holocaust were both similar and in some ways different from those of men. As Martin Gilbert in *The Boys: Triumph Over Adversity* points out, in many camps only a small number of girls survived in comparison with boys, hence more 'boys' went to other countries afterwards, including England (1996:377). In the liberation of Belsen, in 1945, in which the British armed forces found 10,000 unburied dead in a camp without water or electricity and in which typhoid was raging, there were 40,000 starving men and women. One of the consignments that the humanitarian relief forces sent to Belsen early on was a consignment of lipstick, which Lieutenant-Colonel M.W. Gonin described in his report of the time:

> It was shortly after the B.R.C.S [British Red Cross] teams arrived, though it may have no connection, that very large quantity of lipstick also arrived. This was not at all what we men wanted, we were screaming for hundreds and thousands of other things and I don't know who asked for lipstick ... women lay in bed with no sheets and no nightie but with scarlet lips, you saw them wandering about with nothing but a blanket over their shoulders, but with scarlet lips. I saw a woman dead on the post-mortem table and clutched in her hand was a piece of lipstick. (Gonin, 1945:11, cited by Reading, 1999: 481).

Lieutenant-Colonel Gonin agonized about the appropriateness of this response of the relief services. Yet, what we have noted in the gendered articulations of the different stages of the Holocaust is that they involved the stripping away of people's humanity, a humanity which in part includes the cultural scaffolding of femininity and masculinity. Hence, one of the nurses who was a humanitarian relief worker at Belsen noted in her diary how differently the Belsen women began to behave as soon as they were given clothes and make-up (Parkinson, 1945). As Gonin (1945) concluded: 'At last someone had done something to make them individual again, they were someone, no longer merely the number tattooed on their arm. At last they could take an interest in their appearance. That lipstick started to give them back their humanity' (p. 11, cited in Reading, 1999:497).

Yet, sadly, just as in some places gendered aspects of humanity were being restored, in others it was being demolished further through the threat of sexual assault. Women often experienced being raped after the War, particularly by Russian soldiers (Rigler, 1998:157).

Not only were there some differences in the process of liberation for survivors of the Holocaust, historians have also noted that there are differences in the experiences of the aftermath and years following the events. Sarah R. Horowitz (1999) notes that a significant worry among women survivors which was different from that of men was that they would not be able to have children. In addition to the reality of enforced brutal experiments in sterilisation on men and women involving the injection of chemicals and the use of x-rays on their reproductive organs, there was also the lingering fear of infertility stemming from the women's experience in the camps of ceasing to menstruate during their imprisonment.

Silences in gendered historiography

Gendered historical accounts provide us with invaluable insights into how gender was articulated and re-articulated at different stages of the Holocaust. However, this aspect of Holocaust historiography is still relatively recent and there are, consequently, gaps in research and obvious silences. This is not a critisism – as Spender (1985) notes, in a sense all accounts are partial but it is important to recognise the fact in mapping the basis for Holocaust memories. Some of these silences stem from the manner in which feminist historiography has thus far been framed: quite rightly the focus has been predominantly on gender issues in relation to Jewish people. But the result is that there is still a dearth of work done on gender in relation to other groups such as the disabled, the mentally ill, homosexuals, Afro-Germans, and the experiences of Romany and Sinti. Research on the margins of the main gendered historiographies in this respect is also illuminating. Tina Camft (1999) highlights, for example, the complex ways in which Afro-German men and women were both excluded yet included in Hitler's facist world. One Afro-German man described how he had been subject

Gypsies.

to forced sterilization yet was allowed to don a Hitler Youth uniform and march with his classmates. Work on the effects of Nazi policies on the European Romany and Sinti is still relatively neglected – although a quarter of a million were annihilated, with all of Germany's 30,000 gypsies sent to Auschwitz. Gabrielle Tyrnauer (1989) points out that there were few 'gypsy' witnesses to the murders (none were given a voice at Nuremberg Trials). Those Romany, Sinti and other tribes who survived, retained up until more recently a strong oral tradition with few written records. What little research there is shows us the different gendered effect of Nazi racist policies in relation to the Romany and Sinti population. Hence the reason for 'gypsies' being kept in a family camp stemmed from the German racial anthropologist Hans Gunther, who believed that 'pure' gyspies preserved ancient 'Aryan customs'.

> They were rounded up from carnivals ... and concert stages, from Slovak villages and Wehrmacht barracks, from Jewish ghettos, Labour camps and detention centres. In Auschwitz they were permitted to be with their families, wear their own clothes and keep a few musical instruments so as to feed German 'zig-ennerromantic' even while they were being prepared for annihilation. (Tyrnauer, 1989:xvi)

Another muted area and tension within historical research that does consider gender issues is that it tends to conflate gender with women. This again is, initially, understandable, with mainstream historiography ignoring the differences in the experiences of men and women in the Holocaust, feminist historians have sought specifically to document women's experiences. However, understanding the articulations of gender within Nazi genocide is not solely about reinserting 'women's issues'. It is also about remembering the experiences particular to men. It is about remembering the same event, such as the moment of separation of men and women on the ramp at Birkenau, or the rape of Jewish women by Nazi SS in a small Polish town, from different subject positions. As we shall see in the next chapter, genocide is a complex jigsaw; to understand its meaning and impact for men and women as victims and survivors we need to attend to their differences while reconciling and connecting the memories together.

The reception of history

The gaps and silences within mainstream historiography identified here have implications for the social inheritance of the events and its mediation and integration by young people especially. Although young people were aware that the history of the Holocaust taught in schools could be partial or biased, none were aware that this in part might also be partial or biased in terms of the exclusion of gender issues within mainstream or dominant texts on the subject. Thus, young Poles were particularly aware that official history of the Second World War taught to them under the Communist system had been written from a perspective that cast the Soviet Union in a positive light: they were aware of silences and gaps in their historical knowledge concerning the Jewish dimension of the genocide and the atrocities also committed by the Soviet Union. Subsequently, before 1989, they had sought to fill the gaps 'from illegal books, illegal materials that were circulated around' (Eva, aged 30, depth interview, April 1998). There was also a recognition of different versions of history in the US: one young Jewish-American woman recollected her sense of frustration with the version taught in state schools which lacked the details of the Holocaust that she had learnt from Hebrew school.

> We actually had a course in eighth grade about the Holocaust for a whole semester ... in Hebrew school we learned about the Holocaust through the eyes of the Jewish people, but in high school they taught us different perspectives, would teach us the American perspectives. They taught us that other groups were affected by the Holocaust – like the gypsies. There was much more of an overview of the whole war in general and not just the Holocaust. I mean they discussed what the camps were like, but it was also a little more political in some ways. (Zara, aged 20, Washington DC, April 1999)

Another young African-American woman expressed a similar frustration: 'I was surprised how history books really, when they focus on World War Two they don't talk about the killing of the Jews, like my history book, I haven't seen anything' (Naomi, aged 16, New York focus group, April 1999).

In young men and women's discussions of key history lessons and books at school there was no recall of particular details relating to gender issues. Important stories included male protagonists as the key movers of historical events or as the doer of heroic acts, and pronouns were generally gender neutral: 'Jews' 'Polish people' 'the Germans'. This is not suprising given the fact that gendered accounts of the Holocaust are predominantly American published, English language based and fairly recent. In most cases they have not filtered into the school curricula either in the US or in other countries, although a conference 'Women and the Holocaust' at the Museum for Jewish Heritage for American school educators in New York in March 2000 may have signalled the beginning of a shift in this respect.

Conclusion

This chapter began by establishing that historiographical sources about the Holocaust remain important to young people even in the face of popular culture telling stories about aspects of the past. It then considered the differences and links between history and memory and how each at different times has been accorded authority and veracity. The chapter then considered, in the light of this, the ways in which gender features in historical accounts of the Holocaust. Although established Holocaust historiographical literature has generally neglected gender, more recent feminist research since the 1980s, predominantly from North America, highlights the complex ways in which gender and ethnicity were articulated by Nazi policies and practices. Although young people were not aware of these biases, an examination of what and how these sources document gender issues and the Holocaust can provide an important foundation for the consideration of the cultural mediation of the Holocaust in autobiography, in different genres of film and in other constellations of the social memory of the Holocaust such as museums. If in historiography the significance of gender has been overlooked, silenced or marginalised, then how have gender and gender issues been articulated in other cultural mediations of the events? The next chapter looks at the role and patterns of memory transmitted to the next generation through autobiography. It considers cultural patterns in how men and women's stories of their experiences have been handed down; how men and women articulate the experiences of atrocity and genocide in ways that are gendered, and the relationships between the form of the written word and the genre of autobiography, especially to traumatic memory.

3
The Demolition of a Man: Autobiographies

'Me, a man, crying'

(Viktor C, cited by Langer, 1998:362)

'Black milk came out of my breast.'

(Fanya Gottesfeld Heller, 1993:275)

Autobiography and memory

There is now more than half a century of writing about the Holocaust, of which life-writing forms a substantial part, from Primo Levi's *If This is a Man* originally published in 1947 (2000) to the memoirs of the children of survivors such as Anne Karpf's *The War After* (1996). There are people's diaries written during the events themselves, as well as autobiographical accounts written afterwards. There are men and women's perspectives as victims, survivors, perpetrators, bystanders, witnesses and rescuers of different religious and national identities. Conventional media studies scholars would not usually include an analysis of the genre of autobiography as part of a study of representations of the past, leaving this instead to the those within the fields of literature or history. But, I would suggest, a less orthodox and restricted approach is required here in order to understand the complex constellations of cultural mediations that construct social memories over time, especially since survivors' life-writings constitute a key element in handing down the events of what happened, as evidenced by the development of young people's socially inherited memories of the Holocaust (Interviews and Focus Groups, USA, April 1999; Poland, April 1998; Britain, 1998, 2000). Life-writing as a medium for communicating the past is also at the interstices between the individual and the social or public domain. As Nicola King (1996) points out, autobiography is the point where individual memories are reworked in their broader social and cultural contexts (p. 50–62). Which of these autobiographies is more remembered than others and how the authors tell what happened is an important part of understanding how these individually gendered stories relate to broader gendered structures and gendered socially inherited memories.

This chapter focuses on a selection of autobiographies by Jewish men and women victim-survivors to explore what they tell us about the social inheritance of what survivor Primo Levi (2000) referred to as 'the demolition of a man' (p. 32). The chapter considers how the medium of the written word renders gender and atrocity a part of our socially inherited memory of the Holocaust. I draw on broader literary and gendered theories of autobiography and life-writing to explore what particular texts reveal about the ways in which individual and social memory and forgetting are constructed in ways that are gendered. I focus, mostly, on published written testimonies, rather than those only available in archives, because their availability means that they are more central to peoples' social memory of the events, as well as being accessible to readers of this book. I examine Jewish men and women's experiences of going into hiding, experiences of the lesser-known camp of Stutthof (near what was known as Danzig, now Gdansk) and the death and work camps at Auschwitz-Birkenau, in what was German occupied Poland. This is not to deny the validity of accounts by Jewish people in other camps, or accounts by non-Jewish survivors. Neither it is to suggest that we should only focus on the accounts of victims and survivors; to look at written accounts by perpetrators, rescuers or witnesses of the Holocaust, is also crucial to our understanding and would form an interesting basis for additional research.[1] The decision to focus on particular accounts by victims and survivors rather than others is to provide a point of focus that allows for an in-depth analysis, as well as a cogent framework for comparison. The main texts I consider are primarily those that were mentioned by young people in the US, Britain and Poland as important to them and which are well known and easily available in English: *The Diary of a Young Girl*, by Anne Frank (Frank and Pressler, 1997), Elie Wiesel's *Night* (1982) and Primo *Levi's If This is a Man* (2000). To ensure the inclusion of at least some subaltern memories of the Holocaust, though, and to bring together, to reconcile men and women's memories of the events, I have also included analyses of less well-known published accounts by women survivors, including Fanya

Gottesfeld Heller's *Strange and Unexpected Love: A Teenage Girl's Holocaust Memoirs* (1993), Rena Kornreich Gelissen's (1997) *Rena's Promise A Story of Two Sisters in Auschwitz:* as well as unpublished testimonies such as Charlotte Arpadi's life-story lodged with the U.S Holocaust Archives, Washington DC.

Theoretical approaches to autobiography

Autobiographies by Holocaust survivors share, in many ways, the conventional features of autobiographies, including chronology, description, characterisation, dialogue and narrative voice (Langer, 1995:41). Earlier theoretical approaches to autobiographies read them as narrative sources for gleaning historical facts; later on, this approach was supplemented by a perspective that emphasised the importance of analysing the psychology of the author. More recent theoretical trends within autobiography studies, however, stress the textuality of the writing, suggesting that we read autobiography as a construction, attending to the language and metaphors, the omissions, gaps, juxtapositions and narrative emphasis which the author uses to give meaning to their experiences (Anderson, 1997; Smith, 1987). This is also the approach increasingly used by Holocaust scholars examining personal testimony and literature. Sarah Horowitz (1988) points out, for example, that the men and women who write Holocaust autobiographies have had to go through an important process of selection and analysis in deciding what to record. Their life-writing, like other autobiographies, should not be read simply as raw material for us to plunder for the facts (p. 371).

The late 1980s and 1990s also saw the emergence of approaches within autobiography studies that included consideration of the question of gender (Bell and Yalom, 1990; Neuman, 1991), sexual difference in autobiography (Hughes, 1999), work on women's life-writing (Anderson, 1997; Smith, 1987) black women and autobiography (Braxton, 1989), masculinity and autobiography (Broughton, 1999) and feminism and autobiography (Cosslett, Lury and Summerfield, 2000). Although Holocaust scholar Lawrence Langer (1998) warns us against over-emphasising the role that gender played (p. 352), there is a growing recognition of its significance. Sarah Horowitz suggests that rather than a gynocentric approach to Holocaust life-writing, or one that privileges gender, we look at the details of how women and men construct testimonies of their experiences in terms of insignia that are trying to convey aspects of their identity which include a sense of pain and loss in relation to both their gender and their Jewishness. She gives the example of a description by Itka Zymiontowicz after her liberation in which she describes her lack of menses, her lack of undergarments under her tattered liberation dress, followed by a description of her camp-issue wooden clogs and the tattooed number on her arm. Horowitz reminds us, 'survivors' reflections are inevitably gendered' but 'gender does not constitute the totality of one's experience' (Horowitz, 1998:371).

Although, Holocaust life-writing does share common features with other autobiographical forms, there are also crucial differences to which one must be attentive. Lawrence L. Langer (1992) writes of the Holocaust being 'a communal wound' that we must learn to feel (p. 205). It is as if for survivors to recall and narrate what happened they must inhabit two worlds – the deep memory of the violated conventions of the camps and the common memory of family and home in the present. To understand, the reader must seek to enter with the writer the world of deep memory. When the subtext of the story echoes for us too as a communal wound, then we will have begun to hear the legacy of the unheroic memory and grasp the meaning for our time of a diminished self' (Langer, 1991:205).

Part of the 'diminished self', I argue, concerns the violation of gendered boundaries and identities, but to understand the complexity of these processes we must also remember that the cultural and historical context out of which autobiographical narratives about the Holocaust spring is qualitatively different from most other life-writing. Not only is the written word as a cultural form particularly significant within Judaism, but part of the genocide and annihilation of Jewish people involved the public burning of books by Jewish authors and Nazi dissenters. For a Jewish man or woman to write the story of their victimisation and survival of annihilation and mass murder thus assumes a weightier significance in comparison with conventional autobiography. For the survivor, the book is not just a book, it is a life: it symbolically replaces books burnt and cultural and social memories destroyed; it provides a testament in the face of Nazi lies and contemporary Holocaust denial, creating a memorial, ensuring the author's 'life' remains within the socially inherited memory after they die. It is also a book of death: within each story of a life survived there is the mute reminder of the literally millions of stories of lives untold and abruptly ended because they died as result of disease, suicide or starvation, or were murdered in the ghettos, work and death camps, transports and marches.

What survivors articulate in autobiography, in this respect, is configured through contradictions particular to traumatic memory arising from atrocity that have been well documented within psychiatry and psychotherapy. Psychiatrist Judith Herman (1992) writes:

The ordinary response to atrocities is to banish them from consciousness. Certain violations of the social compact are too terrible to utter outloud: this is the meaning of the word unspeakable ... Atrocities, however, refuse to be buried ... remembering and telling the truth about terrible events are pre-requisites both for the restitution of the social order and for the healing of individual victims. ... The conflict between the will to deny horrible events and the will to proclaim them aloud is the central dialectic of psychological 'trauma'. (p. 1)

Herman also stresses how 'traumatic events call into question basic human relationships. They shatter the construction of the self that is formed and sustained in relation to others' (Herman, 1992:51). While all autobiographies make public the connection between the individual and the group (Swindells, 1985:121), the loss of self and relationships as part of many survivors' experiences is an important part of their writing, with the writing then acting as part of the restitution and reconnecting process necessary to rebuilding the shattered self in the post-Holocaust world. Traumatic memories, as opposed to common memories, are generally a central part of the narrative in Holocaust autobiographies, with the rise of the Nazis and the impact of the War forming the chronology and geography of the story. Hence reading Holocaust life-writing simply by using established approaches to autobiographies and/or in terms of purely using a gendered lens in which women are seen as 'doubly estranged' from language and culture (Smith, 1987:48) would be to miss the complex meaning of the communal wound in a way that is both disrespectful and intellectually clumsy. The approach I suggest is a complex one that looks at the ways in which narratives of the Holocaust are articulated through contradictory mechanisms, subjectivities and tropes that are related through cultural background, gender and, ultimately, traumatic survival. A reading of Holocaust autobiographies in which we are attentive to gender, in this way, provides us with an understanding of how the dismantling of gender was part of the humiliation and victimisation that victims and survivors experienced. What their words tells us is important to our understanding of genocide, and its social inheritance within culture. Survivors express in their autobiographies traumatic experiences in terms of the demolition of a complex contradictory identity that includes gender, as well as gendered difficulties faced after liberation in the process of trying to reconstruct a post-survivor self. I begin by considering the overall patterns of memory, in terms of the broader context of whose life-stories are more dominant or more marginal within the social memory of the Holocaust.

The familiar and the strange

One notable aspect of personal testimony literature on the Holocaust is that the most well-known accounts are by men. Accounts by Elie Wiesel, Primo Levi, Jean Amery and Viktor Frankl were all mentioned by young people in focus groups in the US, Britain and Poland, while those by Charlotte Delbo and Ida Fink were not (focus groups, Poland, 1998; US, 1999; UK 1998 and 1999). These are also accounts by survivors rather than by perpetrators, bystanders or rescuers. Sarah Horowitz argues that accounts by women have been more prone to falling out of print; they then become less available for classroom use and subsequently how the Holocaust has been taught and remembered in this respect has been largely based on accounts by male survivors (Horowitz, 1998:369). Mixed gender anthologies tend to give more space to the work of men: out of 33 contributors to Lawrence Langer's (1995) *Art From the Ashes* anthology, only four are women. However, the problem of books being allowed to fall out print was also one faced by male Holocaust survivors in the first few decades after the war. Primo Levi's *If This Is a Man*, initially turned down by a number of major publishers, was accepted for publication in 1947 by a small company that printed just 2500 copies. The company went bankrupt and the book went into oblivion until 1958. It was only since then that it gained worldwide readership, selling more than half a million copies, with translations into eight languages (Levi, 1998:137).

One personal testimony of a victim written at the time by a woman was mentioned consistently in focus groups in the US and Britain and has gained world-wide recognition, with the sale of over 15 million copies worldwide (Huttenbach, 1998): *The Diary of a Young Girl* by Anne Frank. Initially published in 1947, after the Second World War, several sections that dealt with Anne Frank's sexuality were cut because 'it was not customary to write openly about sex, and certainly not in books for young adults' (Frank and Pressler, 1997:vi). One critic has suggested that the diary became accepted and popular as far a field as Japan because it was about a girl, rather than a woman, and because of its air of sanctity (Reisz, 1997:41–3). It is notable that the vulnerability implied in the given title – *The Diary of a Young Girl* (my emphasis) contradicts Anne's own identification of herself as a strong female adult – ' I know that I am *a woman, a woman* with inner strength and a great deal of courage' (Frank and Pressler, 1997:260, my emphasis). What is also notable is that the diaries end with Anne's discovery by the Nazis and it is only through an Afterword that the reader learns that she was transported to Auschwitz-Birkenau and later was moved to Bergen-Belsen, where she died in the typhus epidemic in the winter of 1944–5, a few months before liberation by the British Armed Forces. In this respect it could be argued that the book became so popular precisely because the reader does not have to face the horrors of the camps themselves. It is also questionable whether the book would have become so accepted worldwide if it had been written by an Orthodox Jewish girl: an equivalent diary written by an orthodox Jewish boy, Moshe Flinkter who also went into hiding, has never gained the same recognition (see Flinkter, 1971).

As well as factors relating to the subjectivity and role of the author intervening into the hegemony of particular memories articulated within the medium of the word, it can also be a question of the form that the life-writing takes. Another teenage girl/woman's victim's account by Charlotte Salomon was little known outside The Netherlands until its exposure at the Royal Academy in the form of an exhibition in 1998 (see Salomon, 1998 and www. jhm.nl 11.1.99). In contrast to Anne Frank's diaries, Charlotte Salomon's work defies convention in its form (a mixture of text, paint, crayon and pencil on paper and tracing paper) and in its overt confrontation with controversial gender-related issues. Salomon's work addresses the predominance of female suicide in pre-war Jewish families (Felstiner, 1997:14–17). It also includes a vivid description of a young woman's feelings in exile being forced to share a bed with male relatives (Salomon, 1998:no. 804) and the problems of a young woman fleeing the Nazi horrors who then faced sexual harassment from other exiles (Salomon, 1998:nos 810, 811).

Forgetting rape

The social inheritance of the memory of genocide within culture, this suggests, becomes constructed and sedimented through a matrix of influences that includes the role of the author within history (as victim, survivor, perpetrator, bystander, witness or rescuer) and their gender and ethnicity as well as the cultural medium of expression. Further, I would suggest that to ensure social cohesion, those stories that are in keeping with a particular set of gendered cultural values are more likely to become part of our collective memory than those that are not. Those stories that question, challenge or disrupt present gendered structures and roles are more likely for some time to be marginalised, left unarticulated, or only covertly expressed in cultural mediations of traumatic events. Part of this also involves particular contradictions associated with trauma and survival: survival not only of the individual but also relationships within the family and broader community. The silencing of particular gendered memories often serves the purpose of enabling such survival in the shorter and longer term. We find several examples of this in the autobiography of the Holocaust survivor Fanya Gottesfeld Heller in *Strange and Unexpected Love: A Teenage Girl's Holocaust Memoirs* (1993). More than fifty years after the events, Gottesfeld Heller was able to speak publicly about the fact that it was not uncommon for the Gestapo to force their way into Jewish homes and rape teenage girls and women while their fathers or parents were forced to watch (Gottesfeld Heller, 2000). This element of Holocaust memory is one that has been largely collectively repressed – by survivors, by relatives and by researchers (Ringelheim, 1998). It was thus not until half a century afterwards that the story of a particular raid by the Gestapo involving rape was told by a relative to Fanya Gottesfeld Heller and was then related by her in her autobiography.

> Unable to find me, Gottschalk and his henchmen left and went looking for me at the home of one of my aunts. When they didn't find me there, they raped her and forced her husband to watch. The rape had to be kept secret because if the Gestapo found out about it they would have killed her immediately, since Germans were forbidden to 'fraternise' with 'subhuman' Jews. My aunt told a few members of the family but they didn't believe her – they didn't want to hear or know about it. She never told her children, and for that reason, I have not disclosed her name. (Gottesfeld Heller, 1993:81)

Even fifty years on, when Fanya Gottesfeld Heller courageously includes this story in her autobiography so that it entered socially inherited memory, she was asked 'why do you have to dredge up the past?'. One woman editor even refused to review the book (Gottesfeld Heller, 2000).

The silencing of rape within Nazi genocide springs from several factors. In part it stems from the contradictory nature of racist Nazi policies at the time in which sexual contact between those defined as Jews and Aryans was punishable by death. Denial is also a common reaction by others to women who experience rape – hence the story is both unable to be told at the time and later survivors' families become unable to hear it. As Sarah Horowitz's points out, we are more able to narrate and accept memories that we feel comfortable with (Horowitz, 2000). A young man may talk, for example, of how he tried to save his father but not mention how they were unable to stop his mother being raped or his sisters being taken away and murdered. Similar patterns emerged in work by Judith Zur in her research with Quiche Maya widows who survived La Violencia by the Guatemalan government when death squads bombed and murdered villagers it defined as 'subversives'.[2] But it is also, I would suggest, that it is more acceptable to tell stories that re-establish social cohesion, part of which includes the familial relationships between men and women, rather than tell stories that threaten or perpetuate gendered breakdown. To talk about and have accepted a memory of rape in the context of the Holocaust is to admit that in the attempts to annihilate another 'race', genocide includes the brutal use of sexual violence against women. For the individual and cultural community to re-establish individual and social cohesion and survive, the memory had to be repressed. With genocidal rape, although both men and women may have been in different ways victims, its memory threatens to tear men and women apart, for included in its memory is both the brutalisation of women by men and the unspeakable emasculation of husbands, fathers, brothers and sons forced to bear witness, as well as their guilt and shame at being unable to protect 'their' women from the enemy. Rape in genocide constitutes the ultimate demolition of established gender conventions and roles; in the aftermath it threatens to divide us, men from women. The silence or difficulties of articulation of this aspect of the past, I would suggest, have a function: they are indicative of the social need to recreate relationships between men and women. In this way, Gottesfeld Heller's journey and its articulation in autobiography voices how the cultural (dis)articulation of the memory of rape as part of genocide has been individually and collectively policed for reasons of personal and social survival.

Forbidden love

Part of the gendered fabric of the past may also include forbidden love or sex. As with rape, the memory of this, in other ways, may also threaten social reconstruction in the present and hence is repressed by the individual and their family to ensure the social cohesion of the broader cultural community. Gottesfeld Heller describes in her autobiography her romantic link with a Ukrainian Gentile called Jan which was tacitly encouraged by her mother and father to aid her survival. The articulation of the memory of this long-repressed, complex relationship, which at first was platonic and then became physical, is central to her chronology of hiding and survival in her autobiography. To narrativise her memories of the events that followed the murderous raid by the Gestapo and Ukrainian militia on September 26–7 1942, in the *shtetl* of Skala, involved attempting to resolve through words the contradictions and conflicts of her victimisation and survival in terms of both ethnicity and gender. This is chronicled largely through the development of her relationship with Jan, the Gentile who saved her life, but who was later accused by her family of murdering Fanya's father during liberation of the area by the Soviet Army. Jan loved her – he had hidden her, fed her, bathed her, saved her from both the Nazi occupiers and the antisemitic Ukrainian villagers who bayed for her blood in her various hiding places, including a barn and a pit in the ground under a hen coop. With the liberation by the Soviet Army, Fanya was free, but was torn between her feelings of gratitude to Jan, her sense of loyalty to her family and the threat to her own personal goals should she marry a lower-class Ukrainian Gentile. For Gottesfeld Heller, the conflict of remembering, as a survivor is not experienced in terms of a gender-neutral identity as a Jewish person but is articulated by her in terms of the losses and conflicts within her identity as a Jewish woman. She encapsulates this in the articulation of the memory of an image of birth turning into death when she tried to imagine a life with Jan as his wife and her future role as the mother of their children.

> How could I condemn my babies to grow up in Poland or the Ukraine, the graveyard for millions of Jews? No, not a graveyard, for there were no graves. The Jews had been burned to ashes, and the ashes had turned to dust which was in the air we breathed and the water we drank ... I saw myself holding a baby to my breast, and my breast and the baby were black with the ashes of their murdered relatives. Black milk came out of my breast. (Gottesfield Heller, 1993:275)

What is narrated here is a gendered legacy. Fanya Gottsesfeld Heller survived but with the internalised traumatic memory of genocide that contaminated her ability to imagine a gendered future as a wife and mother – both her and her baby are covered in ashes. Thus, although 'liberated', the imagination of the self as a 'normal' mother is impossible where the memory remains visceral through being articulated out of the place/land where atrocities occurred. Antisemitic mass annihilation has infected an imagined maternity: white milk is turned to black ashes, nurturing and giving life is inverted to death. She then describes how the conflict of these subjectivities is resolved by a marriage, quickly arranged, to a young Jewish man, Joseph, and a tacit agreement to forget.

> He was told that I was a very nice girl, intelligent, educated, and from a fine family, but that I'd had an affair with *a goy*. 'You know,' he said to me, 'if you tell me that you're a virgin, I'll buy you the nicest Persian lamb coat.' I told him, 'you can save yourself the coat.' He said nothing more and never asked me about Jan, not then and not ever, and I respected him this. (Gottesfeld Heller, 1993:278)

Her survival requires the recreation of a stable role and identity as a wife and the re-establishment of this within the Jewish community, but this is dependent on forgetting how she was forced to step beyond the gendered and religious subjectivities and boundaries of the time. Hence her particular trauma, in terms of the conflicts, sense of loss, betrayal and shame she felt as a survivor and as a woman who survived through having a pre-marital sexual relationship with *a goy*, a Gentile, were dealt with for decades after the War by a collaborative familial discourse of silence. It was not until 1969 that she decided to voice the memories privately through therapy; even then it took two years before she felt able to mention her experiences in the War. It was to be another 22 years before her story entered our collective memory through the publication of her autobiography. The result, however, in terms of public reactions to the book, were 'letters and calls of disgust from other survivors'. Overall, she said, 'there was a lot of disapproval for these memories ... the discussion of sexual encounters during the Holocaust continues to be taboo even among open-minded and intelligent scholars.' (Gottesfeld Heller, 2000).

Stripping and reclothing

Like Gottesfeld Heller, Charlotte Arpadi, a survivor of Stutthof Concentration Camp in the northern part of German-occupied

Poland, as well as several other work camps, also felt unable to record her experiences for forty years. Although, not published, her written account, now on public record in the US Holocaust Museum archives, is illustrative of the painful struggle for expression she felt as a female survivor.

> Forty years have passed since the liberation and all this time I was reluctant to talk about the ghetto and camps. To my family I just wanted to be acknowledged as a wife and mother, not the survivor. To my friends and co-workers I wanted to be just Charlotte, without anybody's perception to be influenced by my experiences. Still, there hardly have been situations at home or at work in which memories of those years would not surface. When our son, Peter, at 18 months, had to be hospitalised I consoled myself that he was surrounded by love and care in contrast to the children in the camp. When I was teaching nursery school and for some children parting from their mothers brought tears, my thoughts turned to those who perished alone. (Arpadi, 1991:77)

What she writes of here is a sense of what Langer has called 'maternity infected with atrocity' (Langer, 1991:16). Arpadi narrativizes the way in which, although she seeks to forget her experiences as a survivor, her traumatic memories mutely force their way into her present subjectivities of wife and mother. Part of Charlotte Arpadi's humiliation and victimisation as a Jewish woman involved the stripping away and inversion of culturally and socially defined roles and expectations of femininity. At the beginning of her account, for example, she describes how on the night of 29 November 1941, the men were separated and taken away from the women who remained with their children, the sick and the elderly. In that moment, 'everyone thought that it was the men who would be liquidated.' (Arpadi, 1991:21) The expectation was that the Nazis would respect usual gender boundaries: people believed that they would murder Jewish men but would allow those perceived as caregivers and the vulnerable to survive. In fact, the situation was the reverse: the women and the vulnerable, including the elderly, children and babies, were the first to be taken to the forest and shot, while the men were taken to work camps. Miraculously, though, Charlotte survived and escaped. She describes later how, when interned in Korben work camp, stripped of the usual signifiers of femininity, the women used their tiny speck of rationed margarine as moisturiser 'to preserve still a shred of our dignity'. (Arpadi, 1991:55)

Towards the end of the War, having survived near-starvation, thirst, freezing temperatures, illness and hard labour, Charlotte was liberated only to face one night an attempted rape by a Jewish man in a shared house in Lodz. On another occasion, she was molested by Russian soldiers at night (Arpadi, 1991:64). Charlotte Arpadi's experience as a survivor thus included the shattering of usual gender boundaries and expectations, the dismantling of the cultural and social aspects of gender, as well as the experience of sexual assault and vulnerability specific to her gender. For Arpadi, although she was 'liberated', this did not include being liberated from the threat of sexual assault.

After the War, Arpadi's describes how self-rehabilitation involved reconstructing a gendered self out of particular symbols and cultural attributes of femininity, as well as particular roles and expectations of herself as a woman. She writes for example, of her delight on receiving a package from her parents that included a lipstick: 'I still can remember how a mere lipstick could have brought me such joy. I had taken another step forward normalising my life and adjusting to civilisation,' (Arpadi, 1991:70). Later she holds on firmly to her roles as 'wife' and as 'mother', but this is always experienced in painful contradiction with a self as a victim–survivor in which these were denied, disrupted and stripped.

Rena Kornreich Gelissen's (1997) remarkable story of survival, entitled *A Story of Two Sisters in Auschwitz: Rena's Promise* has both similar and different contradictions and tropes. She describes how she survived 3 years and 41 days in Auschwitz and Birkenau, promising her increasingly depressed sister Danka, in the face of daily selections for death, that if Danka were selected she would go to the gas chamber with her so that she would not die alone. The story includes elements common to many Holocaust survivors – descriptions of a horrendous journey in a cramped cattle truck with no light, air, water or sanitation facilities; being stripped, shaved, starved and used as forced labour; descriptions of the cold, the lice, the rats, disease, the beatings, and daily deaths. Also common to autobiographies by other women survivors who survived Auschwitz and Birkenau is a central narrative of the loss of a complex identity that includes traumatic memory wounds that were experienced in terms of being both Jewish and female. Her story begins with a description of life in, Tylicz, Poland, in a loving Orthodox Jewish family. 'Every few weeks Mama would take off her wig and I would shave her head, as is customary in Orthodox homes ... I dreamt of the day that I would have my head shaved as a solemn vow to my husband.' (p. 10).

One of her first memories is of her first boyfriend who was a Gentile and whom she was subsequently forbidden to see anymore by her father. He had offered to convert to Judaism in order to marry her, but she refused him on the grounds that it would devastate her parents. In November, 1939, she described how the men's holy books were burnt and their earlocks and beards cut off by the Germans (p. 24). Thus, at first, it seems as if it is only the Jewish men who will be victimised. Like Fanya Gottesfeld Heller, the village families also thought the women were safe because of the Nuremberg laws, 'any Aryan having sex with a non-Aryan could be punished by death, and many of the Jewish families thought their daughters were safe because of this concept of *Rassenschamde*, or "race disgrace"' (p. 29). However , when German soldiers tried to raid the house and rape the women inside, this belief was quickly proved erroneous. Rena Gellissen escaped to Slovakia but was later transported to Auschwitz where, for her, the literal stripping and shaving shatters her complex Orthodox Jewish woman's identity she described in the beginning.

Nevertheless, Rena Gelissen's narrative then centres on emphasising her survival through difference, particularly in the retention of her gendered difference. Unlike many other prisoners who ceased to menstruate in the camp, she describes how she continued to menstruate, even in Birkenau, where the retention of this aspect of womanhood was experienced in terms of both sexual shame and potential death: 'Will I be in the shaving line on a Sunday, embarrassed in front of the men? Will today be the day I cannot find anything to stop the flow and the SS decide to beat me to death for being unclean?' (p. 105). She is not a man since she menstruates; she, like the other women, must wear flimsy dresses, unlike the men who had uniforms with jackets and trousers (p. 134). She is also not like the girls with the 'clean, white pressed aprons'. These 'broken souls', with their 'bottomless eyes' who were the experiment victims, tortured until they died or were vegetables, 'They are no longer human beings, having long ago ceased to be girls or women' (p. 148). She is also not like the women selected for sterilisation (p. 183).

This creation, narration and preservation of the 'not-like' survivor-self is also established in relation to a mute absence in her narrative. This is expressed in terms of the absence of Jewish and non-Jewish men, from whom they were largely separated, but also in terms of an absence of the missing (murdered) mothers, and missing Jewish

mothers in particular, who suddenly, painfully and briefly burst into
the narrative:

> We arrive at Emma's kommando in the morning to find fifty middle-
> aged women going with us to work. We gape at them as if they are
> aliens from another world. It is strange to see women in their fifties;
> they usually select any women in their forties or older for the gas ... It
> is terrible to see elder women without kerchiefs on their heads and as
> bald as we are. For a moment I think how Mama would have felt if
> she'd been forced out in public without her wig or a babushka.
> (p. 164).

After being beaten by a guard for resting, she finds reason to survive by
trying to restore gendered Orthodox Jewish norms, organising kerchiefs
for the mothers. But the next morning the 'mothers' have gone. 'As hard
as we have all become, these women have touched our hearts and made
us feel again, but the wounds are deep and sore to the touch.' (p. 171).
After this, 'there's no sorority of sympathy or understanding' (p. 177).

Gelissen also narrativises a sense of survival through sustaining
some identity as a woman by establishing at various points in her story
her difference from men through the brief contacts with male prisoners, who formed the overwhelming majority in both Auschwitz and
Birkenau. An example of this is when, once transferred to the safety of
the laundry, she includes the memory of a mild flirtation with a male
prisoner, Marek, who asked her if she had ever had sex, to which she
blushed and said she was a virgin. 'We're in Auschwitz and you are
embarrassed? There is laughter in his voice ... I am also amused by this
thought. With everything we have been through, with everything we
have seen, I am still self-conscious.' In this way we are reminded of the
relational construction of gendered identity and the sense of self that
Rena described at the beginning. In her account, then, the story is told
as one in which despite everything, this was not lost entirely (p. 210).
At the same time, in the language she uses to describe herself and the
others – the term 'girl-women' is used in the camps – there is a sense of
gendered identity particular to the experience. In this way, the story
establishes both its difference from the present and its commonality:
she retains accepted forms of femininity (blushing) and ends with an
almost fairytale gendered convention in which she is rescued – not by
a knight in shining armour – but by John Gelissen, commander of the
Red Cross work team no. 10, whom she later marries (1997:266).

Complex masculinities

What we have seen in women's life-writing so far is that what is and is not articulated will, in part, be multilectically constructed in relation to, by and through social structures and ideas in a present time and place about acceptable gender roles and boundaries, as well as our ideas in the present time and place about past gender roles and values. What enters collective discourse about the past is also multilectically constructed by our present social roles and identities relating to ethnicity and religion. To relate a story of a sexual relationship between a Jew and a Gentile destabilises handed-down memories of the world at that time and challenges the bivalent paradigm that the world can be unproblematically divided and categorised on clearly defined good/bad, ethnic and religious lines. What is articulated after genocide is also constrained by the need to survive, which, for us as human beings, includes the necessity to re-establish trust and connections with others. What is silenced or articulated is dependent on the degree to which the memory threatens to support or undermine the re-establishement of gendered 'norms' and roles, as well as the social cohesion of – in this case – the post-Holocaust Jewish community. A dominant trope in women's autobiographies concerns the stripping and reclothing of gendered subjectivities. This is also evidenced in both similar and different ways in the autobiographies of male survivors.

In Elie Wiesel's (1982) *Night,* he opens his story, set in the little town of Sighet in Transylvania, not with a description of himself but with a description of another man called by the townspeople 'Moshe-the-Beadle' 'as though he had never had a surname in his life'. (p. 1) Moshe was poor, clumsy, barefoot, rarely spoke, a foreign Jew, though accepted by the established Hassidic community because he was ' a past master in the art of making himself insignificant, of seeming invisible.' (1982:1). Moshe is contrasted in the narrative to Elie's father – 'a cultured, unsentimental man' (p. 2) who is respected by the Jewish community and 'more concerned with others than with his own family' (p. 2). Elie then introduces himself – as a twelve-year-old boy, the only son, deeply religious, who weeps when he prays and who wants to learn the Zohar, the Cabbalistic books, the secrets of Jewish mysticism. In this way, the pre-Holocaust narrative establishes a remembered world of men centred on the contrasting characters of Moshe, Elie's father and Elie himself, while the women – his mother and three sisters – are voiced but muted, woven into the fabric of the background, making meals, lighting fires. The beginning of the atrocities start when Moshe, as a foreign Jew, is expelled from the village with all the other foreign Jews. He survives to return to the village, a changed man who no longer talks of God but tells stories of the mass murder he has witnessed, only to find that he is not believed: his stories are dismissed as those of a madman. When all the rest of the Jews are rounded up into the big ghetto, Moshe-the-Beadle warns them a last time before fleeing and disappearing; his presence is, from then on, felt as an absence in the narrative, a silent question that remains forever unanswered. Soon afterwards the family, along with the other Jews of Sighet, are moved to the 'little' ghetto, taking up the houses and beds of 'the absent ones '– those that had been deported three days before.

In this way, the subtext of Elie Wiesel's opening chapter suggests the rich complexities of his identity, as an Hassidic Jewish boy, configured through and between not just the contrasts of gender but also between contrasting and complex masculinities articulated by class and nationality. His identity is remembered relationally between his 'native', Jewish, publically active, unsentimental, cultured father and the 'foreign', surnameless, poor, weeping Moshe, supported by the family background of the women. In this way, Moshe's invisible, emotional, clumsy, surnameless state is recollected as prefiguring in some ways what Elie and his father later experience. As the normal societal structures are broken down, so too are the established boundaries of his father's masculinity, 'My father wept. It was the first time I had ever seen him weep. I had never imagined that he could' (Wiesel, 1982:16). In Auschwitz, Wiesel describes how the men of Sighet were stripped of their names, and pursued a strategy of not drawing attention to themselves. One man who made himself known by his masculine strength, they learnt, had to put his own father's body in the crematorium. Similarly when, prior to this, Elie Wiesel was deported along with his family, he recollects how a woman predicted the fires of Auschwitz-Birkenau. Her screams, in the crushed confines of the cattle truck, terrified everyone to the extent that she was beaten into silence by the young men in the transport. As with Moshe-the-Beadle, the narrative subtext of these earlier scenes suggests that what happened to the marginal subalterns of the community – the poor, the foreign, women – pre-figured the annihilation to come.

The world divided

Once the Jews of Sighet leave the transport on arrival at Auschwitz, the men and women are separated. It is the last time Elie Wiesel sees his mother and sisters, and after this his world becomes almost entirely male. Running throughout his account is, then, a terrible silence, a muted absence of the other half of his world, the world of women and girls of whose fate neither he nor the reader is told at that stage. The one woman configured in his memory after this is a young woman passing as an Aryan who helps him with a few words in German. His sense of self is remembered in relation to a masculinity in the camps increasingly articulated as bestial and brutal. His greatest fear, consequently, is that he will be separated from his father, but later, on the death march from Buna Labour Camp to Buchenwald, his greatest fear is that he will abandon or forsake his father. When his father becomes very ill, the dilemma, Wiesel recalls, was whether he should help his father at the cost of his own life or leave his father to die. He recalls the argument put forward by one prisoner. 'Listen to me boy. Don't forget that you're in a concentration camp. Here, every man has to fight for himself and not think of anyone else. Even of his father. Here, there are no fathers, no brothers, no friends. Everyone lives and dies for himself alone' (Wiesel, 1982:105). This is the male survivors, equivalent of Rena Kornreich Gelissen's 'no sorority of sisterhood'. Caring, filial duty is annihilated, presented as resulting in possible death, while survival is articulated in terms of the necessity to practice an extreme form of masculinity offered by the man with 'the great hairy hand on my shoulder' (p. 105).

After his father dies, Wiesel, in a state of numbness, ceases to think of his mother or his father and is transferred to the children's block with six hundred others. Just before liberation, for the first time since the beginning of the book, he refers to himself as a child again, rather than as an adult: 'We children stayed flat on the ground'. After liberation, his subjectivity shifts and he includes himself in the group of adult males.

> our first act as *free men* was to throw ourselves onto the provisions. We thought only of that. Not of revenge. Not of our families. Nothing but bread.
>
> And even when we were no longer hungry, there was still no one who thought of revenge. (Wiesel, 1982:109, my emphasis)

What Wiesel's account suggests is that liberation for him as a male survivor involves a particular set of conflicts, related to his gender as well as his identity as a Jew, which we are entreated to enter, to understand and remember. The expected role of men at the time, and to some extent today, is to protect and look after women and children. Nazi policies meant they were unable to do so. The traumatic subtext of loss, pain and guilt prevalent here stems not only from being a survivor while others have died, I would suggest, but also from being a boy-man who has survived unable to help, protect or even find out what happened to the women and the vulnerable who disappeared from his life. He is even then denied the fulfilment at liberation with the other 'free men' to seek revenge against their Nazi perpetrators, to be angry, to return the violence done to them in the manner expected of men . What Wiesel narrativises is an agonising sense of the impossibility of return to or even growth into the expectations of 'manhood'. Elie Wiesel and his fellow survivors were 'free men' and yet so driven by hunger that bread was their first priority, not revenge. After that, he repeats the trope with the 'young men went in to Weimar to get some potatoes and clothes – and to sleep with girls. But of revenge, not a sign' (p. 109).

The penultimate memory described by Wiesel is when, having eaten his fill after liberation, he becomes ill from the food and spends two weeks suspended between life and death. Placed near the very end of his chronicle of survival, the memory suggests that he was literally and psychologically sickened from being forced by Nazi-induced starvation to seek food rather than revenge. He ends the autobiography with a description of himself, not configured within a complex set of relations to others, as at the beginning of the story, but in relation to his own reflection in the mirror.

> One day I was able to get up, after gathering all my strength. I wanted to see myself in the mirror hanging on the opposite wall. I had not seen myself since the ghetto.
> From the depths of the mirror, a corpse gazed back at me.
> The look in his eyes as they stared into mine, has never left me. (p. 109).

For Wiesel, then, unlike Rena Kornreich Gelissen, for example, there is an enduring sense of alienation from his gender and from masculinity, articulated as a psychic split. But, like Fanya Gottesfeld Heller, there is also an internalisation of atrocity and death. This is not described in terms of an imagined future-gendered role as a father but is articulated as an isolation felt forever afterwards symbolised by a dead male self: 'the look in *his* eyes' staring into the eyes of an (un)gendered survivor self-'mine' and 'me'.

With Elie Wiesel's life-writing, part of the legacy he articulates and hands down to us is the contradictions and difficulties of being stripped of his complex relational identity as an Orthodox Jewish male and his attempt to recuperate an identity as a male survivor. He leaves with us in his written account a sense of struggling forever afterwards with the feelings of being suspended between worlds, in terms of his gendered identity. Wiesel at liberation is neither boy nor man in the terms offered to him in the camps and in liberation. The self that looks back from the past is dead, along with his family and village and the gendered Jewish identity that he negotiated within it.

Demolishing manhood

We see some echoes of these tropes in Primo Levi's autobiographical work, *If This is a Man* (2000). The title itself suggests the underlying uncertainty regarding what being a man means after the Holocaust. Early on in his account, having been sent by Nazis from a detention camp at Fossoli, near Modena in Italy, by transport train to a work camp at Monowitz near Auschwitz, in German-occupied Polish upper Silesia, Levi writes:

> Then for the first time we became aware that our language lacks words to express this offence, *the demolition of a man.* In a moment, with almost prophetic intuition, the reality was revealed to us: we had reached the bottom. It is not possible to sink lower than this; no human condition is more miserable than this, nor could it conceivably be so. Nothing belongs to us any more; they have taken away our clothes, our shoes, even our hair; if we speak they will not listen to us, and if they listen, they will not understand. They will even take away our name: and if we want to keep it, we will have to find in ourselves the strength to do so, to manage somehow so that behind the name something of us, of us as we were, still remains. (Levi, 2000:32 my emphasis)

One could argue that Levi uses the phrase 'the demolition of a man' generically to mean all humans. Certainly on one level it is. To demolish is to raze to the ground something that has been constructed and built over time. Levi describes being starved of food and water, shouted at in German, shaved, stripped of his documents and clothes, disinfected, reclothed in a prison uniform and tattooed with a number. The men become muted and unable to look at each other. However, as with Wiesel's *Night* there is an enduring silence that dominates the text which stems from the moment of the separation of the able-bodied men from the women, children and elderly men.

> What happened to the others, to the women, to the children, to the old then we could establish neither then nor later: the night swallowed them up, purely and simply. Today, however, we know that in the rapid and summary choice each one of us had been judged capable or not of working usefully for the Reich; we know of a convoy no more than 96 men and 29 women entered the respective camps of Monowitz-Buna and Birkenau, and that of all the others more than five hundred in number, not one was living two days later. (Levi, 2000:26).

The question of where the women went, as for Wiesel, remained unanswered for Levi and the other male prisoners. This horrific loss within the narrative again mutely reminds us that one of the central roles expected of men in Italy from where he was deported, and embedded within the expected 'norms' of different masculinities, is providing for the protection of women and children. It is not until 200 pages later in the narrative that this silence is broken with the story told by candlelight by a young woman called Olga. She relates how, out of all the 300 women, children and elderly that had disappeared that first night at the camp, all had died except for five women survivors (Levi, 2000:207). Levi's legacy to us is the reminder that genocide demolished the established conventions of being a man.

Thus, embedded in Primo Levi's memories, as with Elie Wiesel's account, is the experience of a particular kind of shame for the male survivor that stems from his reduction to a passive prisoner constantly driven by nothing but the desire for something to quell his raging hunger and thirst. He writes:

> To destroy a man is difficult, almost as difficult as to create one. It has not been easy, or quick, but you Germans have succeeded. Here we are docile under your gaze; from our side you have nothing more to fear; no acts of violence, no words of defiance, not even a look of judgement. (p. 156).

He contrasts himself, stripped of his manhood, to another form of masculinity represented by him in another man. He tells the story of how they were forced to bear witness to the murder of a man in the form of hanging because he had assisted in carrying arms into the camp in an attempted rebellion. This man: 'must have been tough. He must have been made of another metal than us.' After the man is hanged they fall upon the pot of soup and eat: 'we satisfied the daily ragings of hunger, and now we are oppressed by shame' (p. 156).

The liberated man

However, unlike Wiesel's account, Levi's return as a survivor to a sense of identity that includes gender is articulated through a different set of contradictions. As the Soviet Army drew near, the Germans abandoned his camp on 19 January 1945, but the stronger inmates, including Levi, found and lit a stove and mended the window of their hut. As a gesture of thanks, the weaker men gave them some of their bread. Levi suggests that it was 'the first human gesture that occurred among us' and significantly 'the beginning of the change by which we who had not died slowly changed from Haftlinge [prisoners] to men again' (Levi 2000, 166). To Levi, then, the return to a sense of manhood began with acts of kindness, not revenge. This relational sense of masculinity is foreshadowed by the memory of an earlier encounter with an Italian civilian worker, Lorenzo, who brought him extra rations for no reward. Levi describes this as a 'feminine' relationship (Levi 2000:125) and it was through the 'feminine' Lorenzo that 'I managed not to forget that I myself was a man' (p. 128).

Once Levi was 'liberated' by the Russians he was washed by two 'robust' Russian nurses 'to make us new men consistent with their own model' (p. 194). He quickly learnt that in their imposition of a Soviet version of manhood, his identity as a Jew was to be silenced. When he tried to tell a Polish lawyer the story of his experiences in Auschwitz, he noticed that the lawyer described him to the crowd not as an Italian Jew but as an Italian political prisoner. When he asked the lawyer why, he replied that it was to protect him because the War was not yet over. After this:

> I felt my sense of freedom, my sense of being a man among men, of being alive, like a warm tide ebb from me. I found myself suddenly old, lifeless, tired beyond human measure: the war was not over, there was always war. (p. 227).

In this way we are reminded of the fact that the fragile rebuilding of the man, Levi, as a survivor is deeply imbricated with his experiences and identity as a Jew. As the presence of women in the narrative returns this is remembered as offering renewed possibilities for the rehabilitation of his Jewishness, yet in ways that are remembered as forever after destabilised by a post-Holocaust world with its tattered boundaries of ethnicity, gender, language and nationality. He encapsulates this in his account of an encounter with two Jewish women from Russia who laughed at him when he said he too was Jewish. One woman said that he could not possibly be Jewish because he spoke Italian rather than Yiddish like them: 'In her country things were much clearer: a Jew was a Jew and a Russian was a Russian' (p. 286).

As in some accounts by women survivors, Levi suggests that for single women the war was not over either but for different reasons: he describes on several occasions the threat of sexual assault that single women faced, with a near-riot at one point as Italian men tried to prevent Russian men invading the place where the single women survivors slept. (p. 341). The event offered another opportunity on his journey from prisoner/survivor to being a survivor with a complex shifting identity. The narrative asserts that the reconstruction of the aspect of masculinity the Nazis destroyed was in part reconstructed for Levi through a re-identification with himself as an Italian (and non-identification of himself as a Soviet citizen or a Russian) in which he helps fulfil a role protecting women (of all nationalities) from harm. This sense of rehabilitated identity is fragile, however, and is retained only through the psychological rejection of survivors worse off than himself. This is encapsulated in the story of Flora, who had provided forced sexual services in the camp. Levi describes how, after liberation, he feels changed but she was trapped by her victimisation and he therefore could not 'identify' himself to her as a fellow survivor who knew her (p. 335). What Levi thus relates is restoration through the re-establishment of a complex set of social relations and subjectivities constructed by defining himself through by processes of identification and non-identification in which gender was a significant part.

When Primo Levi describes the final journey home to Italy after a circuitous journey by train east and back again via several other countries, the 'single women' were kept separate from the men and couples in their own trucks for their safety. Only once do we glimpse a harmonious memory of young men and women happily working together in the form of young Jews who were setting out for Israel and confidently attached their hired truck to the back of the train. When Levi describes crossing the border and entering US army occupied European territory for the first time, the women and men – in a reversal of the German's initial separation of the sexes – are, to Levi's surprise, kept together in the same room, this time to be deloused with DDT. He ends the chapter with an almost comic return to chivalry, with a knockabout punch-up from one husband who refuses to let his wife be touched by an American in the process of being deloused with DDT: 'Woe betide anyone who touched his woman. After a few minutes of silent and gentlemanly combat, the officer fell to the ground with a bleeding nose; the girl, shaken and pale, was dusted all over according to the regulations'. (p. 374).

Conclusion: the genocidal jigsaw

In her work on narrativisation (life course) and fictionalisation (self as character) in women's autobiographies, Marie-Francoise Chanfrault-Duchet argues that gender identity is an important constituent of the woman's life-story:

> It intervenes in the main structures of the narrative: the life-course, the key patterns and the anecdotes, and, finally, the closed meaning system (shaped by the thematic configuration and the connotation system), as part of the identity conveyed and taken up by the subject, in reference to accepted models of female identity. (Chanfrault-Duchet, 2000:74).

What we see in terms of autobiographies of Holocaust survivors is that gender, too, is an important constituent in Jewish people's narrativisation of events and in the self as character. This is true for both men's and women's accounts. The articulation of their memories of the events through the cultural form of autobiography provides us with an important cultural legacy in understanding gender and genocide. When we look at both men's and women's accounts alongside each other (rather than separately, neglecting one gender for the other) we see that they are part of the same shattered and shattering gendered genocidal jigsaw: the rape of a woman also involves the unspeakable shame of her husband forced to watch; the murder of women and children leaves a legacy of absence for the men selected to work. Further, although there are differences in the articulation and reconstruction of the gender for survivors, there are also elements that bridge their accounts. In both men's and women's accounts, for example, much of the narrative centres on coping with terrible hunger. Levi writes, 'The Lager camp is hunger, we ourselves are hunger, living hunger.' Out of this hunger in both men's and women's accounts there are recollections of 'fantasy cooking' in which recipes were told and retold. The women of Terezin, having access to paper, provided us with a legacy of their recipes. As Cara de Silva (1996) notes, some are muddled and incomplete, with ingredients missed out or steps inverted (p. xii). This she suggests is testament to illness, disorientation, an unsettling interruption, or the discovery that a contributor's name was on a transport list. She also points out that while one might assume more women than men did this 'fantasy cooking' since on the whole they would have been responsible for cooking back home, there is at least one example of a recipe book created by men in the Second World War – by prisoners of war in a Japanese camp (p. xi). Lack of writing materials at camps such as Auschwitz accounts for there being no written record from the time of fantasy cooking (Marguilies cited by De Silva, 1996 xxix) but even then 'fantasy cooking' certainly took place as Levi's account demonstrates: 'Bela is describing his Hungarian countryside and the fields of maize and a recipe to make meat-pies with corn-cobs and lard and spices' (Levi, 2000:80).

Yet, it is not simply a recipe that Bela is remembered as describing, but a recipe out of, and symbolising attachment to, a particular country and place – his home in Hungary. Likewise, the recipes of the women of Terezin, suggest that they were written mostly by Jews of Bohemia and Moravia (De Silva, 1996:xli). The religious split in town ran straight through the populace's Sunday menu: the Jews had Wiener Schnitzel, the Gentiles has roast pork with sauerkraut and dumplings (Wechsberg, 1966:14). With this we are reminded that through the commonality of hunger sprang imagined and remembered meals in which men and women of all backgrounds tried to hold on to a fragile fragment of their pre-Holocaust complex identities. This points to the fact that there are important liminal points in the survival identities of men and women: one way of dealing with the demolition of men and women to a hunger beyond our imagining, was to elicit the retention of some memory of identity through recipes and meals.

Complex contradictions of gender and ethnicity intervene into the articulation of individual survivors life-writings, as well as their re-articulation or dis-articulation of our collective memories. The contradictions are embedded in the stories handed down to us by Jewish men and women who were victimised by the Nazis and is also evidenced in the stories they articulate concerning their survival and recuperation. This analysis of a selection of autobiographies also suggests that while there were some common gendered experiences, their articulation in life-writing is polyvocal: gendered contradictions were negotiated differently for each survivor (and each of the victims). There were also commonalties that crossed gender boundaries. It is, I would suggest, through an exploration of the ways in which these aspects of identity and their various contradictions are articulated in personal memories of survivors that we will be enabled to understand with more depth 'the communal wound' of the Holocaust.

What I have not addressed here, however, is how gender in the autobiographies of victims of other social groups and ethnicities is represented, as well as gender in the memories of perpetrators, bystanders and rescuers. We should be mindful that these too form part of the gendered jigsaw of socially inherited memories of the Holocaust.[3] It is, I would suggest, through being attentive to the complexities of people's different experiences of genocide and the different ways in which they write their stories that we, as men and women, begin to understand and become reconciled to the depth of who and what has been, forever, lost to us, what is being remembered, and why.

Finally, it is important to recognise that being attentive to these complexities within autobiography and history in isolation is not enough: the written word is better understood as a part of a chain of media involved in the construction and configuration of socially inherited memories. Autobiography and historical texts are in continual re-articulation with other cultural forms through which the past is also handed down. Memories of the Holocaust are inherited through a complex constellation of cultural mediations that include a range of other mass media, including visual, sound and memorial landscapes. In the next chapter, I address how we can begin to understand the articulation of gender and memory within the medium of film.

4

Moving Memories: Propaganda, Documentary and Holocaust Feature Films

'And if Moses appeared to see a film made about his life – he'd also say "but that's not me".

(Frank Reiss, survivor of Theresienstadt, 2001)

Film and memory

Perhaps it is no accident that the word 'usher' – which nowadays we associate with the person who shows us our seats in the cinema – has its etymological roots in the phrase 'the keeper of the door to the bones'.[1] Though the practice of gathering in the darkness of the tomb of our ancestors around their bones to listen to genealogies is less common,[2] in late capitalist mass-mediated cultures people gather together in the dark cave of the cinema to watch on the flickering screen, among other stories, the filmed memories of various pasts. This chapter explores gender and the making and configuration of socially inherited memories in the medium of film. I look at how gender is articulated in propaganda film, liberation footage, documentary and feature films about the Holocaust.[3]

Filmed 'memories', according to a national survey in the United States on popular sources and uses of the past by Americans, now form an important part of how we learn about history: Eighty per cent of respondents said they had recently watched movies or television programmes about the past, in comparison with 53 per cent who said they had read a book about the past (Rosenweig and Thelen, 1999:15–16). Within the socially inherited memories of young people who took part in the focus groups and interviews I conducted in the US, Britain and Poland between 1998 and 2001, in all cases at least one feature film, or in some cases several feature films and unspecified documentary films, were recalled as raising awareness of or contributing to an individual's already established historical and cultural understanding of the Holocaust. Film was to said to make events 'more real' or in some way to bring home the facts in the history books. As one respondent put it: 'Reading about it in text books didn't really er show you what it was about. It was written in, you know, text book form. It was very dry and boring, but when I saw the pictures or films, that really made it seem more real (Jane, aged 22, focus group, Washington DC, April 1999).

Another American student said that films 'showed what happened' in terms of the atrocities of the camps, in contrast to history books that seemed too abstract and general:

> [W]e were learning about the history of World War Two, you know, the history of why it happened and how Hitler approached to um get his goal to um be in power and that was one of the ways to um eliminate Jews. I guess at that point the teacher was like, 'you know let's see this movie cos its – it shows what happened', like really what happened, how um people was in a concentration camps, I mean what they did to the Jews and yeah, 'cos in the history text book they just talk about how Hitler wanted to, you know, take over the world and stuff'. (Cindy, aged 16, focus group, New York, April 1999)

The role of film in raising post-Holocaust awareness of the events is not surprising given that the number of moving images related to and about the Holocaust, and our access to these has increased enormously with the diversification of broadcasting and the advent of satellite and cable television resulting in the development of specialized channels, including those for history. Janice Hadlow from Channel Four Television in the UK has estimated that on any evening in the UK it is now possible to see at least one programme related to the Second World War and the Holocaust (Hadlow, 2001). Although, as the previous chapter shows, the written word is certainly one of the most important media for passing on to subsequent generations the events of the Holocaust, film and television programmes also figure strongly in providing translations and versions of past events.

Particular films have had almost universal appeal and have changed the articulation of the memory of the Holocaust. NBC's TV drama *Holocaust* gripped viewers in the US and was subsequently shown in many European countries: broadcast for the first time in 1978 in the United States and subsequently many countries elsewhere, including West Germany in January 1979, it reached an estimated total of 220 million people (Insdorf, 1989:4). Stephen Spielberg's 1993 *Schindler's List* was watched by one-quarter of the inhabitants of the UK. Since then at least twenty films that deal directly with the Holocaust have been released in the US alone, with the influence of *Schindler's List*, according to one critic, evidenced by these recent films emphases on stories of survival (Sklar, 2000:11). According to Trude Levi, a survivor of Auschwitz and Holocaust educator in the UK, it also opened the doors of schools and universities to survivors wanting to talk about their experiences and personal memories of the events in an effort to help educate young people (Levi, 2001). *Schindler's List* also figured highly in young people's memories, and it is this film, in the final section of this chapter on feature film, that I analyse in more detail. First, though, I consider the theoretical and critical approaches taken by a range of critics and scholars to films and the Holocaust. I then look at some examples of Nazi propaganda films: film as witness of the atrocities, taken by the Allied forces at the end of the War, as well as later documentary films.

Critics and Holocaust films

Film and television programmes about the Holocaust are generally perceived by critics as more controversial and problematic in relation to history and memory than written autobiographical accounts. Perhaps in part, this is because of the special place given to books and the word rather than the visual in Jewish culture – but it is also, I would suggest, because there is a greater wariness of the commercial imperatives underlying feature films especially. Some survivors and writers on the Holocaust, notably Elie Wiesel, have suggested that some films seem 'an outrage to the dead' (Wiesel, 1989:xii). Critics have suggested that feature films in particular universalise and vulgarise the events (Doneson, 1987:119); that they resort to moral simplification (Langer, 1995:166); and that they trivialise and romanticise what took place (Indsdorf, 1989:4).

At the same time, film and television are recognised by many as major forms through which Holocaust history enters collective memory: Doneson (1987) argues that in the US, before the Holocaust became a properly taught subject in schools, film was a key part of how people learned about the events (p. 8). Likewise, Andreas Huyssen argues that many of the post-Holocaust generation find out about the events initially through the media of film and television (Huyssen,

1995:256). Jeffrey Shandler's (1999) study, *While America Watches: Televising the Holocaust* (p. xvi) argues that the viewing of programmes about the Holocaust on television has pulled the subject into the everyday thoughts and feelings of millions of viewers; it is the fact that we are able to view it at home, amid the domestic family environment, that makes this possible. Responses to controversial feature films that have used comedy or farce include the recognition that they may be providing an important memory of the events for the younger generation, as suggested by the Director of the Anti-Defamation League in his endorsement of the controversial comedy, *Life is Beautiful* (1999):

> It is clearly necessary to be very careful how one approaches this sacred subject. *Life is Beautiful* does just that by employing comedy in a very careful and instructive way. Its success in Italy and Cannes, and undoubtedly in the United States, may well pave the way for the next generation's effort to keep the memory alive. (Abraham H. Foxman, National Director of the Anti-Defamation League and a Holocaust survivor, www.adl.org/opinion/ film-fable.html 29 October 1999)

It should be stressed, however, that it is difficult to generalize, since the scope and variety of films and television programmes related to the Holocaust are huge. Annette Insdorf's filmography in *Indelible Shadows: Film and the Holocaust* (1989) includes 174 fiction films and 110 documentaries with Holocaust-related themes produced in the English language by the late 1980s (Indsdorf, 1989:267–76). The Imperial War Museum in the UK, in a conference on the subject in 2001, included Nazi-made films for propaganda; films as a form of witnessing the liberation of the camps made by the Soviet Army and Allied Army film crews; later film documentaries, including Claude Lanzmann's (1985) *Shoah* and documentary programmes for television such as Michael Darlow's (1975) *Genocide,* as well as the dramatized accounts of the events as feature films and television series. Films have been produced in many different languages, and in a variety of styles and genres, ranging from blockbuster high-budget Hollywood films to small projects shot with hand-held video cameras. I look at the articulation of gender in a small selection of films from a range of genres.

Shooting obscenity

Some of the film footage that we inherit related to the Holocaust that has been used and reused within later documentary and feature films was produced during the time that the events themselves took place, by the perpetrators themselves, and within the context of Nazi cultural policies that were gendered as well as 'raced' (Reading, 1999). As Jewish people were removed from the cultural sphere in Germany as early as 22 September 1933 (Goldhagen, 1997:137) they were at the same time assaulted through a barrage of antisemitic propaganda that depicted Jewish people and Slavs as genderless subhumans threatening the continuance of the Aryan 'race'. One headline screamed, in August 1938, 'Pregnant Sudenten German Mother pushed off bicycle by Czech subhuman in Ostrava' (Bielenberg, 1984:36). In the films produced for propaganda purposes, German women such as Leni Riefenstahl were active producers making films such as *Triumph of the Will* (1935) with its discourse of nationalism articulated through an emphasis on the power of masculinity and male comradeship (Taylor, 1979:182).

Screening policies in Nazi Germany in relation to film and TV were based on the idea of a vulnerable Aryan female in need of state protection. One of the most insidious of Nazi propaganda films, *The Wandering Jew* (Fritz Hippler, 1940), had billposters that ordered German women to view a special version of the film from which the final bloody slaughterhouse scene had been cut:

> Since additional original material of Jewish animal slaughters will be shown at the 6 pm performance those of a sensitive disposition are recommended to see the 4 o'clock performance. Likewise, women will only be admitted to the 4 o'clock performance. (Cited in Taylor, 1979:203)

In Nazi propaganda, while Aryan women were treated as the vulnerable cell-bearers of the next generation of Aryans, Jewish people were stripped of the cultural scaffolding of gender (Reading, 1999). Popularized film stereotypes of Jewish people almost always were associated with Jewish men, rather than Jewish women, as in *Jud Suss* (1940, Veit Harlan) a Nazi propaganda feature film, ranked the sixth most popular film in Nazi Germany (Tegal, 2001).

The all-male SS film crews shot for propaganda purposes images of 'Jewish life' in the Nazi-created ghettos to record the conditions in which people lived, neglecting to say that the squalor was in fact Nazi induced. Thus footage from the Lodz (Litzmannstadt) ghetto taken in 1939 was used to portray Jews as overcrowded, unhygienic and dirty in Fritz Hippler's *The Wandering Jew* (1940) a film purporting to be a documentary (Taylor, 1979:191). The film was shown in the occupied territories, including the German-occupied city of Lodz, in 1942 (Charman, 2001). Gendered aspects of Jewish life were recorded for propaganda purposes to show Jewish people in a negative light: *The Chronicles Of The Lodz Ghetto*, written by people in the ghetto at the time, describes how, between 8 and 10 June 1942, in Hospital No. 1, Moylim (Circumcisers) were compelled under orders to perform circumcisions on baby boys while being filmed by Nazi film crews (Dobroszycki, 1984:203).

While such films were used to perpetuate antisemitism in Germany and its subsequent occupied territories, the act of filming was also employed as a form of humiliation of those people targeted by the Nazis. Whereas documentary film is often viewed as facilitating the public sphere or public good, in Nazi Germany film crews intimidated their subjects as part of Nazi policy. SS officers often carried their own photographic equipment to record still images of their activities. Images of Jewish men being symbolically stripped of their earlocks and beards by Nazi soldiers in Police Battalion 101 in Poland were photographed by officers and their images displayed afterwords so that others could order copies (Goldhagen, 1997:245–6). Likewise, we have handed down to us images of Jewish women from the Mizoc ghetto stripped naked, with a pregnant woman running to join the huddle waiting to be executed because a Nazi officer from the Einsatzkommandos captured it in film (Goldhagen, 1997:154). Men and women were effectively captured and shot twice: imprisoned in ghettos and camps and captured in photographs and movie films; people were shot at from the barrel of a gun while being shot by a film camera. Within these prosthetics of Nazi atrocity are embedded gendered experiences that arise from the particular combination of the event itself and the act of filming by male SS film crews. These are important to recognize as part of our understanding of the gendered dimensions of genocide and its memory and mediation. Stripped naked, both men and women are vulnerable, yet for women (as discussed in Chapter 2) there was the underlying real experience and /or threat of sexual assault. The camera itself in this context becomes part of this violation of women's bodies. To be captured as a woman running naked while pregnant in front of the gaze of a cameraman is qualitatively different from running naked as a man. Likewise, embedded in the Lodz ghetto film shot of a Moylim performing circumcisions of boys is the Nazi male violation of a part of Jewish men and boys experience (see Dobroszycski, 1984:203). The Nazis were also keen to film the pain and torture of their victims, capturing on celluloid 'surgeries, castrations, induced infections and diseases, wounding and maiming, eventual evisceration and decapitation. (Dworkin, 2000:161). There is something obscene and pornographic about filming private acts of human beings without their consent or in filming human beings being humiliated and degraded before being murdered. In some cases, according to Andrea Dworkin, the Nazis film crews forced Jewish men at gun point to sexually assault children (Dworkin, 2000:163).[4]

Even when what is asked of people or what is being filmed seems quite ordinary, what is on celluloid is perverse once we understand the film in terms of the broader context of its production and history. For example, a short film Der Fuhrer Schenkt Den Juden Eine Stadt (*The Fuhrer Gives a City to the Jews*) (1944) was shot in the Theresienstadt ghetto to convince the outside world of the positive conditions and facilities provided by Germany for the Jews. Survivor of the ghetto, Zenka Ehrlich (2001) has described how the film was made after a massive 'beautification programme' in the camp just after a Red Cross visit in June 1944 for which fake cultural and health facilities were set up and overcrowding in the barracks and living quarters was dealt with by the deportation of 7000 people to eastern death camps. The film includes footage of the 'ordinary lives' of men and women: men making and mending shoes; women chatting, knitting and laughing between the bunks in the barracks, and a family sitting down for meal. Yet, the 'family' recorded with its 'mother, father and children', had never met each other until the moment of filming (Becker, 2001). Zenka Ehrlich, who was filmed by a Nazi film crew at the camp at Theresienstadt swimming across a river in order to demonstrate that Jewish people were pursuing ordinary recreational pursuits and had time for leisure, said people performed 'their roles' under threat of being sent to the east (Ehrlich, 2001).[5] Many people afterwards were sent to their deaths anyway (Yad Vashem, 2001). We witness the filmed footage of the ordinary gossip between women; women knitting on their beds and looking after babies and children, or boys and men working in the shoe factory, knowing that the enactment of 'normality', in part gendered, was the only currency the people had left to trade for their lives. Not only is the record on celluloid the only one we have of the majority of these people, but the Nazi sham disarticulated people's identities and gender in ways that were typical of the genocide. Embedded in the coerced act of motherhood on film, for example, is the absence of the woman's life and family prior to her deportation to Theriesienstadt, as well as the enduring absence of her in death. The film invokes questions that cannot be easily answered: we do not know if the woman in 'the family' really was a mother or what happened to her real children. The normal dialogical possibilities collapse because we know that the people were soon to be murdered.

The production of such propaganda films was also within a context in which victims and bystanders were prevented from filming or recording their own images. The photographer Karl Lutz, for example, noted in his diary that he had his camera confiscated in Hungary when he tried to capture a group of Arrow-Cross thugs beating up a woman on the street. He had a revolver pointed at him and his camera and film confiscated (Yad Vashem Archives 01/3475).

Witnessing murder

Other filmed material handed down to us and forming part of our moving cultural memories is that obtained at 'liberation' at the end of the war and in the weeks of its aftermath, filmed by the Soviet Army in the liberation of the camps in Eastern Europe and by the US Signal Corps and the British Army Films and Photographic Unit in the liberation of the western camps. The most well known of these – the *Chronicle of the Liberation of Auschwitz* (1945), filmed by four cameramen of the Soviet Army several weeks after liberation (Swiebocka 1995:44) is shown to visitors, in the cinema, in the museum at the death camp at Auschwitz and also forms part of the footage on display in the US Holocaust Museum. At the time, though, this was not seen as credible footage by the Western Allies: according to Christian Delage, 'the Americans had to see what their own camera-men shot before they believed Soviet films taken at Auschwitz' (Delage 2001). In the aftermath of the War, the British Army Films and Photographic Unit and the US Signal Corps subsequently filmed the liberation of Western camps, such as Belsen, in February and March 1945. As with Nazi film crews, the Allied film crews were all men. This was certainly not untypical generally for film production of the time: while women had entered areas of journalism and photography in the Soviet Union, Europe and the US they were still to enter the profes-sions of film and documentary making as documentary cameramen and directors. Movie cameras were cumbersome and heavy, and film crews were considered by the British and the Americans as part of front-line troops in which women were not included. Women were present, however, as photographers and journalists of the time: Margaret Bourke-White accompanied US forces into the camps at Erla and Buchenwald, and Lee Miller was one of the first people into Dachau on an assignment for *Vogue* (see Zelizer, 1998:88–9). Reporters Marguerite Higgins, Martha Gelhorn and Iris Carpenter were also present at the liberation of the camps. Women were present as victims and survivors, as witnesses and as guards; women were also present in the liberating forces, as nurses and humanitarian workers, in relief organisations in camps such as Belsen (Gonin, IWM, File 85/38/1; Elvidge, IWM 89/10/1; Rudman, IWM 94/51/1).

Yet despite this, Barbie Zelizer (2001) notes that women are not present in the same way in the photographic record of events: in still images they were either over-gendered (shown with traditional domestic and maternal markers) or gender was absent, with women 'depicted in the atrocity photos in ways that neutralized their gender' (p. 256). With moving images, however, the articulation of gender in relation to atrocity in some films taken by the liberating forces is more complex, partly because of the film as medium and partly because of contradictions of the genre: witness films are documentaries, and in this respect are seen to have a special relationship to the real, to provide in some way a referential record (Corner, 1996:10). Yet at the same time, witness films were shot with particular government and army objectives as part of the defeat of the enemy. A good example of this is in the film produced by Sidney Bernstein, *Memory of the Camps*, shot by British army film crews in 1945 and assembled in 1946. Five of the six original reels survived and were kept unseen for decades in the Imperial War Museum archive in London. An edited version of the film was transmitted on the UK's Channel Four News on 20 December 1983, primarily as a 'lost' Alfred Hitchcock film since he oversaw the original editing and assembly of the film. The original idea for the film, however, came from the psychological warfare division of SHAEF (Supreme HQ Allied Expeditionary Force) and was intended as an Anglo-American project for German audiences to show them the horrors of Nazism carried out in their name. However, the US withdrew from the project on July 9th, 1945, and made their own film *Die Todesmuhlen* released in the US zone of Germany in January 1946. According to one source, the British film *Memory of the Camps*[6] was never released because of the difficulties within Germany in the first nine months of liberation: the British were anxious that such a film was not appropriate in post-war conditions in which many Germans were homeless and starving as a result of allied bombing (Sussex, 1984:93).

The film opens with cheering crowds and a speech by Hitler. It cuts then to scenes of tranquil farms and orchards around Bergen-Belsen. We see scenes from the camp at Belsen at the time of liberation, then scenes at other camps, including Dachau, Buchenwald, Ebensee, Mauthausen and Therla, intercut with a close-up shot of a map showing the location of the various camps. The script for the original version shows that it also included scenes from Auschwitz shot by Russian cameramen, but this was the sixth reel that was lost (Concentration Camp Film, IWM. A70. 515/1–5). Women are most present at the beginning in the footage of the liberation of Belsen. Here, they are shown, in keeping with Zelizer's analysis of still images of liberation, predominantly in the resumption of domestic roles – cooking, washing, tending children. They are also shown as anonymous corpses, as perpetrators of atrocity (camp guards) and witnesses (German inhabitants). Men are predominantly the uni-formed liberators and the foreign witnesses in this section. The footage is anchored throughout with a voiceover by Trevor Howard.

However, the film also renders some complex and startling images of the camps in which gender is configured in ways that contradict the predominant images that came to be handed down. For example, prior to corpses being pushed into pits with bulldozers, for several days the British army organized the ex-SS and Nazi women guards to move corpses themselves, by hand. Women ex-prisoners are shown in the film shouting and screaming at their previous torturers, shaking their fists and weeping as the corpses are dragged past. The images of naked corpses being dragged by ex-guards are far from genderless. In Belsen, the majority of corpses are clearly female, their breasts sagging, their long hair dragging on the ground. In another scene we see female ex-prisoners washing. The camera shows their bodies, quite beautiful, amid the devastation, and the women smiling. The next shot shows a woman dressing, followed by a man shaving and a woman with curlers in her hair. We also see women as active participants in humanitarian roles: one scene shows a woman ambulance driver setting off with some patients. The sequence ends with the more well-known image of the liberation of Belsen (footage shown in the US Holocaust Museum, for example) with a mass of corpses being bulldozed into pits and the huts set on fire to prevent the further spread of typhus.

The rest of *Memory of the Camps* is more familiar in its rendering of gender and atrocity. Footage of Dachau shows uniformed male prisoners and men peering at the camera from out of their three-tiered bunks. We see images of a gas chamber, shots of victims' belongings in the clothing depots. In Ebensee the images are of starving, naked, shaven-headed men displayed for the camera. The film, overall, also predominantly stresses how traditional gender roles were kept intact. For example, in shots of the hospital set up near Bergen Belsen we see nurses helping child survivors to eat. The narrator says: 'most of them had been saved by the women inmates who had given them their food.' While undoubtedly this did happen, testimonies show that what women also experienced was being unable to save their children or to maintain their usual role as mothers and nurturers (Nitzan, 1998:117; Small, 1998:88–9).[7] The one aspect that we see, briefly, in the sequences after Belsen, and which disrupts the narrative is film of the 'brothel' at Dachau where, through a wicker fence we glimpse, as if they are virtually untouchable, the faces of women raped as sex slaves inside. As we see a close-up of a young girl smiling in what appears to be relief at her liberation, the narrator says: 'as the women died they were replaced with women from the women's camp at Ravensbruck'. As in Primo Levi's encounter with the ex-prisoner from Auschwitz who had been used as a sexual slave (see Chapter 3), the film goes no further in its articulation of this aspect of the Holocaust. No footage is included of Ravensbruck women's camp. We see no more of the women who were used in the 'brothel'. The film archive at the Imperial War Museum has no holdings of any film taken by the liberating forces at Ravensbruck Women's Camp. Although, of course, this is not conclusive that none was shot, it is significant that none is easily available to public memory, particularly as there is footage of all male camps.[8]

What is also significant about *Memory of the Camps* is that the Jewish identity of prisoners is rarely mentioned. The narrator stresses the variety of nationalities present in the camps. At Dachau the narrator declares: 'Here were 32,000 men of every European nationality' (Commentary and Shot List, IWM. A70. 515/1–5). Again, during film of the corpses in pits at Bergen-Belsen, for example, the voiceover states, 'We will never know who they were – whether they were Catholics, Lutherans or Jews.' What is notable here is that there is a difference between the narration anchoring the visual images of the film and the details of gender and ethnicity which were included in the original written *Secret Caption Sheets* recorded by army personnel and held in the Imperial War Museum archives. The *Secret Caption Sheet* for the Army Film and Photographic Section's shots of Belsen includes the comment: 'The inmates called by the Germans "Political Prisoners", were of all religions and countries, *mostly Jews*, whose only crime lay in the fact that *they were Jews'* (*Secret Caption Sheets*, A700/300–700/312: IWM. p. 31, my emphasis). The caption sheet for the same day notes that, before liberation, while it was mostly male prisoners who were responsible for burying the dead, when the men 'collapsed exhausted, the work was carried on by young girls and women'. (*Secret Caption Sheets*, A700/300–700/312. IWM. P.31). Particular images have also not been handed down to us for technical reasons. The commentary from the *Secret Caption Sheets* for Sandbostel camp, 14 May 1945, states:

> It is impossible to shoot the many interesting scenes in the impro-vised hospital without additional lighting. The same applies to the interior scenes of great interest in the camp itself. The human laundry (where German female labour is used to wash the internees' before they are taken to hospital), the interior of internees huts being cleaned by women, the cleaned out cells and the kitchens, to mention a few possibilities. (*Secret Caption Sheet* 2716. A700/334/1. 14.4.1945)

Particular scenes were also censored for political reasons: The Supreme Headquarters Allied Expeditionary Force – Rear also removed footage in which ex-prisoners attacked their former guards.[9]

Memory of the Camps raises important questions about the differing capacities of still and moving images taken by the liberating armies to witness atrocity in ways that allows for the gendered complexities of genocide and for the specific identities of its victims, perpetrators and witnesses. It also raises the question of why the film was left unseen for so long. Perhaps in part is it because in *Memory of the Camps* we *do* see the gender of the corpses (including those who are clearly female) and we do see gender articulated in more various ways, and because of this it was thought to be too controversial to be shown? A corpse being dragged by her hair, her breasts scraping on the ground, retains even in death her humanity in a way that a pile of jumbled corpses being bull-dozed does not: she could be our mother, our sister. An anonymous jumble of corpses, in contrast, articulates atrocity while providing a sense of distance between ourselves and the victims in a way that the gendered image does not. As Luc Boltanski(1999), in *Distant Suffering,* explores, lack of detail and particularity allows for detachment by the spectator even from real suffering and atrocity (p. 15, 32). *Memory of the Camps* also indicates how our inherited memories of genocide are wrought with silences and contradictions as a result of the context of production: what was articulated in writing – in documents – in the words of the cameramen (as witnesses) did not always find its way into the film itself. Where particularly difficult gendered aspects of atrocities were included (such as the 'brothel' at Belsen) they are quickly retreated from to show other (now more familiar) images of atrocity of starving male survivors. After the Nazis genocide, I would suggest, visual legacies that were reminders of the differences of people's experience were muted in the interests of re-establishing social cohesion between nations, ethnic groups, and men and women.

Realizing attrocities

Later documentaries about the Holocaust vary enormously, from Yorkshire Television's depiction of a survivor's return to Auschwitz with her son in *Kitty: Return to Auschwitz* (1989) to Claude Lanzman's nine-hour epic *Shoah* (1985). As with witness documentaries, and unlike feature films, later documentaries have embedded within them what John Corner (1996) describes as a claim that a special relationship to 'the real' is in some way being achieved. Unlike witness films, however, later documentaries are not shot from the position of the liberating armies. Perhaps because of this, unlike fictionalised or dramatised accounts in feature films, reactions to the use of documentary film to realize memories of the atrocities are generally positive. James Young (1988), for example, in *Writing and Rewriting the Holocaust: Narrative and the Consequences of Interpretation* addresses how documentary can provide an appropriate language for expressing experiences of the Holocaust. With victims and survivors speaking a range of languages, in *Shoah,* he points out, questions are asked by Lanzmann in French, translated into Polish, Yiddish or Hebrew and retranslated back into French, with English subtitles. 'It is almost as if no single language were finally adequate to the task. At least part of the text here is both this repetition and seeming reformulation of events in language, as well as the events apparent flight from language' (Young, 1988:161). Young adds that, whereas with testimonies in print silence could only be expressed as a blank page, in Lanzmann's *Shoah* silences are accompanied by the visual image of the person who is silent and unable to find the appropriate words. According to Simone de Beauvoir (1985), it is the capacity of *Shoah* to convey 'the unspeakable through people's expressions' that gives it such value in handing down memories of the events (p. iii). Young also points out that filmed testimonies restore the humanity of Jewish people: we see them in colour in their family and home environments, which is very different from the reduction of Jewish people to Nazi-shot black-and-white photographs of hollow-eyed victims (Young, 1988:168).

Yet, Holocaust documentaries are constructs: like all documentaries, they are a mixture of both artifice and evidence (Corner, 1996:2). Their production context, the kind of modalities used, who and how people are privileged in voice and images is still problematic and will articulate certain aspects of memory while silencing or marginalising others. Documentaries as texts are also constructed in ways that are gendered (see Waldman and Walker, 1999). At the same time, Holocaust documentaries are in a variety of ways constructed within the particular context of 'national' memory of the events. One of the most well known documentaries, the first French film about the camps, Nuit et Brouillard (*Night and Fog*), directed by Alain Renais in 1955, screened in Britain in February 1960 and later rebroadcast in 1990 on all French television channels following a series of desecrations of Jewish cemeteries, is fraught with controversy because of this. The film juxtaposes images of a camp in the 1950s with original photographs and film from the liberation. Its focus is on German repression, resistance and deportation of prisoners but in non-ethnic terms. It includes little mention of the antisemitic elements of the Vichy regime. Following the historical trend in France (and other countries) of the time in which the genocide of the Jews was not at the heart of narratives of the Holocaust, the specific extermination policy against the Jews was not really included (Delage, 2001). Neither is there any mention of the annihilation of Europe's Sinti and Romany people. Yet, without this dimension, the history of the Holocaust makes little sense. One part of the voiceover declares: 'With these new cities, the Nazis can win the war. But they lose it. No coal for the ovens, no food for people. Bodies litter the camp' (*Nuit et Broulliard*, 1955).

Mass slaughter is explained as the outcome of the Nazis pursuance of economic domination. This aspect of the film has made some critics and film-makers uncomfortable (Smith, 2001). What does not seem to trouble critics, though, is the film's gendered disjunctures. In the first sequences of the film, virtually all the shots are of men; deportees are referred to by the voiceover as him/he; Kapo's are invariably referred to as he; in a section on medical experiments there is no mention of the forced sterilization of women, although the castration of men is discussed. Then, halfway through the film, there is a notable shift: it begins with close-ups of the identity cards in which we are told 'men and women of 22 nations' died. This is shortly followed by photographs of Nazi families, including their wives: 'nearby the commandant's house, where his wife keeps house and entertains – its like any other garrison to her'. The narrative then includes specific gender experiences such as the use of women as sexual slaves in the Nazi-controlled brothels. Prisoners and deportees are then refered to as men and women, and the film includes photographs of naked women victims. A key moment in the film is the inclusion of shots of hair, taken from liberation footage of Auschwitz: ie the images are anchored clearly, with the narrator telling us, as we see long hair and plaits, that this was women's hair. It is difficult to know the reason behind the shift of discourse in the film from one of the gendered exclusion of women to their inclusion later in the film. The shift is evident in both the voiceover and in the choice of images.

In Claude Lanzmann's *Shoah*, however, there is no such shift: women are consistently absent. The predominant emphasis is on men as survivors, as perpetrators, as witnesses and as bystanders. This aspect of the documentary has not gone unnoticed by both survivors and critics. As Pascal noted in *Jewish Quarterly:*

> I remember sitting in the National Film Theatre when Claude Lanzmann first presented Shoah in Britain at the Jewish Film Festival. At the end of the nine-hour film, a woman in her 70s with a German accent asked Monsieur Lanzmann why no women were present in his film. He answered defiantly and somewhat defensively that his interest was in a particular group of men, but this woman, like the other women in the cinema, was not satisfied. (Pascal, 1998:72)

Undoubtedly, *Shoah* is an extraordinarily valuable film and it is a monumental achievement, but because of this its status as one of the key documentaries about the Holocaust means that its gendered legacy is all the more important to explore. The film focuses on the detailed process of killing and disposing of the bodies of Jewish people at death camps in Poland and on those who participated in and were witnesses to this process. In this respect Lanzmann is right: the people forcibly involved – in the shaving of people's hair, in the digging up of earlier massacre victims shoved hastily into pits, in the pushing of the gassed bodies into the ovens and the piling of corpses on to the pyres – were those in the Special Squads, the 'crematoria ravens', who were all men and mostly Jewish. Not many of the men survived because they were regularly murdered so that they would not be witnesses to the events, as Primo Levi describes in *The Drowned and the*

Saved (Levi, 1988:22–51). Thus, although interviews with men out-weigh women in the documentary 26 to 7, with those interviews with women short and rarely given a voice more than once (unlike the male interviewees who are frequently returned to and allowed to speak at length), it is neither sufficient to dismiss the film on this basis nor to dismiss the gender bias embedded in the very heart of the film. What the film hands down to us, in moving form, is a core feature of the system of Nazi murder: the separation of women, children and the elderly from men; the involvment in the preparation for slaughter and disposal of corpses of women, children and the elderly by Jewish men under threat of their own lives; the use of men to cut the hair off naked women and children, often their own mothers and sisters and neighbours, before they were murdered; the herding of elderly people and ill mothers with children to 'the infirmary', a death pit where the infirm and children were immediately shot in the back of the head.. The women, children and elderly cannot speak, they cannot be present in the film because they were the murder victims in this process and therefore are not alive to tell the story or bear witness.

Such video and film testimonies have advantages over the written word, in that they can convey non-verbal memories, the facial expression, the gesture that accompanies that which cannot be told in words: 'unlike literary testimony, video testimonies can also represent not telling a story, the point at which memory will not enter speech' (Young, 1988:161). The unwritten absence that runs through the survivors' life-writings of Primo Levi and Elie Wiesel (see Chapter 3) are visualised in *Shoah,* in the pauses, in the faces of the men attempting to render memory into narrative, in the images that haunt them of the women they witnessed going to their deaths. The film is an attempt to articulate the awful absence of the women that is the corollary of the role that some male victims and survivors were forced to take in the Nazi death machine. The women's absence is in fact present in the words and faces of the men, as the interview with Abraham Bomba, who worked in Treblinka as a barber cutting off the hair of women to send to the Reich, shows:

On this side the women went in and on the other side was a group of working people who took out the dead bodies – some of them were not exactly dead. They took them out, and in two minutes – in one minute – everything was clear. It was clean to take in the other party of women and do the same thing they did to the first one. Most of them had long hair – some had short hair; like I mentioned, the Germans needed hair for their purposes. (Abraham Bomba (1985) in *Shoah, The Complete Text of the Film,* p. 116)

Bomba was interviewed while cutting hair in an Israeli barbershop that Lanzmann hired for the film. Lanzmann said 'it would have been obscene' to have interviewed Bomba cutting women's hair: what he was doing in the film in this respect was not representational (Lanzmann, 1985a:97). As Stella Bruzzi suggests, the sequence is 'an evocation' because 'it eschews archive footage' and 'will never be evoked' (Bruzzi, 2000:108). What we see before us in viewing Abraham Bomba and other witnesses in the film is not simply the men whom Lanzmann interviewed:. We are invited to imagine and remember in the gaps of their discourse, in the unarticulated pain on their faces, the thousands of women and children who could not be interviewed because they did not survive. In the words of the men, in their silences, in their asides we are hailed to remember the women. In the men's recollections are the absent ones:

Railway workers

They jumped from the cars. What a sight! Jumping from the windows. There was a mother and child.

A Jewish mother?

Yes. She tried to run away. And they shot her in the heart. Shot the mother. This gentleman has lived here a long time; he can't forget it. (Railway Workers, *Shoah, The Complete Text of the Film,* 1985:29)

Understanding documentary films about the Holocaust from a gendered perspective is not about counting heads or giving emphasis to women's perspectives: it is about recognizing that sometimes the gendered facts of Nazi genocide can only be articulated by visual absence, made manifest by the filmed witness of men's words and faces on the screen. As Janet Walker (1999) notes, film and video can provide important ways of remembering the Holocaust that account for 'innovative ways to hang onto historical truths' while simultaneously acknowledging the variability of memory'. Retrospective film and video versions of the events of the Holocaust allow for the elaborations, ellipses and silences, as well as truths inherent in traumatic memory (Walker, 1999:1).

Admittedly, there is not yet the nine-hour equivalent of specifically women's experience, focusing on women who were forced to work in the 'brothels', for example. But there are some subaltern documentaries that do provide women with a voice and image. These are both from the point of view of perpetrators such as *Nazi Women* (2001) and from the perspective of survivors as with Yorkshire Television's *Kitty: Return to Auschwitz* (1989). There is Loretta Walz's film solely about the women's camp at Ravensbruck (1995). Some also depict the role of women as resistors, as in the Belgium film by Myriam Abramowicz and Ester Hoffenberg, *Comme Si C'Etait Hier* (As If It Were Yesterday) which celebrates the daily resistance of women who saved many Jewish children in Belgium. Annette Insdorf (1989) argues that the latter film gives 'special attention to the efforts of women' by its focus on the everyday heroisms of its virtually all-female subjects (p. 230). The soundtrack is predominantly female with focus given to the special role that women had in developing a mutual help network to save Jewish children. The director of the film suggests that women's memories are given a greater role in the film because of women's involvement in its production: 'You see women because women made this film it is the kind of thing you don't see in army films, for example. It was *natural* for us to talk to women as well as men. (Myriam Abramowicz quoted by Insdorf, 1989:230).

To some extent this may be true and it is certainly the case that women are actively foregrounded in this film. They are also not flattened out, or simplified or stereotyped in the ways in which they tend to be in other films. As we saw with autobiographies, who makes the memory – in this case who is involved in the making of a film – can influence the way in which we remember genocide. Would a woman have made *Shoah* in the same way, or even have made it at all? It is also significant to our understanding of the articulation of Holocaust memory in film that none of these films has gained the same prominence in the canon of Holocaust film memory.

Dramatizing survival

With feature films about history, the prime influence, as Pierre Sorlin (2001) notes, is money (p. 29): we cannot talk about cinema unless we also recognize the capitalist imperatives that lie behind it. To some extent this is true of all mediations, but more so with film and nowhere is this more apparent than with feature films. The result is that in order for feature films to reach a mass audience they tend to use established Hollywood conventions in narrative and character, sanitising the events so that real terror, despair and degradation are rarely seen. Lawrence Langer in *Admitting the Holocaust* (1995) argues that in Hollywood versions of the Holocaust events are reduced to a simple story of triumph over tragedy. The terrible moral dilemmas and inability to take comfort that people faced are retreated from and replaced with a safe cheerfulness. 'Moral simplification is one of the many sins afflicting writing about the holocaust' Langer writes (1995:166). Other critics of feature films about the Holocaust argue that they have translated the events into a universal story with American values. The tendencies, argues Judith E. Doneson (1987) have been towards the universalization, democratization, vulgarization and popularization of events (p. 119). In American films the Jewish dimension of the Holocaust is superseded by the telling of the story in a way that emphasises that this could have happened to any ordinary American family. Thus, in the film version of Anne Frank's Diary, made in 1959, when the family is shown celebrating Hanukkah, the prayers are not in Hebrew but in English. Dr Dussel, who in real life was actually a dedicated believer, is turned in the film version into a Jew who is an unbeliever so that he (with the majority of the mass American audience) can have Hanukkah explained to him (Doneson, 1987:119).

These conventions and processes of sanitisation are not gender neutral: universalisation includes the stripping away of the rich variety of gendered roles and experiences and the use instead of gendered stereotypes, framed within the particular conventions of – in many cases – American masculinity and femininity current at the time of the film's production. A key example of this is the phenomenally popular, *Schindler's List* (Dir; Spielberg, 1994), a US production that generated a huge amount of media coverage and raised debates about how best the Holocaust could be represented. A plethora of reviews, commentaries and academic critiques considered virtually every aspect of the film. Positive reactions stressed the educational value of the film and its achievement in reaching such a broad public in so many countries (Alster, 1994; Davies, 1994) : 'Steven Spielberg's inspired tale of the Holocaust leaves a powerful message ... This film deserves every bit of praise that it received. Its still the most talked about movie of our time' (Loshitsky, 15.11.99). Others discussed the reactions to the film in the US after an incident in Oakland, California in which high-school students were asked to leave the cinema after laughing at the portrayal in the film of Nazi violence towards Jews (Rich, 1994; Schwarz, 1994;

Spolar, 1994). Others looked at reactions to the film in Germany (Eley, 1997; Miller, 1994; Niven, 1995). Some discussed the form of the representation (Manchel, 1995, 1998) and why Spielberg had chosen to use black and white throughout most of the movie (Nagorski, 1993).

What is little discussed, though, are the ways in which gender, genocide and survival are articulated within the conventions of the film. First, the choice of story and hero (the rescuer) is significant. The narrative centres on the story of Oskar Schindler, a German member of the Nazi Party who went to Poland during the War to build a business using slave labour, but who had a change of heart and ultimately saved 1100 Jewish people's lives. Yet why Schindler? There were many other 'heroes' and 'heroines' who saved the lives of Jewish people. Irena Sendler, for example, championed the cause of the Jews before the Holocaust and risked her own life many times, rescuing over 2500 Jewish children from extermination, as Joe Steinberg's (1995) latest study shows (pp. 24–6). But Sendler, as a Pole, as a resister and as a woman, I would suggest, is not the right kind of 'hero' for Spielberg and American audiences: with the reconfiguration of alliances after the War, West Germany – and after 1989 the reunited Germany – was a US ally; while Poland, east of the Iron Curtain and part of the Soviet orbit in the Cold War, was the enemy. In American memory, as Eva Hoffman (1998) notes, Poles are recalled as worse antisemites and more to blame for the genocide of the Jews than the Nazis, despite the fact that Poland was under German occupation, with the greatest concentration of German troops than in any occupied country and those who helped Jews did so under threat of execution (Piotrowski, 1998). Hence, I would suggest, the choice of Schindler (rather than Sendler) and the depiction of Poles in the film as virulent antisemites.

Second, the central relationship in the film is not Oskar's with his wife Emile, but Oskar's with the Jewish accountant, Yitzak Stern, and with the sadistic Amon Goethe. At the beginning of the film we see, briefly, Schindler's wife when she visits him in Poland and discovers him in bed with another woman. In the next scene we see her being put on a train back to Germany by Schindler. She is effectively banished from the action of the film: we see nothing of her again until the end, when Oskar has rescued 'his Jews' by setting up a factory in his home town in the Czech Republic and she joins him, helping Jews in the new factory. In the final scene, we see the real Emile Schindler, elderly and wheelchair bound, placing a stone on Oskar's grave in Jerusalem, following on from the 'Schindler Jews today'. In this way, the film replicates what Vladimir Propp in *The Morphology of the*

Folktale (1928) saw as the central elements of the traditional patriarchal fairytale: our hero – Schindler (a seeming villain but who is really good) is assisted in his task by a helper (Stern and black marketeers) and is hindered in turn by villains (Nazis such as Goethe) and Henchmen (Nazi soldiers). At no moment does a woman assist the development of the story. Rather, women in this film are either there to be rescued (Jewish women); there to provide a moral anchor (Oskar's wife) or there to provide sexual interest (cabaret women, Goethe's mistress, Schindler's mistress).

There are one or two exceptions which both disrupt the traditional patriarchal Hollywood narrative and indicate that as well as people being targeted because they were Jewish, Jewish men and women experienced wounds particular to their gender. We see Nazi soldiers humiliating Jewish men by cutting off their earlocks. We see how being a Jewish woman in a non-traditional role incited particular hatred: when a Jewish woman engineer is depicted as proudly telling Amon Goethe that the foundations of a building are unsafe and will need rebuilding, he calls her 'a fucking Jew bitch engineer', and shoots her dead in the back of the head. However, the corollary to these moments is the dominant idea, contrary to much historical evidence (as discussed in Chapter 3) that survival was in large part dependent on Jewish people enacting traditional gender roles and maintaining particular aspects of femininity and masculinity. What enables women's survival in the film in the face of Nazi atrocity is shown as dependent on their ability to conform to acceptable forms of femininity. Thus, Helena Hirshe, the passive maid of Amon Goethe, survives by remaining silent even in the face of repeated insults and violence. Regina Pelman, passing as Polish with false identity papers, quickly learns that to gain an interview with Oscar Schindler she must use her feminine attraction to be accepted by his male gaze. When she turns up at his factory the first time and asks to see him, he takes a look from the top of the stairs, notes her drab and grey appearance, and refuses. When she returns in a glamorous dress and wearing make-up he agrees to see her.

Likewise, what is shown to enable Jewish men to survive is not their education, ability to use languages or their professional status, but only their ability to become skilled manual workers. While in many cases this was true, in others it was their education, their ability to speak several languages, especially German, or their ability to play a musical instrument that enabled them to survive. In most cases, survivors say it was luck. The gross exploitation of men, as physically stronger, in their use as crematoria workers is not included in the film.

When it comes to *Schindler's List*'s dramatization of the Holocaust the tendency is to stick to established gender conventions: women are shown as nurturers, even amid genocide. We do not see the dilemmas faced by those in the camps who had to murder or abandon their new-born babies. In the Spielberg version of events, even in the midst of brutality, starvation and death, mothers remain mothers – they are able to maintain their roles in some form by caring for their offspring or having children and being able to keep them. In *Schindler's List* we see women rushing towards the children, trying to save them. What the film does not explore is how part of people's trauma in the brutality of genocide involves the disruption of normal roles and relationships in which established gender boundaries are broken. Only when traditions are broken that might be acceptable to a contemporary American audience are these included, such as when a woman in Plaszow concentration camp in the absence of a male rabbi acts to marry two prisoners.

Underpinning the film are also elements of what Roland Barthes (1972:129) describes as myth, transforming historical aspects of gender into nature. This is imbricated with what Judith Doneson, in an essay on earlier holocaust films, describes as 'the Jew as female figure': in US films, she argues, Jewish people are generally associated with femininity. The Jewish person is depicted as weak and dependent on the Christian/Gentile, and is seen as 'being incapable of saving himself [*sic*] without the aid of the strong, male Christian' (Doneson, 1978:12).[10] The diversity of Jewish women and men, Polish women and men and German women and men in German-occupied Poland is transformed into myths of 1990s hegemonic American femininity and masculinity that appear to us as natural because they relate to widely held beliefs in our own era about gender and gender relations. Men, for example, are constructed around mythical elements of masculinity. Oskar Schindler is the big man, the hero, and the protective father. Even the momentary use of colour in the film rests on Oskar's paternalistic view of a little girl that he witnesses amid the chaos and murder when the Cracow ghetto is liquidated. Amid a film shot almost entirely in black and white we see her little red coat as she escapes through a door. Later, when the bodies are exhumed at Plaszow concentration camp, where the Jews of the ghetto were taken, Schindler sees again the little girl, this time she is dead and the red coat is the only spot of colour amid the grey. When Yitzhak Sterne is taken to a transport for failing to carry his work papers, it is Oskar who rescues him at the last moment, overriding the authority of the Nazi soldiers and getting the transport stopped. Like a distraught father to his son, Schindler barks, 'What if I had got here five minutes later?' And like an errant son who has failed to heed his father's warnings, Sterne admits he was only taken because he had 'stupidly' forgotten his papers.

In a later scene, with Amon Goethe's maid Helena Hirshe, Schindler is depicted giving her chocolate and listening to her tell him how Goethe beats her. Schindler reassures her that Goethe will not kill her, because she pleases him too much. Then in close up we see Schindler move to kiss Helen himself. She looks at him fearfully: 'Its all right' he reassures her, 'its not that kind of a kiss', and he kisses her gently on the forehead. When the Jewish men arrive in Zwittan, Schindler is depicted standing above them, his arms outstretched like Christ/God made flesh, as he makes a speech reassuring them that the women are on their way and that hot food is awaiting them. When the train full of women is diverted to Auschwitz, Schindler buys them back with diamonds, refusing to take the Nazi official's advice to not 'get hung up about names'. As children are torn from their mothers as they return to the trucks, Schindler yells, 'They are *my* Jews.'

The narrative thus invites us to see Schindler as a go(o)d father, protecting 'his people'. In fact, according to other sources, it was more complex for the real Oskar Schindler, who had less control over deciding who was saved and who was murdered: 'Owing to the immense confusion at Gross-Rosen at that time, some prisoners who had been on the list went to entirely different sub-camps and they were replaced by others, frequently put on the list by accident (Zaglada Zydow Krakowskich, 1996:6). Of those that reached Brunnlitz from Plaszow, their numbers gradually increased 'as others were gradually getting there from the transports passing through' (Zaglada Zydow Krakowskich, 1996:6).

The hegemony of Hollywood overdramatised versions of the Holocaust should not be thought of as total however: *Schindlers List* is not the Holocaust. As with documentaries, there are subaltern memories that are present in smaller-budget non-American films. Particularly in those features directed by women we see that one of the key textual motifs is the childless mother and the motherless child. The Polish film *Ostatni Etap* (The Last Stop) – made in Poland in 1948 and directed by Wanda Jakubowska has as its first dramatic scene the birth of a baby followed by its immediate murder, suggesting that the shared identity of the childless mother was 'the source of many women's relationships in the camps' (Insdorf, 1989:152). Exceptionally, earlier popular mainstream American movies such as *Sophie's Choice* (1982), directed by Alan Pakula and based on the novel by William Styron, though questioned by Elie Wiesel (1983:1–12), among others for its choice of heroine – a beautiful, multi-lingual Pole – do present us with the painful choice many women faced of surrendering their children in order to survive themselves.

Conclusion

Films are a key medium in our social inheritance of the history and memory of the Holocaust. But moving images, like any other medium, present us with a retranslation of events; whether propaganda, liberation footage, documentary or feature films, they are not historical documents. Part of this retranslation, within the particular context of the genre, includes particular ways in which gender is articulated. Propaganda films made by Nazi perpetrators reproduced a discourse of nationalism that was gendered, as well as 'raced'. They were produced from within the particular discursive context of SS film crews and embody a gendered context that involved the humiliation by SS film crews of men and women in specific ways. Liberation films were produced within the discursive contexts of men witnessing the aftermath of the Holocaust from the national positions of armies from US, Britain and the Soviet Union entering the camps in which gendered identities were in some instances simplified to render the themes of witnessing and atrocity and at other moments articulate gender in complex ways. With later documentaries, such as *Shoah*, although criticized by some for not equally including women, the genre allows for visual absence to articulate the mute absence of women who were murdered. With mainstream feature films, such as *Schindler's List*, commercial imperatives tend to result in the use of patriarchal narratives and conventional gendered stereotypes of masculinity and femininity. Although the latter is still undoubtedly valuable in enabling an introduction to history for the post-Holocaust generation, this reading suggests that we need to be aware of how feature films may fail to articulate those aspects of the Holocaust and the processes of genocide that are the most painful to remember: the disarticulation of established roles and gendered identities.

Overall, as with autobiography, the more well-known socially inherited memories of the Holocaust handed down through film tend to be those that in particular ways help re-establish or confirm gendered roles and identities, and thus help maintain social cohesion. In this respect it is important to approach films about the past, even 'documentaries' of the events, in ways that are critical of how these memories may be being mediated. As with the written word, though, films should not be considered as discrete cultural entities but as part of a complex constellation configured through and in relation to other mediations of events. This is especially evident in the context of the museum. Historical texts, autobiography and some of these films, particularly those taken by the Nazis and 'liberation' footage, are now increasingly handed down as part of the past in various public or community memories of the events represented to us in museums and memorial sites dedicated to the Holocaust in many different countries. It is to this aspect of the public, institutional and state-sanctioned cultural mediations of social memory that we turn in the next chapter.

5
The Absence of Women's Hair: Memorial Sites and Museums

> For death is not only biological and personal, but also cultural. The dead look different at different times and in different places
>
> (Simpson, 2001:3)

Museums and public memory

Whereas 'the spectacle of the new' was what attracted people in the nineteenth century, now we flock to exhibitions about the past (Samuels, 1994). Museums play an important role in the creation of 'public' memory, acting as the locus for a power struggle between the State, the people and, increasingly, corporate capital over what historical stories are remembered (Wallace, 1996:vii). Throughout the countries of Europe, since 1945, many of the sites relating to wartime murders and atrocities were preserved and made into memorial spaces and museums. In Poland, the Council for Preservation of Monuments to Resistance and Martyrdom created 225 memorials after the Second World War (Browstein, 1992:23). Concentration and Extermination Camp sites were preserved and developed to include an archival resource base for individuals and organisations. In Poland, the Polish National People's Council, held in Warsaw on 31 December 1945, determined, following deputations from survivors, that Auschwitz be designated a place of martyrdom. Two years later, on 2 July 1947, the Polish parliament declared that the extermination camps at Auschwitz and Birkenau, with all their buildings and installations, should be preserved, and a museum established (Smolen, 1995:246). The memorialisation of the Holocaust in the form of museums has also extended beyond the boundaries of wartime German-occupied territories. With the creation of the State of Israel, Yad Vashem: the Holocaust Martyrs and Heroes Remembrance Authority, was established in 1953 by an act of the Israeli Knesset (see www.yad.vshem.org.il). In the USA, 15 years after President Carter's administration established The Commission on the Holocaust, the US Holocaust Museum was opened (Linenthal, 1997:1). The USA has museums with Holocaust-related themes in many States including Michigan, Texas, New York, Pennsylvania, Maryland and California. There are museums and permanent exhibitions in the Southern Hemisphere, including the Sydney Jewish Museum, opened in 1992, and the, Japanese Holocaust Centre in Fukuyama City, opened in 1995. In the UK, Beth Shalom, the first small Holocaust museum was opened in Nottingham in 1995. In April 2000 a permanent exhibition on the Holocaust, was opened in the Imperial War Museum, supported by 12.6 million in Heritage Lottery Funding.[1]

The popularity of these museums and memorial sites indicates that, increasingly, they are an important part of the polylogical development of people's socially inherited memory of the Holocaust. This is evidenced by the numbers of visitors. The US Holocaust Museum in its first year alone attracted two million visitors at about 5000 a day (Linenthal, 1997:338). The Imperial War Museum's Holocaust Exhibition had 10,000 visitors in one week in its first year, and in less than its first year had admitted 140,000 people (Bardgett, 2001:5). The State Museum at the preserved Auschwitz-Birkenau concentration and extermination camps, now a UNESCO World Heritage site, was visited by more than 21 million people between 1947 and 1992 and has 600,000 visitors per year, one-third of whom are from overseas (Smolen, 1995:263). The Japanese Holocaust Centre had 10,000 visitors in its first year (www.urban.n.jp). In the USA, although only a quarter of the respondents had visited a concentration or extermination camp, most had visited either the Museum of Jewish Heritage in New York or the US Holocaust Museum in Washington (focus groups, Washington and New York, 1999). In Poland, all respondents had visited an extermination site at least once, many more than once (focus groups, Gdansk, Cracow and Lodz, 1998). In the UK one-quarter had visited concentration camp sites in Germany, but few had visited the Belsen room in the Imperial War Museum or the new Holocaust Exhibition (focus groups, London and Leicester, 1998, 2000). In both Britain and the USA some respondents had also visited Yad Vashem in Israel.

Framing museums and memorial sites

The role of memorial sites and museums in handing down the memory of the Holocaust has not gone unnoticed by critics and Holocaust scholars. Research on Holocaust memorial sites and museums has explored questions about the place, role and appropriateness of the Holocaust museum or memorial in modern culture (Milton, 1991). Drawing on Jurgen Habermas's (1987) statement in *Eine Art Schadensabrichling* that 'Auschwitz has changed the basis for the continuity of the conditions of life within history' (p. 163), Andreas Huyssen suggests that museums concerning the Holocaust provide something solid in a world in which temporality and space are collapsed and fact and fiction are blurred. Scholars have also addressed the ways in which national agendas have shaped the memory of the Holocaust presented to visitors in the museum environment and in memorial sites. Thus Huyssen (1995) argues that there are significant differences in the ways in which museums in different countries represent the Holocaust. In Germany, the absence of the Jewish presence was articulated in memorial spaces as a traumatic burden within East and West German national identities (Herf, 1997; Maier, 1980) In Israel, the memory of the Holocaust was both the end-point and starting-point of its history; and in the Soviet Union and the former Eastern bloc before 1989, the ethnic specificities and antisemitic dimension of the genocide was silenced in the simplistic representation of Nazi oppressors versus international communists (Giteman, 1997; Huyssen, 1995; Steinlauf, 1997; Young, 1993). In Poland, especially, the memory of the Holocaust continues to be an 'embattled terrain' of Jewish memory, Polish memory and the memory of the West (Browstein, 1992; LaCapra, 1998; Hoffman, 1998:3). In the UK, Tony Kushner has critiqued the previous, much smaller, exhibition at the Imperial War Museum for its anglicisation of the events and its presentation of the Holocaust from the perspective of the British liberators rather than the victims and survivors (Kushner, 1997). At the same time, Richard Crownshaw (1999) reminds us that although this may have been the dominant meaning of the 'Belsen' exhibition, the visitor 'might see meanings there other than those intended by the museum' (p. 297). As James Young (1988) argues: 'In every country's memorials, in every national museum and archive, I found a different Holocaust and at times I found no Holocaust at all' (p. 172).

   What studies have not addressed, however, are the ways in which, as well as articulating with nationality and ethnicity, the shaping of public memory articulates with gender. As Hooper-Greenhill (2000) suggests, in relation to museums generally, subjectivity in the museum environment includes gender as well as nationality, class, ethnicity and sexual orientation (p. 111). Although the history of the Holocaust in the museum context may be clearly articulated through ethnicity and nationality, we also need to ask how these differences between museums are also rendered through various approaches to gender. How do sites of memory invoke people's gendered experiences of genocide? How do objects and artefacts articulate with differing discourses of femininity and masculinity to construct gendered identities in Holocaust museums? Is there a gendered Holocaust canon or narrative within museums that gives voice to men and women in different ways? Are artefacts, films and photographs in Holocaust museums shorn or attached to the gendered stories that may explain their provenance or inclusion?

This chapter explores some answers to these questions through an examination of the differing configurations of gender and socially inherited memory in memorial sites and museums in the national contexts of the US, Britain and Poland. It looks at how gender is articulated and left unarticulated in the memorialisation of the Holocaust by the Polish state in the Nazi death camps at Auschwitz-Birkenau. The chapter explores gender bias and exclusion in the official American public memory of the Holocaust created through reconstruction and narrativisation of the events in the US Holocaust Museum in Washington, and how intimacy and context have created greater gender balance, as well as silences, in the Jewish-American memorialisation of events in the Museum of Jewish Heritage in New York. Finally, there is an analysis how gender balance and articulation of experiences specific to men and women have been created in the British public memory of the events in the Holocaust Exhibition at the Imperial War Museum in London. I base the analysis on research visits to these memorial sites and museums during 1998–2001.

Artefacts in Auschwitz

There are many memorial sites in what was German-occupied Poland during the Second World War, but probably the most renown is the extermination camp that is now the Auschwitz-Birkenau State Museum situated near the town of Oswiecim in Southern Poland. The concentration camp at Auschwitz I was established under the direction of Heinrich Himmler in 1940 as a place of slow death for Poles and for people from concentration camps within Germany. The much larger extermination camp, Auschwitz II or Birkenau (Brzenzinka), began to be built in October 1941, with a women's section after August 1942. Local Poles living in the area were deported and barracks were established. Approximately forty smaller sub-camps – the first one built at Monowitz – were also established in the vicinity. These were forced labour camps and were termed Auschwitz III. After 1942, Auschwitz-Birkenau became the main extermination centre for Jews and gypsies. Of the people that died there, 90 per cent were Jewish and had been brought there in overcrowded cattle trucks not only from Germany but also from the German occupied territories of Austria, Sudentenland, Greece, Yugoslavia, France, Belgium, Holland, Norway, Lithuania and the USSR, as well as the Axis countries and their allies – Italy, Czechoslovakia, Hungary, Romania and Bulgaria. There are various estimates of the numbers murdered at the killing centre at Birkenau, but recent statistics confirm that between 1.2 to 1.5 million perished (Niewyk and Nicosia, 2000:194–5) The estimates have varied because the majority of men, women and children sent in transports after 1944 were gassed on arrival, with no formal records of their names made. Those people deemed capable of work on arrival were stripped of their clothing and belongings, shaved, tattooed with a number and used as slave labour. Of the people who were given numbers, 'few lived longer than six months; they died from starvation, disease, rigours of hard labour, beatings, torture, and summary execution – by shooting, hanging or gassing' (Smolen, 1990:17). The main form of murder was by mass asphyxiation with lethal chemicals released from Zyklon B pellets in underground chambers designed to resemble showers. In the largest of these, up to 1500 people could be murdered at any one time. Each chamber had its own crematorium in which up to 4,416 bodies could be turned into ashes every 24 hours. The remaining bodies were stacked and burnt in the open air. Before being burnt, all 'valuable' items were removed: hair was shaved off for manufacture into yarn and other uses; false teeth and crowns were extracted from people's mouths to be melted down; prisoners' belongings were sorted and shipped back to the Reich. The murders reached a peak in the summer of 1944 when around 400,000 Hungarian Jews were gassed over two months. The process was speeded up by extending the railway line up to the gas chambers (Smolen, 1990:17–19).

In January 1945, as the Soviet army was approaching, the Nazis removed 60,000 prisoners from the main camps and subcamps, force-marching them hundreds of miles into camps in Germany. When the

Soviet army arrived at Auschwitz on 27 January there were only approximately 7,000 men, women and children still alive, emaciated and ill. Some of the survivors requested that the place become a permanent memorial to the sufferings of people imprisoned there and to those that had died. On 2 July 1947, a resolution was passed by the Polish parliament to preserve the camps at Auschwitz. The Museum at Auschwitz-Birkenau was the first to be established on the site of a death camp. In 1956 the remit of the Museum was extended to include the conservation of artefacts and buildings, scholarly research and education (Smolen, 1990:261).

Although officially announcing itself as a 'museum', with a café, a coach park, and even a hotel nearby that tourists can stay in, Auschwitz as a site of atrocity, as Webber (1995) stresses:

> is also one vast cemetery, a place of pilgrimage, where people come to lay flowers, light candles, say their prayers, observe their silences … the totality of Auschwitz is a monument to itself. We don't have a word in our language adequately to describe what this place is. (p. 283)

The 'museum' at Auschwitz consists of the two main preserved sites at Auschwitz I and Auschwitz-Birkenau II. The two sites are very different. The former is where most people visit, and consists of brick-built three-storey prison buildings, with semi-paved roads and some trees. On approach, there is the car park packed with tour coaches, a small hotel and a 'museum' cafeteria selling hot meals. Visitors enter through the gate passing under the words *Arbeit Macht Frei* (Work Makes Free) and enter the main museum building which includes a bookshop selling publications about the Holocaust and a cinema showing a film entitled *Chronicle of the Liberation of Auschwitz* which visitors may view for a small fee. The film uses footage taken by Soviet cameramen some weeks later, in the aftermath following liberation of the camp by the Soviet Army (Swiebocka, 1995:44). Visitors are then free to take their own routes among the prison buildings, the gas chamber, the infamous block 11 or death block, which includes standing torture cells a couple of feet square in size. There is still the death wall where people were shot, the gallows where prisoners were hanged. Inside the buildings – some of which are open to the public – the walls are lined with photographs of victims. There are displays of artefacts and people's belongings found stacked in their hundreds of thousands in Birkenau: shoes, false limbs, walking sticks, reading glasses, pots and pans, toothbrushes, hairbrushes, shaving brushes, suitcases painted with people's names, and, stacks of tresses of human hair.

For 45 years the mass murder of Jews was given little prominence in the exhibitions. The memory of the genocide against the Jews, central to the history of the extermination camp at Auschwitz II, was highly marginalised (Browstein, 1992; Hoffman, 1998:3; Young, 1993;) After 1989, with the collapse of Communism, an international Council for the Museum was established which includes representatives of the Jewish communities. Exhibitions that simply promoted communist ideology were closed down and new exhibitions revised and created (Webber, 1995). However, the displays and organisation of the exhibition rooms were, and still largely are, organised around the identity of European nationality, which in effect fragments and distorts the antisemitic purpose that underlay the death camp. This was and also is the case with Romany ('gypsy') memory: there is little recognition given to the specific sufferings of Romany people (Bandy, 2000). As Harold Tanner reminds us:

> The fate of the Roma paralleled the tragic fate of the Jews, who were also imprisoned and exterminated. They were tortured, used for inhuman scientific experiments, and put to death in the infamous gas chambers. One of the worst of the camps, Auschwitz, held sixteen thousand Roma at one point. By August 1944, only four thousand Roma remained. After a visit by Himmler, the last imprisoned Roma were led to the gas chambers. (Tanner, 2000:www.geocities.com/Paris/512/Paraimos.htm)

The memory of people's Jewish or Romany identities is largely subsumed within discourses of nationality.

At the same time, at Auschwitz-Birkenau the organisation of public memory around nationality is also articulated in ways that are gendered, both overtly and mutely. There were and are some specific places where the sufferings particular to gender are overtly voiced: in Block 10, for example, we see the gynaecological chair used by Professor Carl Clauberg to conduct experiments on Jewish and Romany women to devise a method for mass sterilisation. We see photographs of row upon row of women with children, awaiting extermination. Some artefacts are mute reminders of the intimate aspects of gender: piles of shaving brushes, each one worn and different, bespeak their male owners. Other artefacts mutely remind us of men' and women's public and private roles: bundles of men's striped prayer shawls remind us of Jewish men's religious roles in the synagogues of their home towns and *shtetls*; pots and pans, spoons and knives remind us of the women who packed them in haste before deportation, imagining that at their final destination they would not be met with death or slave labour but, instead, would somehow continue their lives as wives and mothers cooking for their families.

The green field at Birkenau

In contrast to the 'museum' at Auschwitz, the 'museum' at Birkenau, a few kilometres down the road, is vast, bleak and treeless: memory here is articulated quite differently. Visitors approach along a barren road and the disused railway that goes nowhere except directly to the remains of the death chambers. Visible from the distance is the red brick-built administrative building and archway. A map in three languages, Polish, Hebrew and English, describes the divisions of the camp: women (Jews and non-Jews) men (Jews and non-Jews) and the Romany (gypsy) camp, where men, women and children were kept together. The prevalence of the memory of European nationalities has gone here. Visitors enter through an archway and walk along the ramp where, after travelling days without food or water, people were unloaded and divided – able-bodied men from women fit for work from women with children and the elderly. Inside, there are grass compounds surrounded by barbed wire and watchtowers and ditches. There are the remains of rows of some of the wooden windowless stables used as barracks, with three-tier rough wooden bunks crammed inside on mud floors. There are the vast latrines, sixty seats long, and beside the huts the death carts used for shifting the corpses of those who had died from starvation and disease in the night. As far as the horizon, like anonymous memorials, stretch row upon row of the remains of the brick chimneys in the centre of each hut. The railway line and ditches built and dug by the prisoners run up to the massive gas chambers and crematoria with their ovens. There is a pond into which human ashes were dumped. There are the ruins of the undressing rooms riven with moss and lank grass. Huge flat plain steps in stone form a monument by the crematoria and gas chambers to the victims.

The monument is inscribed: 'Forever let this place be a cry of despair, and a warning to humanity, where the Nazis murdered about one and a half million men, women and children, mainly Jews from various countries in Europe. Auschwitz-Birkenau 1940–1945'. The scale of the place is vast. The site articulates viscerally the memory of these factories of death: no visitor can leave without realising the full horror of Birkenau II – a purposefully planned industrial plant designed to reduce hundreds of thousands of human beings to ashes rapidly and 'efficiently'.

When visitors look at the map in front of the camp and then walk the compounds, particular aspects of gender and ethnicity are present but unvoiced, embedded silently within the remains of the empty buildings and mud and wire. Visitors walk the difference/the distance between the men's camp and the women's camp. They see that the women's camp[2] is smaller than the men's: what is mute and left unarticulated within the memory of the camps are the reasons why they were different sizes. This is not to argue that the museum *should* tell visitors why, but that, read in relation to other sources it is possible for visitors to gain a deeper understanding of why the women's camp should be smaller. Felstiner argues, for example, that only one-third of women were selected for slave labour rather than immediate death, while, in contrast, two-thirds of men survived the immediate selection and were sent to the men's camp to do slave labour (Felstiner, 1997:206).[3] The *Auschwitz Chronicle*, based on the archives of the Auschwitz memorial and the German Federal Archives, shows, for example, that of the plundered property taken from victims which was discovered by the Soviet army on liberating the camp, there were 348,000 men's suits in comparison with 836,515 women's dresses (Czech, 1990:xviiii). There is, as Felstiner points out, little careful, gendered, statistical analyses of murder and survival statistics at Auschwitz. But she argues that, based on a number of secondary sources, as well as calculations from transport lists and survivor and perpetrator testimony, at this point more women than men were selected for immediate death (Felstiner, 1997:269–70). What is also not articulated is that conditions at the time in the women's camp, according to the autobiography of the Commandant Rudolf Hoess, were so much worse than in the men's camp: 'The women's camp, tightly crammed from the very beginning, meant psychological destruction for the female prisoners, and this led sooner or later to their physical collapse. From every point of view, and at all times, the worst conditions prevailed in the women's camp' (Hoess, 2000:137).

As described in male survivors' autobiographies (see Chapter 3), to understand the gendered inheritance of genocide within different cultural mediations and memorial sites we need to be attentive to what is not said, what is mute in representation as well as that which is articulated. As for Primo Levi (2000: 26) and the men separated from the women, the children and the elderly at Birkenau, the fate of the women selected for death, who disappeared into the night, remains mutely embedded in the earth beneath the visitors' feet.

These contradictions of silence and articulation are rendered in similar ways in relation to the memory of the Romany. On the museum plan the information tells the visitor that Romany were kept separate from all others, from Jews, from Poles and from Russian prisoners, and that unlike other groups they were not divided by gender, but kept together in families. As we walk the bleak space of the Roma family camp, we tread the 'difference' between Roma and all others; but we are left again with a sense of disarticulation, of what is not said or recalled. What is not articulated in the grass and the wire of the 'gypsy' camp is the reason why Roma were kept together: the initial policy by the Reichsfuhrer SS was to preserve 'pure' gypsies of the 'two main tribes' and their customs as examples of descendants of the original Indo-Germanic race. The initial plan was to 'collect them together for research purposes with a view to putting them in reservations. They were to be precisely registered and preserved as an historic monument' (Hoess, 1995:125). However, in July 1942, the Reichsfuhrer SS Heinrich Himmler visited the 'gypsy' camp and afterwards ordered that the those capable of working should be separated and the rest killed.

> The gypsies capable of work were transferred to another camp. About 4000 gypsies were left by August 1944, and these had to go to the gas chambers. Up to that moment, they were unaware of what was in store for them. They first realised what was happening when they made their way, barrack-hut by barrack-hut towards Crematorium I. It was not easy to drive them into the gas chambers. (Hoess, 1995:126–7)

As the visitor makes his or her way through the extermination camp at Birkenau, these silences and disarticulations within the memory of the camp break down the usual dialogical relationship that a visitor or mourner would experience with the dead in a normal cemetery. A specific example of this is what appears at first sight to be an ordinary field of grass some way off from the main barracks complex. The information board beside it states that this was the field in which thousands of people's ashes were dumped. Here the visitor experiences a sense of overwhelming horror at the total breakdown of a societal order that usually includes in the memorialisation of the dead some visible marker of people's identities. As human beings, whoever we are, whatever our cultural background or gender, we all share the common fact of death, yet the processes of dying, death, disposal and the memory of us that lives on normally will be articulated, as are our lives, through particular subjectivities that include gender and religion. We may be buried and given a commemorative stone, or cremated and given a plaque that will include our name, our birthday and very often words related to the roles we have fulfilled in our lives, 'a loving wife and devoted mother', 'a loyal husband and hard-working father'. In the memory of the dead in a graveyard or cemetary, a gravestone or plaque will usually in some way articulate the gender of the dead person when they were alive. But this is not so at the green field at Birkenau. In the ground of ashes in which fragments of bone remain there is embedded a fundamental element of genocide. At Birkenau people had been singled out for death on the basis of their gender and their 'race'; yet, in death and after death, in the green field all aspects of identity have been obliterated; there is nothing left to distinguish one murder victim from another. At the field at Birkenau no one had a funeral that was a matrix of expected roles and customs. Cremation is forbidden in traditional Jewish law, yet Jewish victims were burnt and ground to ashes. A male rabbi should have led Kaddish, the prayer for the deceased but, since there were no funerals, no prayers in the usual manner could be said. No family could sit shiva, mourning for seven days; no memorial candles could be lit (Mukherjee, 2000). The green field reminds us that Nazi genocide disarticulated gendered Jewish religious and cultural signifiers even in death. In the Jewish cemetary in Lodz, for example, one of the oldest in Europe: 'Women and men as well as children of both genders were buried in separate plots. Even in the cholera victims' field women and men usually lie in separate rows. At least to the end of 1942, these rules were observed' (Muszynscy and Muszynscy, 1995:90–1).

On male plots in Poland before the War commemorative stones for men were often a book, a shelf, or a bookcase, indicating that the deceased was a learned, respected man; on women's graves, symbols of nurturance were common, such as a pelican with young; symbols of candles or candelabra were almost exclusively on the graves of women as their job was to light the candles for the Sabbath (Muszynscy and Muszynscy, 1995:100). But, there could be no gender-specific markers at Birkenau, and no Orthodox Jewish family members were buried in separate plots because there were no bodies to bury. The process of Nazi genocide meant that at Birkenau, ashes stripped of all forms of identity were trampled into the land or dumped in the river:

> During the period when the fires were kept burning continuously, without a break, the [human] ashes fell through the grates and were constantly removed and crushed to powder. The [human] ashes were taken in lorries to the Vistula, where they immediately drifted away and dissolved. The ashes taken from the burning pits near bunker II and crematorium IV were dealt with in the same way. (Hoess, 1995:199)

For the Roma, too (though they often also took on the dominant religion of the region in which they travelled) particular Romany approaches to death, funerals and forms of mourning were denied. No word could be sent to all relatives, as is usual, through the *vurma* (fixed contact points) and thus no family member could obtain forgiveness as is usual from the dying. On the night of the Zigeunernacht, when 4000 Roma at Auschwitz were killed, there could be no washing and dressing of the corpses to prevent *marime* (spiritual contamination). There could be no wearing of red or white or black by mourners, or throwing of coins and earth into the grave, because there were no graves. There could be no funeral meals and declarations of the end of mourning. There are no thorn bushes or stones placed to protect the living from the *marime* spirits that the dead can emit. And sixty years on, we remain puzzled as to why the *porrajmos* (the devouring – the name given for the Romany genocide) – is so little spoken of, not knowing that part of the reason is that among many Roma the name of the dead should not be mentioned in case they return to haunt the living. When visitors view the 'belongings' on display in the barracks in Auschwitz I they may not know that this too is an affront to Romany custom; disrespecting the belief that in this world we own nothing, we simply borrow it while we are here and on our deaths our belongings should be destroyed or sold to non-Romany (Lee, 2000).

At Birkenau, then, the gender and cultural background of victims and survivors are present in the post-war map; silenced in the gaps between the buildings and disarticulated in the field of ashes. For a moment, the visitor, in visceral memory, at the site of the atrocities themselves, witnesses in the breakdown of the usual dialogic aspects of memory, in the sense of absence, in the horror of disarticulation, one of the meanings of genocide.

Accidentally a boy

Thousands of miles from Auschwitz-Birkenau, far away from the atrocities themselves and decades after the events took place, are other Holocaust 'museums'. One of the most famous of these is the US Holocaust Memorial Museum – a combined museum, archive and memorial, opened in 1993. Significantly, the museum is sited in the nation's capital and near major symbols of American democracy – the White House, the Washington Monument and the Jefferson Memorial. Part of its mission, like that of many Holocaust museums,[4] is the use of the memory of the events to provide for a more inclusive present and future. Thus the museum seeks to encourage its visitors 'to reflect upon the moral and spiritual questions raised by the events of the Holocaust as well as their own responsibilities as *citizens of a democracy*' (US Holocaust Museum, Visitors Guide, 1999, my emphasis). The Director of the Research Institute of the Museum, Michael Berenbaum, has stated: 'In America, we recast the story of the Holocaust to teach fundamental American values – pluralism, democracy, restraint on government, the inalienable rights of individuals ... freedom of the press, of assembly, of religion' (quoted in Gourevitch, 1999:2). However, also significantly, how gender is articulated in the museum is not all-inclusive, 'pluralistic' or wholly 'democratic'; as we shall see, it recasts the story of the Holocaust in some ways that are gender biased and unbalanced.

The building itself, designed by architect James Freed, attempts to communicate to visitors the feel of forced movement – disruption, alienation, constriction, observation and selection (Linenthal, 1995). The dark grey steel, riveted girders, red-brick walls with patterns based on those at Auschwitz, echoes of watchtowers and ghetto bridges were designed by Freed so that the building itself is a 'resonator of memory' (Weinberg and Elieli, 1995:25). Care was taken down to the smallest details: the light fittings in the lifts are copies of the lights in the gas chambers; the seat covers in the conference room are in stripes of blue and grey like those for prisoners' uniforms; the carpets are beige with grey specks like ashes. The museum is a 'narrative history museum ' in which there is the imposition of 'a necessary sequence' in the arrangement of the exhibits (Weinberg and Elieli, 1995:51). Visitors follow a predetermined route, as they would a film or a book. This is unlike 'collecting museums' in which visitors are free to enter and exit different collections as they wish. In the historical narrative museum artefacts and exhibits 'derive their meaning and significance' within the context of the narrative' (Weinberg and Elieli, 1995:51).

The visitor's journey begins by taking a lift up to the start of the permanent exhibition on the fourth floor, *The Holocaust: Nazi Assault 1933–1939* . The exhibition narrative consists of text, newspapers, film clips, artefacts and photographs that chronicle the Nazi rise to power from 1933 to 1939, showing the increasing persecutions against Jewish people and other social and ethnic groups who did not fit into the Nazi Aryan ideal. The third floor, *The Holocaust: 'Final Solution' 1940–1945* chronicles the removal of Jewish people from their homes, their reloca-tion into ghettos and camps, forms of resistance, mass murder by the killing squads, life in concentration camps and the gassing of Jewish people in the 'Final Solution'. The audio presentation *'Voices from Auschwitz'* is on this floor. The second floor, *The Holocaust: Last Chapter* chronicles the resistance and efforts of those who tried to save the Jews, the liberation of the camps in 1945, the War Trials at Nuremberg, the American experience and the particular experiences of children. It chronicles life for survivors after the war in displaced person's camps, the emigration of Jewish people and the creation of the State of Israel in 1948 following the partition of Palestine by the United Nations in November 1947. Survivors tell their stories through the film *Testimony*. It also has a hall of remembrance, America's national memorial to the victims of the Holocaust, and the Wexner Learning Centre in which touch-screen computer stations allow people to pursue their particular interests. On the ground floor there is a space for major temporary exhibitions on aspects of the Holocaust and the Wall of Remembrance commemorates, with 3000 tiles made by American schoolchildren, the 1.5 million children that died.

Whilst waiting for the lift for the fourth floor, visitors are invited by a museum official to choose an 'identification card' from two boxes labeled 'males' and 'females'. From this they learn the name, age, occupation, origin and fate of one person caught up in the Holocaust. Visitors are free to choose whether they pick a male ID card or a female ID card. However, my observation over five days was that the overwhelming majority of people chose an identity card that matched their own gender. On one of my own visits I chose a male ID card – Emanuel (Manny) Mandel, born May 8, 1936 in Riga, Latvia, from a religious Jewish family. Later that day, in the Ladies Rest Room, a 13 year old girl asked 'Who are you?' – referring not to the real me, but to my 'Holocaust Identity' suggested by my ID card. She was surprised when I told her I was a young boy: 'Oh. How come you're a boy? Did you pick from the wrong box? You see I'm a girl so I chose a girl. Look. See? Alice Lok. I was born in February 7, 1929. Budapest. Hungary. I'm

Jewish. Well actually I'm Christian – Alice is Jewish. She was in Auschwitz' (Girl visitor, aged 13, US Holocaust Museum, April, 1999).

This encounter raises several issues concerning subjectivity and remembering in the museum aenvironment. First, the curator/designers and visitors assume an ability to practice flexible identifications in terms of remembering religion, nationality, age or ethnicity: the American-born Christian girl assumes the identity of a Hungarian Jew for the day. But, in contrast, curator/designers and visitors assume the practice of fixed and unchanging identifications in terms of remembering gender. Gender is perceived as something essentialist and 'natural': one 'naturally' picks male or female depending on one's sex ('I'm a girl so I chose a girl'). One would only choose otherwise by accident – 'Did you pick from the wrong box?'. The design of this part of the museum could have been that the male and female ID cards were kept together, so that visitors randomly picked the identities of either gender. Or, the museum could have chosen to make other divisions immutable – children and adults, for example. The decision to divide the identification cards into male and female is thus not without significance. The ID cards carry the motto 'For the Dead and the Living we must bear witness' – the connotation is not only that whether one was male or female during the Holocaust mattered but also that whether we are male or female as witnesses to their memory also matters. The identification card boxes hail us as males or females from the start of the narrative history of the Holocaust. Our dialogic memory of the events begins with us having to make an explicit choice about identification based on gender. But this 'choice' is within the social experience of gender as something 'natural', fixed, given and difficult to transgress. This structures the visitor's reception of the past and the identification between ourselves as visitors to the museum and the 'real person who lived during the Holocaust' (ID card wording). On one level this can be interpreted as an evocation of what we learn on the third floor of the 'selections' for life and death in which men and women were separated. However, as we shall see, this resonance is, in parts, mystified and left incomplete. This is not unique to the US Holocaust Museum and is not untypical of representations of the past in museum environments generally, as Gaby Porter (1996) has suggested. It is the result of a complex rendering of gender in which masculinity and femininity in the museum environment tend to be constituted in discourse through a set of hierarchical opposites. The roles of women in history tend to be constructed in ways that are relatively passive, shallow, undeveloped, muted and closed; while men's roles tend to be active, deep, highly developed, fully pronounced and open. Certain gender differences are not made explicit and, with some notable and important exceptions, women's presence in some places of the narrative is muted, while men's presence, in most places, as victim, perpetrator, resister and rescuer in a variety of ways tends to be dominant. Overall, the Holocaust in the US Holocaust Museum is narrated through a gendered hierarchical dichotomy articulated through photographs, video, text, artefacts and the relationships between these different media.

Undeveloped and unpronounced

The first artefactual exhibit of the US Holocaust Museum on the fourth floor is a display of prisoners' uniforms. Such objects, with provenances of both women and men, are important signifiers of ethnicity and gender (Hooper- Greenhill 2000:111). All except one of the 'prisoners' uniforms are in fact the familiar uniforms of male prisoners: trousers and top, with the dominant stripes of dark blue and grey. It is this fabric design – based on the uniforms of male prisoners – which is used as a resonator of memory on museum chairs. What is left unarticulated is the fact that there are fewer female uniforms in existence because more men than women were selected for slave labour rather than death (Felstiner, 1997:208). Women selected for immediate death would not have needed uniforms. Many women selected for labour did not wear uniforms, either (Ringelheim, personal communication, 6.9.01). However, there is no textual explanation as to why only one sole woman's dress in paler, narrower stripe is present in this tower of men's uniforms. Many visitors would not necessarily know that men and women wore different uniforms. As a result, artefacts deeply imbricated with gender – clothing – which belonged to men are used as signifiers of the experiences of both male and female prisoners, but without making the gendered context or the men's provenance of the artefacts explicit. As Hooper-Greenhill stresses, the provenance of artefacts is important – it provides the context and makes transparent the stories behind them (Hooper-Greenhill, 2000:14). In the display of uniforms, and at points elsewhere, the critical provenance of the artefacts is left undeclared. By doing what Porter (1996:113) describes as mystifying the process of production, this serves to obfuscate underlying meaningful, educational and memorable gendered structures of discourse and provenance, suppressing women's presence and experiences.

The construction of women's roles as passive and undeveloped is illustrated by the pronounced focus given to the spaces and places that men inhabited. Thus, while we see, for example, on the fourth floor, with the rise of Nazi power the public acts of humiliation and the actions of the stormtroopers on both Jewish men and women, we do not see the everyday humiliations for Jewish women arising from their interactions with ordinary German women in the domestic or private sphere. To many highly assimilated German-Jewish women, rejections by German women, very often whom they had known for years, were as painful as the public humiliations by stormtroopers on the street. Obviously there are no 'visible' reminders, in the form of photographs, of these aspects of everyday life. But it is a question of finding other ways – through artefact or text for example – of being attentive to the importance of telling particular stories related to private spaces, the domestic and familial as well as those which are publically recorded through newspapers, photographs or films. This is important: as Claudia Koontz's research shows, it is there 'at the grassroots, in a social world inhabited by women' as much as in the 'extravagant insanity of Hitler's megalomania that the steps towards genocide were made' (Koontz, 1987:xxxv).

However, artefacts tend to construct women in this early section of the museum's historical narrative as objects rather than subjects or producers of discourse. A section on the Nuremberg Laws includes, for example, a special edition of the propaganda paper *Neue Sturmer* with a short textual translation of the German that reads: 'Why do Jews massively and systematically perpetrate race defilement against German women?' 'What are the consequences of race defilement for German women and German girls?'. Yet what if we included in the picture reference to the fact that German women were also the active producers of this propaganda (as well as Jewish men depicted as perpetrators and German women as victims in it)? We know that Gertrud Scholtz-Klink, the chief of the Women's Bureau under Hitler, wrote her propaganda book, *The Woman in the Third Reich,* which is still readily available, in the 1930s (Koonz, 1987:xix). Over a million German women subscribed to her journal (p. xxxiv).

There is little differentiation made between men' and women's experiences in the deportation figures, in the descriptions of the ghettos and camps, and in extermination figures. There is no mention of the fact that in many ghettos there were more women than men but that the structures of the Nazi – imposed Judenrats emulated the Jewish prewar all-male kehallas. And while the Oneg Shabbat – the recording of ghetto life in Warsaw – is mentioned in the museum, no mention or use is made of material from the study of women conducted at the time as part of this (see Dobroszycki, 1984; Unger, 1998; Ofer, 1998)

In the descriptions of the process of selection for death, narrated on the third floor, camp exhibits and text boxes tend to use the word 'prisoners' when they mean male prisoners, or the word 'camps' when they mean specifically male camps. The text for the section *Who shall Live and Who shall Die?* along with a photomontage of Jews from Hungary on arrival at Auschwitz, followed by a photomural of two long lines of women and men, reads: 'On the arrival platform, an SS officer conducted the selection – the sick, the elderly, pregnant women and young children were sent to the gas chambers. Male and female prisoners deemed capable of work were sent in another direction for an assignment of Slave Labour' (US Holocaust Museum). The text suggests that if you were not sick, elderly, pregnant or a child you would not be selected for death and that an equal number of men and women were deemed capable of work. Yet we know from accounts by survivors discussed in the previous chapters of this book that this was not the case, and that more women were sent for immediate death because their role as mothers and carers meant that on the whole they stayed with their children (see Chapters 2 and 3).

While specific acts against men as men are shown, the parallel story of what happened to women is often left unanswered or untold. An example of this is the section on *Lidice: Resistance and Reprisal* on the second floor. The Germans suspected Lidice inhabitants to have wounded Reinhard Heyrich, Chief of Security Police and Governor of German-occupied Poland, on 27 May 1942. The main text reads: 'All the adult males were shot on June 10 and the women were arrested and imprisoned in the concentration camp.' Each subsequent text reference and photograph refers to the murder of the men. There are no photos of women at all in this section and no voices of women. We are told nothing more of their fate. Did they survive the concentration camp? We know that the men were all murdered; but the visitor is left wondering what happened to the women.

With other social and ethnic groups, gender is also articulated unevenly. For example, on the fourth floor, when it comes to homosexuals, the text reads: 'The vast majority of homosexual victims were males; lesbians were persecuted to a far lesser extent.' Some recent research suggests that the extent of persecution of lesbians has been camouflaged, in part, by the fact that women who were lesbians tended to be imprisoned and labelled not with the pink triangle for homosexuality, but were labelled and thus identified with a black triangle, usually designating the Nazi category of 'asocials' – a group that included criminals as well as political prisoners of both sexes (Fuchs, 1999:x). Elman suggests that scholars still tend to ignore or minimise the fate of lesbians under Nazi rule because of their own biases (Elman, 1999:9). Although the subject is rarely discussed, a number of testimonies suggest that lesbians were especially chosen to be raped in the Nazi-created brothels. Erich H., a gay survivor, notes, for example, that 'the Nazi's especially liked to put lesbians to work in the brothels. They thought it would shape them up' (cited by Elman, 1999:16).

Another example of the uneven representation of gender in relation to different social and ethnic groups is in a section on the Romany, which includes a display of a woman's dress, a 'gypsy' wagon, violin and hair combs. The text reads: 'the woman who wore these combs was forcibly sterilised – a common fate for gypsy women in Nazi Germany.' The visitor is told little more than this. Although about one-quarter of Europe's Romany, Sinti and other tribes were murdered, there are few voices of witnesses or survivors. It is arguable that there are fewer sources in relation to the 'gypsy' genocide, yet there is material available. Lodz, for example, had its own ghetto for Roma and Sinti; all of Germany's 30,000 'gypsies' and part-'gypsies' were sent to Auschwitz where, unlike most of the other predominantly Jewish prisoners, they were kept within family groups and allowed to wear their own clothes, as well keeping their musical instruments. This was due to confused German policy against the Romany and Sinti that combined an element of 'zig-ennerromantik' with preparations for their eventual annihilation (see Kenrick and Puxon, 1972; Galinski, 1983; Hancock, 1996; Ramati, 1986; Lewy, 2000; Milton, 1997; Tyranauer, 1989).

Women's voices are muted in depictions of the liberation of the camps and the aftermath. We see the liberators as men – Allied soldiers, Soviet soldiers; visitors are told, 'The liberation included African-American and Japanese-American soldiers'. The film footage of Bergen-Belsen includes depictions of women victims and survivors showering, cooking, washing and combing their hair. The problem stems from how we represent and narrativise 'liberation'. If we represent this as one moment in time, taking the military perspective of liberation, the narrative representing the past will exclude relief workers and medical workers who provided the tools and practical support for survivors' rehabilitation – liberation in practice. We are not told, for example, that women were also present as humanitarian workers, providing essential nursing care and humanitarian aid. At Bergen-Belsen, for example, archive letters from women in the Imperial War Museum, London, show that while British women aid workers did not initially visit the camp, 'as it was considered too horrible' (by the British commanding officers), a letter home from Miss Impey, a nurse, to her family describes how out of the 62 relief workers 41 were women who bathed survivors and helped organise clothing, food and medical aid. Five hundred German nurses had also been drafted in to provide additional nursing support (Impey, 1945). Lieutenant Gonin, in his report on the liberation of Belsen, wrote that each night, when the relief workers and military met, 'the problems particular to the ladies would be discussed, first, about eleven o'clock they would be dismissed. Gin, brandy and champagne would appear and we would finish our business by twelve or in the morning (Gonin, 1945).

We see photographs of women SS guards (perpetrators) – there were 26 female SS at Belsen out of a total of 70. We also see them as victims/survivors. It is notable, therefore, that although the Allied women relief workers were initially hailed by the British press as the 'Heroines of Belsen' (Gonin, 1945:3; see also Zelizer, 1998), women taking an active role as practical 'liberators' and those survivors who also quickly took an active role organising soup kitchens and clothing distribution are so muted in the later public memory of events articulated and represented at the US Holocaust Museum. Part of the difficulty, I would suggest, in representing and therefore handing down this aspect of the aftermath of atrocity concerns the relative invisibility of women's work. The 'drama' of the story tends towards the dominant public record of events provided through military films of liberation rather than the repetitive, daily, ongoing 'un-heroic' work of rehabilitation. We also know from the previous chapter that it was difficult for technical reasons to record on film some of these latter activities – such as the 'human laundry' – where survivors were washed and disinfected at Bergen-Belsen (see Chapter 4). These aspects of the story, in order to be included in the public memory of events, would need to be represented in the museum through other means, such as artefacts and documents.

Hearing voices

Although sex differences are signalled through the separation of male/female ID cards as essential in terms of experience and identification at the start of the visitors' narrative journey, the museum, on the whole, does not then make key gender differences explicit in the narrative, nor are women's and men's experiences given an equal prominence. There are, though, a couple of important and notable exceptions to this. The first is the audio theatre on the third floor of the museum, *Voices from Auschwitz*. This consists of a glass-walled room next to the main exhibit of the extermination camps where visitors can enter and sit down to listen to taped voices of survivors experiences. It is one of the few places in the museum's narrative where one is not overtly channelled as a visitor – one can pass by the room without entering and in this sense the room is experienced initially as a narrative 'diversion'. However, although the room, unlike most exhibition spaces, is sealed off from the rest of the narrative one can see other visitors through the glass walls, and if there are few other visitors some voices permeate the walls. One cannot hear clearly, however, unless one enters the theatre itself.

The voice content of the room includes experiences of women not articulated elsewhere. One survivor, Helen Waterford, says, for example 'The women with children ... when they had children, there was no help. They had to go ... you go to the other side, and you only think "oh they are with the children ... they will be taken care of". That's what we thought, all of us' (Helen Waterford, audio theatre, US Holocaust Museum). Another, Hana Bruml, recalls: 'As we came and we undressed, we had to go through a hallway, naked except in the shoes. An SS came by and looked at our bellies ... if some of us might be pregnant. If they saw anybody pregnant, they pulled them out' (Hana Bruml, audio theatre, US Holocaust Museum). And Cecilie Klein-Pollak remembers: 'We didn't receive not even an underwear or brassieres or panties, just that one dress' (Cecilie Klein-Pollak, audio theatre, US Holocaust Museum). We hear in the *Voices from Auschwitz* aspects of the Holocaust that are rarely mentioned:

> I think it was the greatest shock for all of us because nobody menstruated anymore. That was over ... we had the whole, um, orphanage of Jewish girls from Paris, girls of 15 years old ... they were very upset when they were not menstruating. Everybody very young was, uh, concerned, but then it was a blessing. What would we have done? We had nothing. We had no underwear. We had nothing. (Helen Waterford, audio theatre, US Holocaust Museum)

For the first time, in the museum, we are asked to remember the specific experiences of women – the anxiety and blessing of not menstruating; the shame of being seen naked by SS men; daughters seeing mothers naked for the first time; mothers and daughters once shaved being unable to recognise each other.

It is not insignificant that the designer/curator of the audio theatre, Joan Ringelheim, the Director of the Department of Oral History, has conducted pioneering historical research on women and the Holocaust, edited the proceedings of the first conference on the subject in 1983 and has published widely on the subject. She has noted the importance of reintegrating the split that we have in social and personal memories between the Holocaust and gender (Ringelheim, 1998). At the time of the development of the museum, as Director of Research for the Permanent Exhibition, Joan Ringelheim wrote memoranda and research briefs on women on many occasions, although she had to be careful not to be seen to push the women and the Holocaust issue too much because it could be seen as promoting her own research (Joan Ringelheim, personal communication, 1999; 2001).

Photos from the Shtetl of Eishishok

Another place where women are present in equal numbers with men, where their presence is articulated and embodied in ways that capture the richness of their everyday pre-war lives, is in the display of photographs in a three-storey tower from the shtetl of Ejszyszski (Eishishok in Yiddish) where Jewish people had lived since the 11th century. The photos were mostly taken by Yitzhak Uri Katz and his wife Alte Katz between 1890 and 1941. In 1941, a mobile SS killing squad murdered virtually the entire population of 3500 people. The men were taken by the SS on 24 September and shot by the old Jewish cemetary. The women were taken on 26 September and murdered. Nine hundred years of Jewish life ended in two days. The arrangement and balance of the photographs and the way in which they rise up in a tower that could appear to the visitor like smoke in a chimney make this one of the most moving and informative parts of the museum. Unusually, we know the provenance of the photographs and the photographers. We are also told in a text box that the arrangement was made by Dr Yaffa Eliach who spent her early childhood in the shtetl and who is the granddaughter of Yitzhak and Alte. The context of production provided with the photographs has a powerful rehumanizing effect that includes the restoration of gendered roles and identities. The photographs were taken as part of everyday life, and we see women and men, boys and girls in their own clothes and environment. This is qualitatively different from the anonymity and obscenity of Nazi-shot photographs, which were taken as part of the Nazi process of humiliating the victim further by capturing the moment of torture, pain or death (see Chapter 4). Here the photos are arranged by a survivor with a living connection to the dead. It is here that many visitors, myself included, wept.

Women's hair

Near Washington DC, in storage rather than left with the dead in Auschwitz or on display at the Holocaust Museum, are 9 kilos of women victims' hair. The reason for the absence of women's hair from the exhibition itself, and the debates surrounding this decision, highlight the gendered tensions and difficulties that underlie the construction and mediation of memory within the public institution. Initially, after museum researchers had visited memorial sites in Poland, it had been agreed that part of the museum's exhibition would include the display of human hair. An order had been made on 16 August 1942 by SS *Brigadefuhrer* that all human hair shaved from prisoners should be utilised: 'out of the combed and cut hair of women, hair-yarn socks for U boat crews are to be made, as well as hair-felt stockings for employees of the Reich railways' (Linenthal, 1995:212). The hair was sold to factories for 50 pfennings a kilo and as well as being used for socks, was also used as insulation for houses (which, where the houses still stand, keep the inhabitants warm) (Warszawski, 1996:132). Soviet troops had found nearly 7000 kilos of human hair at Auschwitz. The Museum at Auschwitz sent over the hair to the Museum in Washington. However, some members of the museum committee, which included survivors, objected on moral grounds to the proposed display of the hair. They argued that to display something so personal, something that was part of someone's body, was inappropriate outside the context of where the atrocities had been perpetrated. Others, however, believed that it was important to show the extent of the Nazi destruction process. Joan Ringelheim argued that the hair would provide a much – needed focus for what was done to women (Linenthal, 1995:214). Although the committee voted by 9 votes to 4 in favour of displaying the hair, Dr Helen Fagin, a survivor, convinced the committee otherwise, pointing out that the display of hair would show 'insensitivity and a violation of feminine identity' (Linenthal, 1995:215). In the end it was decided that an enlarged photograph of the hair would be shown, rather than the hair itself. Edward T. Linenthal (1995), in his history of the museum, takes the view that the debate was purely about a clash of different voices – the commemorative and the educational. Yet embedded within the debate, I would argue, are also clashes relating to gender politics, memory and media representation. This is further evidenced by the exhibit itself.

The photomural of the hair is preceded by a narrative that shows enlarged photos and close-ups of arms with number tattoos and a large photo of the male survivors of Salonika displaying the numbers tattooed on their arms. There is a large photograph of male prisoners with tattoos on their chests. The text box accompanying this states, 'many Soviet prisoners of war had numbers tattooed on their chest'. In this way, as throughout the museum, gender neutral words such as deportees, prisoner and survivor are constructed to mean men and occasionally men and women. Women are usually referred to separately as women prisoners, or women survivors.

There is a photograph of women in lines of five who are holding each other for support, with text that reads, 'Initiation into concentration camp life was degrading for women, who had to undress in front of SS guards. These newly arrived Hungarian Jewish women have just had their hair shorn'. Although the explanation does include some articulation of the specific humiliation women felt, the use of the passive verb with no active subject pushes out of discourse the complex gendered dimensions of this experience. Male survivors have described their pain and horror at having to cut the hair off women, sometimes even their own wives and mothers (see Chapters 2 and 4). Women survivors have likewise described the specific humiliation and shame women felt at being shaved by men, particularly when this involved body hair (see Chapter 2 and 3). There are then the particular meanings left unarticulated for Orthodox Jews. To shave a man's earlocks and beard is to emasculate him; to shave a young single woman is to do something that should not be done until marriage. The text accompanying the photograph of the hair states: 'the state Museum of Auschwitz in Poland exhibits hair from about 40,000 deportees. The hair in this photograph represents a minuscule fraction of the total amount shorn from concentration camp prisoners and genocide victims' (US Holocaust Museum, text box).

Since most prior narrative has already constructed prisoners and victims to mean men, unless stated otherwise, we are as visitors left uncertain as to whether this is hair belonging to men and women, or specifically to women. It is in fact the latter, according to Linenthal (1995: 114). This is not meant to question the validity of having a display showing both (especially since men and women were shaved) but it is to highlight the continuing uncertainty as to women's presence/absence in the museum's narrative especially at particular artefactual conjunctures. Since the photograph *is* showing women's hair, then why not say so? – particularly since the overriding objection to its display rests on Dr Helen Fagin's understandable sense that its display would violate particular 'feminine' identity and not simply human dignity? The brief inclusion of some sense of critical provenance for the choice of photograph – saying, this is women's hair but it was not displayed because it was felt it would violate feminine dignity further, would clarify its authenticity for visitors. Indeed, as I silently looked at the photomural of women's hair, an American family next to me debated whether the hair 'was real'. 'They could have just made up that photo,' said the boy. The point is that the hair is absent because it is real and because it originates from the heads and bodies of women who were murdered.

It should be stressed, however, that to raise these issues concerning gender in the US Holocaust Museum is not to question the overall veracity or validity of the project as a whole. It should be emphasised that the museum is still an immense achievement, involving the dedicated work and expertise of many people over many years. It facilitates an important part of our collective remembering and education about the Holocaust and it provides a rightful memorial to the dead. As Joan Ringelheim reminds us, 'the hair is one small part of a much greater whole' (Ringelheim, personal communication, 1999).

On intimacy

There are, though, other ways of articulating gender in the public memory of the Holocaust in the museum environment. One example of this is within Jewish-American memory constructed and mediated at the *Museum of Jewish Heritage: A Living Memorial to the Holocaust*, situated at the tip of Manhattan where, historically, Jews first landed in North America in the seventeenth century. As with the US Holocaust Museum, the placing of the museum is politically significant: it stands opposite the Hudson Bay with the Statue of Liberty and Ellis Island in its sights, reminding visitors of the national discourse of America as the nation state that grew out of accepting refugees from political and religious oppression.[5] The museum was opened on 15 September 1997, after 16 years of debate, discussion and hard work following a Task Force Report recommending that a museum and memorial be built in the City. The building was designed by Kevin Roche and is six sided as a reminder of the six million Jews who died as well as symbolising the Star of David. Like the US Holocaust Memorial Museum, it is an historical narrative museum, with visitors taken on a story told over three floors: 'The World Before, the Holocaust and Renewal'. Artefacts, throughout, are carefully integrated with individual survivor's accounts and the museum as a whole includes more than 2000 photographs, 800 artefacts and 24 original documentary films (Museum of Jewish Heritage, undated).

Its mission, curatorial approach and ethos in key ways are very different from the US Holocaust Museum. Its mission is to 'educate people of all ages and backgrounds specifically about twentieth century Jewish history, before, during and after the Holocaust' (Museum of Jewish Heritage, undated). Unlike the US Holocaust Museum, which also tells the story of non-Jewish victims of the Holocaust, including to some extent Poles, homosexuals, 'gypsies', the mentally ill and disabled, the Museum of Jewish Heritage concentrates on the Jewish dimension of events. The emphasis is on the richness and longevity of Jewish history before and after the events, with the Holocaust contextualised within this. The word 'Holocaust' is in fact not mentioned on the first floor of the museum at all. According to David Liebmann, Deputy Director of Education:

> it's deliberately set up so that you don't come in thinking this is the Holocaust Museum. Very often we are referred to in that way but we are not a Holocaust Museum ... we try to show the humanity and what happened and the humanity often comes from how people lived. How they treated each other, how they faced terrible circumstances and then made it through or didn't make it through (David Liebmann, Deputy Director of Education, *Museum of Jewish Heritage*, interview April 1999)

An important part of the museum experience is the role given to gallery educators: these are women and men, many of whom are survivors themselves, trained in Holocaust education, who provide visitors with support and additional context for the exhibits and people's stories. This emphasis on stories and context, David Liebmann stressed, is a conscious part of the museums ethos. The museum, rather than using theatricality or trying to emulate or imitate the conditions of horror:

> lets the story tell itself ... we are not trying to turn the Holocaust into pornography. It's not an objective occasion. It's not a spectator

sport where we say look here are all these dead people, let's look at them. There are very few pictures of dead people ... it's about people's lives and how they lived during the time – that's the key that makes the difference. (David Liebmann, Deputy Director of Education, *Museum of Jewish Heritage*, Interview April 1999)

The role of the educators, combined with the fact that the museum is much smaller than the US Holocaust Memorial Museum, gives it an intimacy that restores people's humanity. The emphasis on combining objective facts about where, when or how something may have happened, along with subjective accounts, experiences, personal belongings and stories, has resulted in a very different articulation of gender: there is a much greater equality given to men and women in terms of voice, image and complexity of representation.

On restoring context

On the first floor, visitors enter a rotunda – a six sided open space – with a large video screen that continuously plays a video recording of men and women talking about their background, thoughts and feelings about being Jewish today. Visitors are invited to empathise with both men and women, and our identification may shift as in everyday life. The video underscores the rich variety of traditions within Judaism. The rotunda establishes from the beginning the rejection of exclusive and essentialist ideas about Jewish identity and instead visitors are invited to connect with many different kinds of Jewish people, traditions and beliefs. These themes of variety, complexity and flexibility are continued into the main exhibition space on the first floor. Here we see the richness of Jewish life in Europe and the US before the Second World War. There is a strong presence given to the domestic sphere and the family and household and because of this women and girls are included in ways that they would not be if the emphasis was solely on the public sphere. Nevertheless, girls and women are also shown in non-traditional roles alongside more common pursuits: we see a photograph of girls at sewing classes in the 1920s as well as at a technical school before the war. Likewise, when survivors in the video displays talk about their grandparents' and parents' occupations at the time, women talk about the broad range of occupations in which women were involved, including those who were successful in entering professional careers such as medicine. From the start, all artefacts and photographs are provided with a sense of critical individual provenance: visitors are informed in text boxes about the original context and ownership of items and what they may have been used for. This establishes Jewish people as subjects rather than objects of discourse, and constructs women as well as men within this as originators of history and memory rather than mute witnesses of it.

On the second floor, men and women are again fairly consistently given equal voice and image. In virtually every case there are equal numbers of artefacts, photographs, testimonies and points of view given by both women and men. Where there are images or film footage in which one gender is foregrounded, this is then counterbalanced with greater voice given to the other gender in the following panel or exhibit. The artefacts include the intimate and the everyday – a pair of men's shoes, a girl's hair comb made in the ghetto. Always, where possible, artefacts have next to them a photograph of their owner(s) that articulates and makes explicit both men's and women's stories and memories. In this way, generic words – 'victim, prisoner, Jew', are constructed to mean both men and women, and women or men in equal measure. An illustration of this is a display of six prisoners' uniforms, belonging to three men and three women, one from each of the six major killing centres. Underneath one dress, the text explains its provenance: 'on her arrival at Auschwitz Birkenau death camp from Cluj, Hungary, Rose Safiro was issued this ill-fitting threadbare dress that offered little protection from the cold' (Museum of Jewish Heritage, *Killing Centres*).

Specific acts and experiences related to gender are generally made explicit. For example, we are told that on arrival at Auschwitz deportees were separated by sex. Survivor, Lena Berg then remembers how, 'We were told to strip; male prisoners shaved our heads and the rest of our bodies with clippers' (MJH, floor two, *Assault on Humanity*).

Underneath a photograph of women in barracks the text states: 'hundreds of women crowd a barracks originally designed as a stable for 52 horses'. (MJH, Floor Two, *The Nightmare of Existence)* To counterbalance this another photograph showing men returning from forced labour has the text 'detachments of 400–500 men brought back with them in the evening five to twenty corpses.' (MJH, floor two, *Torture and Punishment*).

Photographs of atrocities, rather than being used uncritically in ways that do not disrupt the underlying obscenity of the Nazis capturing their victims on film, are given a sense of critical provenance that enables the visitor to become aware of their own process in viewing the photograph. The photographs become artefacts with stories, rather than simply records of events. For example, underneath an enlarged black-and-white photograph of four women lined up in their under-wear and three other smaller photographs of people being murdered, the text reads, 'A Jewish victim is photographed before being murdered by an SS killing unit in the Ukraine, USSR, 1942'. Another text box reads, 'Jews forced to strip are photographed by the SS before being executed by mobile killing units. Poland 1942. (Museum of Jewish Heritage, Floor Two, *Organising Mass Murder*). The museum translates rather than reproduces Nazi linguistic obfuscations such as Einsatzgruppen – in this case 'mobile killing unit' – making explicit and accessible what happened. The text makes clear the process of photographic production. The SS photographers who with their cameras shot those being shot, are included as perpetrators of abuse: the photograph is thus used as visual testimony of the literal stripping of victims prior to murder, but is also displayed as evidence of the abusive use of photography and filming by the Nazis as part of the dehumanising process that men and women underwent prior to their deaths.

Another technique that the museum uses is to return the gendered humanity of the victim by reminding us of their life prior to the atrocities. After horrific photographs showing stacks of unidentified corpses and a description by Filip Mueller describing how the bottom layer of corpses at Auschwitz-Birkenau consisted of children, the old and sick, there follows a room of 2000 individual photographs and names of men, women, boys and girls in equal numbers which serve symbolically to reverse the Nazi dehumanisation process.

> They had homes and lives. They had families and friends. They had names ... 2000 men, women and children symbolise the many trainloads sent to Auschwitz ...

> They are shown here not as they died, but as they lived – a gesture of respect to the victims and their families and a gesture of defiance to the Nazis who attempted to obliterate their memory. (MJH, Second Floor, Portraits Gathered by the Association of Sons and Daughters of Jews Deported from France)

The liberation dress

The final exhibition on the second floor centres on the dress of a survivor. The dress, stitched by hand from blue-and-white check gingham, has puff sleeves and a tailored waist. It was made by and belongs to survivor Frania Bratt Blum. Displayed in a glass case so that it is visible from all angles, the text box reads: 'Sitting upon her bunk in the recently liberated Dachau concentration camp in May, 1945, Frania Bratt used fabric supplied by the US army to make a dress for herself and her sister' (MJH, second floor, *Frania Bratt's Liberation Dress*). In this way the dress is used to symbolise the restoration of an identity for women after the war – the survivor re-clothed in self-made femininity. The survivor here is represented as actively reconstructing her life, using her skills to produce something useful and beautiful and lasting. The photographs of women and men that accompany this in the section entitled the *Surviving Remnant* emphasise the traditional roles that women took on immediately after the war in terms of marriage and motherhood. One could argue in this respect that the dominant discourse here excludes other roles that women also took on. However, as explored in Chapter 3, in women's autobiographies and accounts of survival they often cite the crucial importance to them of remaking themselves as 'a wife' and 'mother'; the roles enabled them to rebuild their shattered selves/lives after the War. However, what the dress does do is present the restoration of these roles as uncomplicated: it silences the fact that for many survivors the role of motherhood was 'infected with atrocity' (see Chapter 3). The exhibition also does not articulate the complicated restoration of 'masculinity' for many male survivors after the war – as Wiesel expresses in his account, *Night* (see also Chapter 3).

Silences

The final part of the exhibition in the Museum of Jewish Heritage shows what happened after the Holocaust and the establishment of the State of Israel. At the end of the exhibition story visitors step into the light cast across the Hudson Bay, the water glittering, surrounding the Statue of Liberty, symbol of political inclusion and welcome, as well as Ellis Island, where poor immigrants would be kept, processed and sometimes turned back. It is here, though, also, that the museum builds post-war memory on a silence: what is not unarticulated on the third floor is any sense of the consequences for non-Jewish inhabitants in the post-war created Israel; the resulting loss of land, homes and displacement experienced by Palestinian women, men and children and the ongoing unresolved conflict stemming from this.

There are also some notable gendered silences throughout the exhibition. For example, the restrictions imposed on Jewish people in various countries in Europe for hundreds of years cut across and through established gender divisions in which women, both Jewish and non-Jewish, were denied many civil and political rights. Laws denying Jewish people political enfranchisement, for example, would have applied to men but not women, since all women in Europe (and the US), whatever their cultural and religious background, were fairly consistently denied enfranchisement until the early twentieth century. Likewise, there tends to be a denial of the ways in which constructed gender roles intersected with Nazi racist policies, resulting in some cases in different consequences for Jewish men and Jewish women. Thus, in the section *Confronting Persecution*, the text box states: 'The elderly – or those caring for elderly parents could not easily leave'. As we know from earlier historical sources, those who care for the elderly, as today, were disproportionately women, generally single women who stayed behind to care for them while male relatives were able to flee. One of the consequences of this, which is also not articulated, is the higher number of women in the ghettos. Other gender differences are also muted: for example, there is discussion of hiding and passing but, as indicated, the examination of some historical sources (see Chapter 2) shows that boys found it much more problematic than girls to pass as non-Jews because they were circumcised. In Eastern Europe, girls also were more likely to have attended local schools learning Polish or Czech rather than Yiddish and Hebrew as boys did at their local Jewish school. This, again, made passing more of a viable option for girls (see Chapter 2). In these respects, it is as if there is a fear of indicating any difference in terms of experience. Yet, such facts, I would suggest, are part of the complexity that was the Nazi genocide: reconciling ourselves to these facts is part of developing a richer understanding of the past.

Intervening into memory

Overall, though, the Museum in New York articulates gender within the boundaries of its focus on Jewish heritage and the Holocaust in a way that is complex and inclusive. This gender balance in the construction of memory is no accident. Partially it can be explained by the overall ethos in which the museum staff themselves as 'a family' wanted to provide a more intimate and humane experience, along with retaining the complexities of humanity and Jewish identity throughout. Thematically, the family is at the centre of the museum, and with it we witness both the loss and restoration of those severed relationships. David Liebmann also suggested that the gender balance in part is facilitated by the high number of women volunteers in the education department. He concludes, 'it probably was deliberately balanced I think ... where we can show something that is more complicated than it first appears, we try to do that. We don't try to simplify any role, we don't try to simplify any aspect of the Holocaust' (David Liebmann, Deputy Director of Education, *Museum of Jewish Heritage*, Interview, April 1999).

The articulation of gender could also have been very different if it were not for an intervention early on in the choices and design of the exhibition by Marion Kaplan, who was one of the academic advisors for the museum. The Acting Director of the Museum, Yitzchak Mais, at the 'Women and the Holocaust Conference: New Perspectives' (2000) described how, in an early meeting, the curatorial group were looking at the choice of photographs that had been selected for display in the museum: 'Marion Kaplan said "what you have here is males only" – and I replied that I just hadn't thought of this ... after that there was a particular sensitivity to gender because of this' (Mais, 2000). The choice of photographs was then changed to include women and men on an equal basis. This suggests that interventions into the construction of socially inherited memories represented in the public museum environment can and do make a difference.

On the value of mindfulness

One of the most gender-balanced exhibitions, however, is the Holocaust Exhibition at the Imperial War Museum, in London, UK, supported by Heritage Lottery funding and first opened in June, 2000.[6] The exhibition replaced a much smaller exhibition which had been criticised by Holocaust scholar Tony Kushner for marginalizing the Jewish identity of victims and focusing on the liberation of Belsen by British forces. Kushner had argued that the victims and survivors were portrayed from the perspective of the British liberators, leaving them dehumanised and without individuality (Kushner, 1997). The new exhibition, which like the Museum of Jewish Heritage and the US Holocaust Museum, constructs the representation of events as a narrative, aims to 'relate the facts of this cataclysmic event, bringing some understanding of what happened and why' (Crawford, 2000:3). The museum itself is approached via the placement of two artefacts signifying the might of the British forces defending freedom of speech; visitors walk between two grey metal 15-inch naval guns from the Second World War and past a chunk of the original Berlin Wall to the left which carries Cold War graffiti saying 'Change Your Life' in white paint on a huge red tongue sticking out of a giant mouth.[7] As a counterbalance to the weapons of war, the guns are encircled with flowerbeds of English roses. The visitor then approaches the entrance to the permanent Holocaust Exhibition through the main exhibition concourse in which the weapons and vehicles of warfare are displayed: tanks, jeeps, submarines, artillery vehicles and aircraft. On leaving the exhibition visitors exit into an exhibition space overlooking the armoured vehicles and artillery walked through at the beginning. In this way, where the main museum shows 'the efforts and sacrifice of many people, including those Allied servicemen and women who gave their lives to defeat Nazism', the Holocaust Exhibition 'depicts also the nature of the evil which they helped to defeat' (Crawford, 2000:3). The exhibition about Nazi genocide is thus situated as part of the story of modern warfare: the Holocaust is represented as part of the bigger narrative of Britain's involvement in fighting the Nazis in the Second World War.

The central element of the narrative, which uses film, photographs, artefacts and documents as well as video testimony and audio stories related by survivor witnesses, is the destruction of the Jews in Europe. But the museum does also give voice and representation to the stories of others persecuted and murdered by the Nazis, including gypsies, homosexuals, Poles, Soviet prisoners of war, prisoners of conscience, Jehovah's Witnesses and people with mental and physical disabilities and illnesses (Crawford, 2000:3).

The exhibition begins with a brief introduction to some Jewish families before the Second World War and Europe after the First World War. We are then taken through the rise of Hitler, the longevity of antisemitism, the development of the racial state, propaganda and race hatred, Hitler's growing empire and those seeking refuge from it. The third floor ends with photographs of those murdered under Hitler's T4 euthanasia programme. We approach the second floor on stairs built to resemble a ghetto bridge. The lighting grows darker and the exhibition space more restricted as visitors are taken through the invasion of Poland, the invasion of the Soviet Union, the murders of the mobile killing squads, the forced movement of people into ghettos, 'resettlement' to the East, the development of the 'final solution' and deportation to Auschwitz. Visitors are shown the process of killing at

Britain
already
knew
↑

Auschwitz in detail, the camp system and inside the camps. They see how some survived outside of the system through rescue, resistance and hiding; how the Nazis tried to destroy the evidence, the discovery of the atrocities, particularly those by the British at Belsen, and the War Crimes Trials. Finally we watch testimonies on video by witness-survivors.

The exhibition illustrates that it is possible to articulate gender and genocide in ways that are inclusive, complex and generally balanced. The overall representation of men and women in terms of photographic images, survivor-witness representations and artefactual origins is virtually equal. This was notable not only in terms of having an equal number of images but also in terms of balancing the focus, size and prominence of images. This is, then, on the whole, supported by the language used in text boxes, which constructs terms such as prisoner, deportee, and Jew to include both men and women. On the whole, visitors are given the provenance of objects and artefacts which makes explicit the gendered origins and stories behind them. For example, in the section *Thousands Seek Refuge* a photospread in the *Picture Post* in 1938 of Jewish boys rescued as part of Britain's kindertransport operation is counterbalanced with stories and artefacts of two girl survivors. This gender balance is maintained in the exhibition narrative by the use of video and audio accounts by survivor-witnesses, most of whom subsequently came to Britain, which give equal prominence to men and women.

Equal prominence to men and women is also provided through documents and accounts by perpetrators. The translation of the Jager Report in the section entitled *Mobile Killing Squads* shows, in the lists of massacres in Lithuania between 4 July and 1 December 1941, how the Nazis themselves hierarchically ordered the deaths of Jewish people in terms of their nationality, usually distinguishing between men and women and giving murder figures for Jews and Jewesses, as the following shows for 2 August 1941:

170 Jews, 1 US Jew
1 US Jewess , 33 Jewesses
4 Lithuanian Communists
209 [total killed]
(*Mobile Killing Squads*, Imperial War Museum, the Jager Report)

The figures highlight the disproportionate number of Jewish men who were slaughtered in July of that year and how this shifted to include the women in communities as well: for example for the town of Rassasiniani the text read

9–16.8.41. Rassasiniani
    294 Jewesses
    4 Jewish Children
    (*Mobile Killing Squads*, Imperial War Museum, the Jager Report)

The enlarged version of this document, which takes up an entire wall in the exhibition, demonstrates to visitors how the Nazis listed other groups separately, and how they usually distinguished between men and women. On 22 August at Dunaberg the toll massacred included '3 gypsies (m); 1 gypsy (f)' and at Aglona on the same day the murder toll included: 'Mentally sick: 269 men; 227 women; 48 children' (Mobile Killing Squads, Imperial War Museum, the Jager Report). The document is placed next to an enlarged photo of a mass grave of anonymous corpses, thereby anchoring the image to Nazi ideology and race 'science'. The anonymous corpses become invested with a location, a time, and a dis-comforting identity as a Nazi-imposed category: we re-see the dead bodies in the mass as men, women and children murdered on a specific day in a particular place because they were categorised as unworthy of life by the Nazis.

It is not only women as victims that are given equal representation in the exhibition but also women as perpetrators. In the section on the camp system on the second floor, the text reads: 'Over 7000 staff – officers, doctors, administrators and guards – served in the Auschwitz complex. These men and women came from many backgrounds' (Imperial War Museum, Holocaust Exhibition, *Auschwitz*).

This is shown alongside a large photograph and biography of Auschwitz Commandant Rudolf Hoess and a large photograph and biography of Irma Griese, notorious camp guard, who is usually shown in other exhibitions and contexts as an anonymous woman in the background. In this way the often silenced or marginalised memory of women as also responsible for the perpetration of atrocities is integrated as part of the narrative. Likewise, women are included as active participants in terms of being helpers and rescuers, as the story with the artefact of a silver spoon poignantly demonstrates:

Anna Wiechac was a widow with three young children in Krakow. In 1943 she took in a Jewish woman with a five year old girl called Marysia. Each morning the pair left Anna's flat. When they returned at night the woman cooked and set the table with Marysia's silver spoon and fork – all that remained of their previous life. One day they left as usual but never came back. (Imperial War Museum, Holocaust Exhibition, *Hiding*)

Women are represented in their roles as participants in the aftermath following the liberation of the camps. A display case with artefacts from British Forces includes a letter from Sister Kitty Eldridge. The letter serves to connote the humanitarian role women took after the War, rather than solely giving voice to the roles that men played in the liberating forces as soldiers.

The exhibition gives voice and image to experiences specific to men and women which are co-balanced and fully integrated into the main exhibition narrative. In the section *Terror Strikes Poland*, survivor Ester Brunstein describes on video her experience of witnessing in Poland Orthodox Jewish men having their beards and earlocks cut off by Nazi soldiers. Next to the video screen is a large photograph of men having their earlocks and beards forcibly cut off amid laughing crowds. Further on, *Invasion of the Soviet Union* has an almost life-size photograph of a naked girl lying distraught in the gutter. An older woman is tending her and pressing a cloth to her genitals. Another panel shows a woman in her underwear, which is ripped and torn, running screaming down a street. The text box reads: 'Local antisemites abuse Jewish women in the streets of Lvov. Dozens were murdered and women were raped. On 29–30 July, after the Germans had captured the city, 5000 Jews were rounded up and massacred by the Ukrainian militia' (Imperial War Museum, Holocaust Exhibition, *The Invasion of the Soviet Union*).

The Imperial War Museum Holocaust Exhibition includes photographs representing the specific memory of the rape and sexual abuse of women, which we know from women's and men's autobiographies (see Chapter 2) was an important but silenced part of women's and men's experience of genocide and the actions and policies that went before it. The photographs are stills taken from a film which is on display in the US Holocaust Museum behind a privacy wall (Joan Ringelheim, personal communication, 8/24/01). By placing this after the specific atrocities committed against Jewish men, at the heart of the main narrative, it articulates the way in which the experiences and mechanisms of antisemitism were at times different for men and women.

In the section on Auschwitz, entitled *Selection*, which accompanies a large scale model in white that shows the selection process, the text includes the words 'mothers with children'. 'On average 80 per cent of each transport – the old, the sick, mothers with children and pregnant women – went to the gas chambers' (Imperial War Museum, Holocaust Exhibition, *Selection*). This is followed by the section headed: *Dividing Men and Women* in which visitors are told that all prisoners were then ordered to divide into groups of men and women. This is followed by the words from Elie Wiesel's (1983) *Night*: 'An SS non-commissioned officer gave the order: 'men to the left' 'women to the right'. Eight words spoken quietly, indifferently, without emotion. Eight short, simple words. Yet that was the moment when I parted from my mother' (Elie Wiesel, *Night,* cited at The Imperial War Museum, Holocaust Exhibition, *Dividing Men and Women*). Wiesel's words are shown next to a photograph of men and women being separated from each other. This is accompanied by the audio voices of men and women survivors and is followed by a photograph: 'Women and children from the Berehovo transport waiting in the birch grove outside Gas Chamber V'. In this way, the exhibition overtly articulates the way in which pre-war gendered roles (women's roles as mothers) and women's biological role (as bearers of children) led them to the gas chambers sooner than men. This is followed by a photograph of women prisoners chosen for work and the acknowledgement of the specific humiliation for women when they had their heads and bodies shaved by men, but it doesn't include the particular insult that this was felt to be by Orthodox Jewish unmarried women, for whom the shaving of the head was normally symbolic of the married state: 'Female arrivals in Auschwitz after being shaved of all their hair. This was particularly humiliating for women. Some SS men taunted them as they undressed and assaulted them during the process of shaving or the shower which followed it' (Imperial War Museum, Holocaust Exhibition, *Inside the Camps*).

Beside a number of men's striped uniforms there is a prisoner's dress, accompanied by the words: 'Prisoner's dress. Women were segregated from men in different barracks. There were also camps specifically for women. The largest of these was at Ravensbruck, north of Berlin' (Imperial War Museum, Holocaust Exhibition, *Prisoners Uniforms*).The inclusion of only one women's uniform relative to the number of men's is counterbalanced by the text which anchors it and hails the visitors attention to it.

Finally, when we are shown the horrors of massacres and murders in the last days of the war in the section *The Death Massacres,* unusually, the museum includes a specific massacre of women in the north of

German occupied Poland. The eyewitness testimony of Celina Manielewicz accompanies a photograph of corpses in the Baltic Sea, depicting the massacre at Palmnicken in 1945. She was one of only 13 survivors out of 9000 women: 'The whole coast, as far as I could see, was covered in corpses and I too was lying on such a mountain of corpses which slowly sank deeper and deeper'(Celina Manielewicz, Imperial War Museum,, Holocaust Exhibition, *The Death Marches*). Such testimony articulates lesser-known aspects of the last days of the War and clearly identifies, by using gender-specific terms, that women as well as men were massacred *en masse*.

There are, though, some mute spaces and less-articulated areas within the exhibition. One concerns the persecution of Sinti, Roma and other tribes prior to 1933. While we are told of the longevity of the persecution of Jews and the persistence historically of anti-semitism, there is no mention of similar prejudices in relation to 'gypsies' that the Nazis built on. Historical sources show that anti-gypsy laws dated from the fifteenth century in Europe. 'Gypsies' were banished, flogged, branded, hounded out and hunted to death. (Kenrick and Puxon, 1995: 12–13). In German States between 1416 and 1774 148 anti-gypsy laws were passed. In Baden in 1922 and in Prussia in 1927 'gypsies' were fingerprinted (Kenrick and Puxon, 1995:13).

There is also one point early on in the exhibition which articulates gender, antisemitism and Judaism in ways that are confused and confusing to the visitor. This is the section entitled *The Longest Hatred*. On one side the visitor is faced with a glass display case crammed with a broad variety of pre-war artefacts. These include a Torah and a kippah along with a copy of Oswald Mosely's *Tomorrow We Live: British Union Policy* and copies of *The Protocols of the Learned Elders of Zion*. It is not made explicit why these artefacts are put together in this way; the uninitiated might easily be forgiven for thinking that the pre-war British fascists were religious Jews. One could be left with the impression that the *Protocols* were authentic. The meaning of the Torah and kippah are not explained. Opposite the display case is a video which stitches together disparate clips of Jewish people before the War. The video is narrated by an anonymous male voiceover with no provenance provided regarding the film clips we see. The result is the objectification and mystification of the people the video purports to represent.

Overall, though, the Imperial War Museum Holocaust Exhibition articulates the memory of the Holocaust in ways that are gender balanced and inclusive. I would suggest the reasons for this, though not easily proven, concern the structure of curatorial production and gendered shifts within public memories of the events in the late 1990s. The Holocaust Exhibition, supported by a Heritage Lottery Fund, was overseen by an advisory group of five major Holocaust scholars and survivors, all of whom were men, but this was balanced by the Exhibition Project Office which included five women including Suzanne Bardgett as Project Director (Imperial War Museum, 2000:47). The Senior Historian, Steve Paulsson, also had an important impact on the writing and editing of the text for the exhibition. His Canadian background, which has some of the most inclusive laws on gender balance, resulted in a mindfulness towards gender in the text which, perhaps without his input, would not have been there (Bardgett, personal communication, 2001). The exhibition is also the most recent out of those analysed here, suggesting that public Holocaust memory, in terms of its articulation and representation of gender, is something that is evolving and gradually coming to include those aspects of gendered historiography generated since the late 1970s, which were discussed in the first chapter.

Conclusion

Undoubtedly, as other Holocaust scholars have shown, the national, political and ethnic context of different memorial sites and museums in Poland, Britain and the United States, result in the memory of the Holocaust being articulated and represented in very different ways (Brownstein, 1992; Huyssen, 1995; Kushner 1997; Young, 1993). The US Holocaust museum, with its entrance hall of battle flags of US Army Divisions, consciously defines the liberation of the camps as an 'American event' (Weinberg and Elieli, 1995:169). The memories of survivors in the Imperial War Museum are those of people who came to Britain; the active forces given voice in the liberation are British. The Museum of Jewish Heritage establishes from its name, from the very beginning with the voices and images of Jewish people in its Rotunda that its focus is Jewish history and thus the dimension of the Holocaust that is narrated concerns the murder of the Jews. At Auschwitz-Birkenau, the legacy of the pre-1989 Polish communist government's ideological emphasis on the national identities of victims is still visible, though supplemented and written over with some inclusion of the Jewish dimension to the killing centre. Yet, embedded within these differing ethnic and national memories are also variations in the ways in which gender is articulated. In Poland, at

Auschwitz-Birkenau, as a site of genocidal atrocities, the usual dialogical process involved in remembering breaks down and gender is emptied and buried, its memory visible only in the physical line on a map and in the empty remains of the women's camp. At museums more distant from the places of suffering and murder, gender is articulated in other ways. At the US Holocaust Museum the roles of women tend to be represented and articulated in ways that are more muted and underdeveloped in relation to the more active voice given to men's roles and experiences. Our identification as visitors is assumed to be flexible except in terms of gender, but gender resonances are then left mystified or incomplete in places of the narrative , except for particular areas such as the audio theatre. In contrast, both the Museum of Jewish Heritage in New York and the Imperial War Museum's Holocaust Exhibition in London, through a careful balancing of accounts, gives equal voice to men and women as Jewish victims but the London exhibition goes a step further in articulating the memory of the Nazis other victims as well as women's roles in history as perpetrators and liberators.

The result in terms of how we think about the representation and mediation of history and the construction of socially inherited memories is that while the dominant narratives of men tend to confirm and reinforce each other in different national museum contexts, the stories of women remain somewhat disjointed and discontinuous. This in part can derive from the narrative emphasis that a museum gives to the events: telling the part of the story from the perspective of the military liberators can exclude the role played in the aftermath by women as humanitarian workers in practical 'liberation'. Telling the story from the perspective of public records and state media representations can exclude women's roles and experiences under Nazism in private and domestic spaces. Using gender neutral nouns can obfuscate the gender-specific nature of artefacts and places.

At the same time, however, the dominant discourse and narratives within public memories in these different Holocaust museums even in 'permanent' exhibitions are contested. In the process of its construction, curatorial production structures and individual interventions have made a difference to the construction of the public memory of events. The production of Holocaust memory, as the discussions resulting in the absence of women's hair in the US Holocaust museum suggest, is fraught with literal and symbolic gendered tensions. The intervention of even one person can make a difference to the overall representation within a public space – as with the final selection of photographs at the Museum of Jewish Heritage. Further, being mindful of gender and its representation within the memory of historical events is not something essentially linked to either men or women, as the example of Steve Paulsson's input into gender-inclusive texts at British Imperial War Museum suggests. The differing memories of the Holocaust in these various museums and at the memorial site also show how gendered, socially inherited memories are never fully fixed by curators or national perspectives even in the 'permanent' exhibition. In gender terms at least, they are still evolving and still in process.

Within this the readings of different memorial sites and museums also indicate that visitors may make sense of the memory of the Holocaust, and articulate aspects of gender or ethnicity which are silenced through their own dialogic intertextuality, by bringing other texts (books, films, other museums) and experiences (personal subjectivities, imagination, family stories) to the museum to intervene into the narrative. Richard Crownshaw has noted, for example, in his analysis of the old exhibition in the Imperial War Museum, that although the contrivance of the past was indeed Anglo-centrist, we should be aware of the possibility of the 'museum visitor's intervention in British collective memory to remember what it forgets' (Crownshaw, 1999:296). This, I would argue, is also a continual possibility in terms of gender: partial or non-articulation of gendered specificities does not prevent altogether the visitor remembering and adding in to the picture their own version of events.

To explore this further, however, we need some evidence of how these various mediations – the written word, the moving image and the museum environment – that this book has considered in the construction of social memory, are integrated and inherited by people themselves. How do different mediations form our different socially inherited memories of events? Do men and women identify with and remember different aspects of the past? This is explored in the penultimate chapter on young people's social memories of the Holocaust in three different countries.

6
Grandma's Tales: Young People's Configurations of Holocaust Memory

'My grandmother always describes with tears in her eyes the moments when crowds of Jews were taken to concentration camps and how they were killed in the streets and how German soldiers, Gestapo, raped Jewish women.'
Monika,[1] aged 21, Gdansk, Poland. *Written Life History*, April 1999.

'Identity is formed at the unstable point where the "unspeakable" stories of subjectivity meet the narratives of history, of culture.'
(Stuart Hall, 1987:44)

Generations of memories

The Holocaust ended in 1945, but subsequent generations have inherited memories of the atrocities through a range of intersecting and contradictory cultural practices and mediations that include historical sources, autobiographies by survivors, films, memorial sites and museums. These mediations, as we have seen in the previous chapters, hand down discourses about the past that are gendered in complex ways to people in their everyday lives. This chapter considers what people themselves remember of these mediations: it looks at the processes involved in the configurations and generation of socially inherited memories of the Holocaust among young people sixty years on from the events. It explores the connections and disjunctures between people's gendered subjectivities and their identification and articulation of aspects of history. The chapter explores how men and women who have no direct experience of the Holocaust develop historical memories from different media. It looks at the differing connections between men and women and different media forms and contents, and considers whether men and women both equally articulate remembered facts as well as feeling; whether men and women remember different aspects of the Holocaust or make identifications and articulations more readily with perpetrator, victim, witnesses or bystanders.

The chapter draws on field research conducted between 1998 and 2001 in the US, Britain, and Poland in which 52 people, mostly aged between 16 and 35, were asked to articulate in writing and in speech their understanding, knowledge and feelings – their socially inherited memories – of the Holocaust, beginning with the first moment in their childhood when they became aware of it.

The chapter begins by considering the broader context of work on the transgenerational effects of Holocaust memory, the reception of history generally and broader theories from cultural and media studies on media audiences, and people's reception of cultural forms. Drawing on qualitative evidence from the study on social inheritance, it then looks at how memories are made within differing gendered structures of the family and upbringing that at the same time intersect with national and ethnic differences. It reflects on the ways in which men and women more easily recollect the past from different media; the kind of images and stories that have become sedimented and more readily articulated; the gender of protagonists in recollected stories; and people's identification and non-identification with men and women in history. It argues that what we remember is articulated by who we are and who we are, in turn re-articulates, articulates or disarticulates what we remember.

Inheriting memories, using history

Most research on young people's memories of the Holocaust focuses on the effects of the traumatic memory of the events on the children and grandchildren of Jewish survivors. These studies, mostly from a psychoanalytical perspective, consider the transgenerational effects of concentration camp and survivor experiences (see, for example, Marcus and Rosenburg, 1989). Others have considered the ways in which the Holocaust has been handed down and how this affects subsequent life choices and ways of being in the world (Karpf, 1997; Fogelman, 1988). James Young cites a study of soldiers on Kibbutz Ein Ha-Horesh in Israel after the Six Day War in 1967 that shows how their inherited memory of the Holocaust is articulated as constituting their given reason for fighting the Six Day War. As one soldier described it: 'It's true that people believed that we would be exterminated if we lost the [Six Day] War. They were afraid. We got this idea – or inherited it – from the concentration camps (cited in James Young, 1988:145).

Although there is enormous diversity in the articulations of the Holocaust for the second generation, as Aaron Hass's (1990) research on the second generation shows, studies such as that cited by Young (1988) also indicate the ways in which the significance and meaning of the Holocaust are experienced differently by people from shared national/cultural and religious backgrounds. Helen Epstein's (1988) groundbreaking conversations with the sons and daughters of Jewish survivors, *Children of the Holocaust*, likewise indicates that the country and context in which the children of survivors were raised influences the articulation of their memory of events.

However, as with autobiographies of survivors, life-stories by the children and grandchildren of survivors suggest that they inherit memories of the events in ways that are also gendered (Horowitz, 2000). Helen Epstein's (1988) study shows how people's gendered identities play a part in their legacy in a number of ways. Where fathers often withdrew into a prison of silence about their experiences, mothers acted as a memory bridge handing down to their children both their own and their husband's experiences (p. 26). In British journalist and writer, Anne Karpf's (1997) autobiography *The War After*, we see how the handed-down memory of her parents' trauma as survivors of the Holocaust is re-articulated through her own expression of enduring anxieties about her role and abilities as a mother to her own daughter. After her baby was born, Anne Karpf was worried that the baby would not survive if she did not put on weight, and she describes an overwhelming sense of loss from having no heirlooms to bequeath to her daughter. We see how the gendered internalisation of death, as described in survivor Gottesfeld Heller's account (see Chapter 3), is inherited and re-articulated in the experiences and narratives of survivors' children. For example, after the birth of her baby daughter, Anne Karpf writes: 'When B sicked up milk, there were traces of my blood in it, and I read them as my badness. I couldn't even say the word "milk" – whenever it cropped up in a sentence, it amazingly came out as "blood"' (Karpf, 1997:256).

Studies of people's reception of general history also indicate that gender is a factor in the ways in which people more broadly identify with, make sense of, and give significance to the past. Roy Rosenweig and David Thelen, in a study of the popular uses of history in

American life which involved a survey of 1500 people of various ethnic and religious backgrounds, found that for both women and men the intimate and familial past was the most important, but that it mattered more for women than men. When they asked people which of four different 'areas of the past' – that of their family, their racial or ethnic group, the community in which they lived, or the United States – was most important to them, 73 per cent of the women selected family, in comparison with 58 per cent of the men. Overall, women had greater interest in the past than men, participating in taking videos and photographs to preserve the past; investigating family histories; attending reunions; and reading about the past. In some cases women's involvement was markedly greater: for example, more women (68 per cent) than men (59 per cent) visited history museums and historic sites. However, one area in which men's interest in the past was marginally greater than women's (83 per cent compared with 80 per cent) was in relation to watching historically based movies and TV programmes about events in history. Likewise, more men than women (61 per cent compared with 53 per cent) declared that they participated in hobbies or collections related to the past (Rosenweig and Thelen, 1999:15–16).

What neither Holocaust-specific transgenerational studies nor quantitative work on the uses of history explore, however, is how our social inheritance of the past involves complex articulations of gender configured and reconfigured from and through a range of cultural practices and mediations. How do people know what they know? Why do men and women remember some aspects of history and not others?

To some extent we could look for the answers to these questions within media and cultural studies: over the past twenty years audience research has explored how women differ from men in their consumption patterns and practices (Stokes and Maltby, 1999; Thornham, 2000). Dorothy Hobson found that women watched TV differently from men – in a distracted fashion in between childcare and cooking, often relying on the dialogue alone to keep abreast of the story (Hobson, 1982). Janice Radway looked at why women read romance novels (Radway, 1987); Angela McRobbie addressed how and why girls read girls magazines (McRobbie, 1991). However, as Liesbet Van Zoonen suggests, the problem is that most research in this area has focused solely on women. Consequently, as Ien Ang (1996) has pointed out, 'how gender is related to media consumption is one of the most under-theorized questions in mass communications research.' (p. 110). Further, the dominant paradigms within British Cultural Studies tends to result in arguments that either overemphasise the text in determining meanings for the viewer, or that advocate 'a polysemic perversity, in which there are no limits to the boundaries of meaning' (Stokes and Maltby, 1999:14). Yet, as David Buckingham (1993) argues in relation to the media consumption of boys, the reception of media texts is not simply structured by our identities but instead, in complex ways, articulates with those identities (p. 97). Further, despite the fact that memory work can allow us to understand how mediations work, cultural theory has been ill-equipped to deal with how identities, memories and media consumption intersect (Kuhn, 1995). Thus, although I draw on some of the insights provided by audience research and consumption work within media and cultural studies, this is with a view to extending these theories into the specific areas of gender and memory.

The concept used in this chapter to explore complex relationships between mediations, memory and gender (as in earlier chapters to a lesser extent) is Laclau and Mouffe's (1985) concept of articulation theorized in *Hegemony and Socialist Strategy* (p. 105). The concept refers to the process by which relationships between different elements are established in ways that modify identity through articulatory practice. I extend this to suggest that articulation explains how representations of the past in various mediations interlock in specific situations with subjectivities, so that socially inherited memories and memory practices acquire meanings that are within particular contexts gender specific.

The importance of (grand)mothers

According to Hermann Bausinger (1990), if we are looking at people's media consumption we need to take into account the whole range of mediations that people experience. As Ang and Hermes note, media consumption can no longer be 'equated with distinct and insulated activities such as "watching television" "reading a book" or "listening to a record" since people living in (post)modern societies are surrounded by an ever-present and ever-evolving media provision' (Ang and Hermes, 1996). This is certainly the case when it comes to the configuration of socially inherited memories. Young people's socially inherited memories and historical knowledge of the Holocaust have been articulated through a broad range of media, including television programmes, films, museums, history books and literature, comic books, games acted out as children, theatre, concerts, watching football games, visits to memorial sites and the experience of growing up in a particular environment, as well as encounters with survivors, teachers and peers. For Americans and British respondents the internet was also significant.

What was most influential, for respondents particularly as children and especially in terms of providing context and anchorage for the development of their subsequent understanding and knowledge, was the interpretative community in which people were raised and the influence of family members in particular. For young Jews from different national backgrounds and traditions, the memories of the Holocaust were so embedded within their culture and community that there was no 'first memory' of the Holocaust – no moment of non-awareness – rather, its memory was ever present. As one Jewish American woman said: 'I don't think there is actually one exact point when I ever became aware of it. I grew up in a town that was 80 per cent Jewish so the Holocaust and big Jewish holidays and everything that dealt with Judaism is pretty much prominent.' (Deborah, aged 20, depth interview, Washington DC, April 1999).

Another Jewish-American from New York city describes how for her, similarly, there was no beginning to her memory and from nursery school onwards there were assemblies in the school auditorium in commemoration of the Holocaust: 'The gym walls were lined with posters that were blown up. Pictures depicting the Holocaust, with scenes from the death camp, um, children, um, people in labour camps, and ... Of course we would, um, we would sing, and there was always a candlelight ceremony and there was six huge candles, one for each of the million' (Elizabeth, aged 23, focus group, New York, April 1999).

Stories either told or untold by grandparents were particularly influential for men and women who had an inherited direct connection in terms of relatives being murdered, who had escaped or survived, who had grandfathers who had fought in the war or who had been deported to Germany to be used as slave labour. Thus Poles, Polish-Americans, Anglo- and American-Jewish men and women, as well as those who defined themselves as British whose fathers, grandfathers or great-uncles had fought in the Second World War, defined these personal handed-down stories as having significant meaning in the early construction of their memories of the Holocaust. For those with no direct personal connection through family with the events, school was usually cited as the first point when they came across the Holocaust. With those respondents for whom the stories of family members were significant, women generally gave more emphasis to this personal dimension than men: in women's written life-histories they gave more detailed accounts of the stories that were handed down to them before moving on to describing configurations of memories from media such as television documentaries and films. In depth interviews and in focus groups, women respondents also gave greater prominence to the influence of family narratives of how their historical memory of the events had developed. Consistent emphasis was given by both men and women to the role played by mothers and grandmothers (rather than fathers and grandfathers) in telling stories about the Second World War and the Holocaust. In childhood, this would be through overhearing stories told between adults, particularly the women of the family in the home environment. For Polish men and women this role almost always involved the recollection of an interpretative story told by the mother or grandmother and generally invoked by a child's question about a memorial or local topography on the way to school or nursery. As Annette Kuhn (1999) notes in her work on older people's memories of cinema going in the UK, this is not unusual: stories are often told and remembered as part of a mental and geographical landscape. A Pole, whose grandparents were Jewish, described how his grandmother, who had been in a concentration camp during the War, pointed out that where they lived was once the Jewish ghetto in Lodz and that many Jews lived there before the War (Marcin, aged 20, depth interview, Lodz, April 1998). The respondent recalled later on in the interview how it was also his grandmother who explained a monument to him near where they lived:

> I can remember that when I was a child I used to play in one park with some friends. My grandma took me there. She sat on the bench with the other grandmas and I was playing and I can remember it well. There was a monument, um, statue which showed a cracked wall, or something like this and a child standing facing the wall and I just got used to that because I used to live nearby. But I asked her what it was and she said it was to commemorate the prison for children. The German prison for children but I just looked of course … the child – that was the child in the monument that was facing the wall – was naked, in fact it was, um, striking for children, so I think this is why I asked her. (Marcin, aged 20, depth interview, Lodz, April 1998)

A woman from Cracow described how a significant early memory stemmed from the interpretative story attached to a local monument that she passed daily with her mother on the way to school:

> There was a monument I was passing on the way to school. Thousands of times. Three men standing. Their faces of suffering.

Their faces; and they have no hearts. There is a huge hole in the place of the heart ... I wanted to know why there was a hole in their hearts and I asked my mother and she told me. (Agnieszka, aged 23, Crakow, focus group, April 1998)

It is not that mothers and grandmothers essentially have authoritative interpretative roles to play in the early construction of Holocaust memory, but that their place and role with the community and their living memory of the past means they are more likely to be in a position to have acted as a memory bridge for younger people. In Poland, it could be argued that evidence shows that the post-communist legacy of both parents working, combined with most families remaining within a particular locality, resulted in grandparents, especially grandmothers, playing an important supportive role in terms of childcare (Reading, 1992, 1996; Sokolowska, 1977). However, the role played by grandmothers and the emphasis given to their handed-down memories was also significant to American respondents of both Polish-Catholic and Jewish backgrounds.

My first ever recollection of hearing the word 'Holocaust' was from my late maternal grandmother ... She lived in a small Polish-American enclave near NYC ... when I was perhaps 8 or 9 years old, she would make references to relatives in Poland, to World War Two and the Nazis and the Holocaust (she used the word 'ovens'). (Michael, aged 29, written life-history, Washington DC, April 1999).

For some of the grandchildren of Jewish survivors, although their experience was one of immersion in Holocaust history and memory from birth, the sense of the past handed on to them was one of unarticulated loss.

No one in my family openly talks about it – the events – and I think that it largely has to do with the fact that we don't know enough. Or maybe it was because the children of my grandparents, including my parents and my aunts and uncles never felt like it was something that they could openly discuss with their parents. (Elizabeth, aged 21, focus group, New York, April 1999).

The figure of the grandmother was also important in handing down memories or silencing memories of the Holocaust for Anglo-Jewish respondents, as well as some Anglo non-Jewish respondents. One woman described how, although her father had described to her as a child 'numerous times over Sunday lunch' how a relative had survived several camps, as a prisoner of war, it was 'brought home to her – its real meaning – the fact that this was real' by her paternal grandmother (Susannah, aged 30, depth interview, London, 1998).

This role played by grandmothers extended to a sense of their authority over the memories of the past when this was discordant with public or state versions of history. Young Poles recalled that prior to the transition from Communism to democracy in 1989, they grew up with a sense of two versions of the past: a private/family memory which ran parallel with public memory that was endorsed through socialist or communist public institutions such as schools and museums. Grandmothers had the authority to signal to grandchildren which version represented 'the truth' and helped them develop the cultural competence required to negotiate between private family memories and the public versions of events articulated by teachers and books at school and in the mainstream media under Communism. 'I was always told by my grandmother that our textbooks lie, our official materials lie. Television lies absolutely ... But I was always told "Okay you have to learn it and to present the knowledge from the textbooks" and I did and it was easier for me' (Yolanta, aged 28, depth interview, Lodz, 23 April 1998).

Another woman in Gdansk described how it was from her grandmother that she learnt about Russian atrocities in the War: these atrocities were a part of Poland's history that schools did not teach children under Communism. Her grandmother, though telling her this 'other history', would warn her, 'Remember do not tell it to your friends' (Joanna, aged 31, focus group, Gdansk, April 1998).

For the tiny minority of young Jewish Poles or people who define themselves as having Jewish ancestry, as some of my respondents did, the memories handed down by the grandparents and especially the Jewish grandmother acted as a memory bridge to that part of the past that the Communist authorities had resolutely endeavoured to silence. One young man remembered how at school he was taught about the Holocaust but in terms of Poles and Russians being killed and put in concentration camps. When he was 13 he learnt that his Jewish grandmother had been in a concentration camp and she told him about her experiences (Marcin, aged 20, depth interview, April 1998). He did not expand on what she had told him and his narrative later reveals that this was due to his enduring fear and experience of antisemitism. He identified with his grandmother and added that since 1989 people now speak about the Jewish dimension of the Holocaust but at the same time antisemitism remains. He said sadly, 'Jews are not popular in Poland in fact. In fact we are quite disliked. I don't know where it comes from' (Marcin, aged 20, depth interview, April 1998).

Grandmothers in all three countries were recalled as having the cultural authority not only to relate their own stories and memories but also as having the authority to act as a mediator of the memories of husbands who were more reticent or who retreated into silence on the subject of the Holocaust or the War. A 20-year-old Catholic woman from Gdansk described how her grandmother told her about her grandfather's imprisonment in Lublin in eastern Poland. A man from London described how it was his mother who related additional information to him about his father's wartime experiences.

Grandmothers, though, also had the cultural authority to silence some memories, as one Polish Catholic respondent notes:

> The parents of my father survived the war, but they do not want to talk about it. My grandmother is always angry when my grandfather tries to describe some events from the 1940s. I've always been wondering why she doesn't want us to know about their life during the war. (Barbara, aged 20, written life history, Gdansk, April 1998)

Similarly, a Jewish-American woman, who described herself as growing up in a town that was predominantly Jewish, described how, although her Great Aunt wanted to talk about the past and wanted to return to Poland, her grandmother was more reticent and did not want to revisit the homes they had been forced to leave.

> [my grandmother] once got into a conversation at dinner with her sister and they were talking and they said that my Great aunt really wanted to go back to Poland. She really wanted to visit all the camps. She really wanted to see everything – like look for old family homes and everything. My grandmother didn't want to do it – she wanted to put it behind her – I guess that was one of the things that really stuck out to me – she wanted to have absolutely nothing to do with it – she wanted to have no relation with the Holocaust whatsoever. (Krystyna, aged 20, depth interview, Washington DC, April. 1999.)

As Sarah Horowitz has explored in relation to fiction about the Holocaust, muteness is often a symptom of a trauma that cannot be spoken of and, at the same time, other stories are told to fill the void

(Horowitz, 1997). Where grandparents, and particularly grandmothers, refused to articulate the past, the rest of the family instead articulated narratives concerning the War and the Holocaust around less painful topics: this usually centred on a story of survival, good fortune or luck. Thus in one Polish woman's family – in which her grandmother refused to speak about her own experiences – the respondent said how the story of her Great Uncle's life in which he had had the good fortune to survive slave labour in Germany was spoken of, described in detail and recollected frequently by the family.

> But there's um – I would like to say that there's a good side in the story because my, er – my mother's uncle was sent to Germany to work there, during the War and, mm, the story, mm, had a happy end because he had a good family for whom-for which he-had to work was – let's call it good – a good one. And, um, he even married the daughter of the, mm, of those people and they lived happily, mm, of course till he died – [small laugh] last year but – but it was something – they, the person-personality of my uncle was something you know the, er, – we we never called him, er, uncle *ju ju* or some-thing like this – it was always 'uncle from Germany' and and this uncle from Germany it was the whole story and everyone, er, knew the the all the facts connected with his life and it was it was good and we will always remember him – that he had such a luck to survive – it was, it was good. (Barbara, aged 20, focus group, Gdansk, April 1998)

At the same time, the predominant role that grandmothers and mothers played in handing down memories contrasted with the felt or literal absence of grandfathers and fathers. One woman from Lodz described how the meaning of the War for her was expressed in terms of this absence.

> what it [the Holocaust] meant for me, first of all, it meant that I was a very unlucky child because I had no grandfathers. Some people, some friends of mine had one or two and for me War meant that both my grandfathers died during the War. That was all I knew for a long time. Only later when I was old enough, I could listen to the whole story. The War was always something to do with some terror. (Bozenna, aged 28, depth interview, Lodz, April 1998)

For the children and grandchildren of Polish victims we see how the memory of the War and the Holocaust is articulated through a social inheritance that involves both the silence/ absence of the grandfather and the voice/presence of the grandmother. In some families it was the absence of the individual's own father in their present or childhood lives, due to the structure of the family or their father's job, that explained why the cultural authority for the past came from the mother:

> 'I think my mother was most important because my father was a driver – a driver of lorries, so he was absent very often and when he was at home, so, um, he was hard to talk to'. (Agnieszka, depth interview, cracow, April 1999).

> my father erm, in fact I don't have cl-close contact with my father but, er, he, w, he was from centre o-, centre of Poland, er, but I think the most important will be my grandmother and and the my mother, er, and the my grandmother, er, because, er, as she was born in Staniswavu the War resulted in her, er, compulsory move- ment here. (Tomasz, aged 20, depth interview, Gdansk, April 1998).

For young Jewish people, in all three countries, while the authority for personal stories was given to the role played by grandmothers – especially by granddaughters – this was articulated in relation to a much bigger literal and deeply felt absence of a 'piece of their family' and subsequent inherited identity. One respondent from New York estimated that around one hundred relatives of hers were murdered during the Holocaust. 'My family was from Poland – I don't even know from where there are no written records and the elderly have passed on. A piece of my heritage, my identity is missing. Burned somewhere in Poland – may be in a mass grave.' (Elizabeth, aged 21, written life history, New York, April 1999).

This sense of the memory of the past left unarticulated by absence was a common theme among Jewish respondents in different countries. One Jewish-American woman said that although her family members had gone to the US at the turn of the century she was still left with a sense of not knowing what had happened to her relatives in Poland and Russia.

> Sometimes, I mean I know that I came from Russian and Polish ancestry but that is about the extent that I really know of it. I don't know anything else and in some ways it is kind of strange because I think it would be very difficult if I ever tried to do a family tree.

I wouldn't really know many with my family right now. I don't know how much they know of their family. My family is very small here, so sometimes it would have been nice to have been able to have that history and to know more people, but as it is so tiny but sometimes, it is kind of dis-connecting I guess. (Zara, aged 20, depth interview, Washington DC, April. 1999).

What Michel Foucault (1979) has described in relation to sexuality as the ways in which the unsaid or unsayable makes itself present in discourse even though silenced, is notable in the ways in which young Jewish respondents experienced, within their social memory of the Holocaust, the urge to speak around the absence of people for whom they have no record.

most of my family came from Germany, but they came, um, I believe in the late 1910s, early 1920s, but, um, my great-grandmother and great-grandfather came over and certainly they left family behind, brothers and sisters and parents an- and that whole family. We have no record of them so we're assuming that most of those were probably killed ... um, so i-it's always been there and it's always been talked about and there's always been in the back of our mind, what if they hadn't come over, you know (Jennifer, focus group, Washington DC, April 1999).

The gendered cultural inheritance of the memory of the past by the post-Holocaust generations in the US, Britain and Poland, which stresses the cultural authority of women in the family, especially grandmothers, contrasts directly with a study of the ways in which memory has been inherited by the sons and daughters of fathers who were Nazis in the Third Reich. A number of autobiographies published in Germany (see Gauch, 1979; Day, 1980) look at the legacy of gendered authority in the handing down and the reception of memory in post-war German families. They show, according to an analysis by Susan G. Figge, that surviving Nazi fathers 'used their cultural author-ity precisely to suppress their children's inquiries into the past (Figge, 1990:195). Sons located narrative authority for the past in the figure of their fathers, while daughters always contrasted the father's narrative power with the silence and verbal disenfranchisement of their mothers: 'If we ask the question, who tells the stories by which we live and interpret our lives, the sons answer 'the father'. The daughters answer 'the father, not the mother' (Figge, 1990:195). With my respondents in the US, Britain and Poland, when the cultural authority of the father was linked with Holocaust memory this was located in the specific context of watching television with father's present.

> My first memories are probably in high school as well, um, *soon* I ca-I can connect more with, er, memories of World War Two movies because my father watched alot of military movies, so I kind of connect it with that. Um, I think my first introduction was in high school, in school, but the actual memories of connecting it to actual the tragedy of the Holocaust was during those movies, watching those movies with my father. (Michael, aged 29, focus group, Washington DC, April 1999).

British men and women recalled watching the *World at War* series with their fathers, and sometimes being made to watch it by them. Slightly older respondents remembered watching *Holocaust* and their fathers providing additional interpretations and what we can call 'authorial anchorage'. Another described how her father had a collection of video's related to the Holocaust that she was forbidden to watch but that she did watch once in secret with her friends. Polish men and Polish-American men additionally stressed the importance of 'father' figures in handing down memories of the past: their local Catholic priest was remembered as important in handing down stories, very often as important as the role played by family members (Luke, aged 49, focus group, Washington DC, April 1999; Michael, aged 29, focus group, Washington DC, April, 1999).

Men's images, women's words

For young people in all three countries, as well as interpersonal communications Holocaust memory was articulated through a variety of media texts and cultural mediations in heterogeneaous, intersecting and contradictory ways. The written word, especially literature, was remembered as providing a real sense of the meaning of the Holocaust for all young people. Young Poles, recollected their knowledge as linked to works by Polish author/survivors, such as *Pozegranie z Maria* by Tadeausz Borowski and *Medaliony* by Zofia Nalkowska. For young Americans it was Elie Wiesel's *Night*, and for young British men and women, Anne Frank's *Diary of a Young Girl* were the key texts. For people whose national or cultural backgrounds resulted in the experience of a contradictory inheritance articulated in private and public discourses, the form of the written word provided a way of narrativising a connection between the two worlds. For young Poles after 1989, books about Jews and the Holocaust became available in ways that they had not been before that date and this provided them with a way of reconnecting the duality of the past that had developed under Communism (focus groups, Gdansk, Cracow, April 1998). A British woman described how she remembered images from the Holocaust after watching a short documentary at school at the age of 12. The film had shocked her and she said that the images remained for many years in a separate part of her mind, outside of her everyday experience, so that she did not connect them to the Europe that she knew and the Germany that she later went to live in for some months as a young adult. The medium that helped her to integrate the images from the film into her broader knowledge, understanding and feelings – her socially inherited memory – of our century was the book. It was through reading history and autobiographies of survivors that she became able to make the connections (Susannah, aged 32, depth interview, London, November 1998). Young Jewish-Americans also emphasised how their own collections of books on the subject enabled them to negotiate the different histories they received about the Holocaust at home or in Jewish Saturday school in contrast with American public school.

There was a number of different gender positionings in terms of the importance given to discourses about the past in different cultural forms. Women overall positioned reading as key to their development of their understanding and integration of the Holocaust; men, in contrast, positioned moving images as important, often beginning their written accounts with a first memory recollected from watching television documentaries and feature films on the Second World War (rather than specifically the Holocaust) at home. 'My first experience about the War was, I got to know, that there was something like world War and when I was watching TV and it was a film ... it was supposed to be watched by young people and this film influenced my first ideas about the war' (Marek, aged 20, depth interview, Lodz, April 1998). Young men also described how these films provided gender-defined roles for them as children which they would then act out in games that they played at school. They said that since male roles tended to dominate the films, these games were generally a boy's only experience. 'Mainly boys [played the games]. There were some female characters in the film. There was a Russian girl whose name was ... but in fact now, um, unless there were some girls who *really* wanted to play this game.

And they could take part' (Marek, aged 20, depth interview, Lodz, April 1998).

Women, in contrast, did not remember playing War games at school as significant to cultural memory practices. It was given only a passing reference in their written accounts, and was rarely mentioned in focus groups and only occasionally in depth interviews. Exceptionally, some British women recollected articulating as a comic walk and salute the character of Adolf Hitler: 'At school we used to take the mickey out of Hitler, like going round like that and click your heel and things like that' (Mandy, aged 20, focus group. London, November 1998). These impersonations were usually perceived as a transgressive memory practice. One said, for example, how she 'got into real trouble once at school for doing the Hitler walk' (Helen, aged 20, focus group, London, November 1998).

The actual content remembered from Holocaust films and still images was also differentiated on gender lines. While women more often described photographic images of child victims, men more often described watching a moment of direct violence as significant to the development of their memory: 'so this woman was holding this guy's, you know, arm and, was refusing to let go – so, er – and an SS officer like just shot 'em right in the head and the bullet and the blood was coming out man, you know? Be, they just left there to die, so it was really touching' (Todd, aged 16, focus group, New York, April 1999). 'I remember just, er, one film because I was a a little child, you know? And I remember it was when he was, he was, er, he was dressed in a paper – paper bag or something like that, and he was, er, he was shot and he covered with with blood – and, er, that's what, er, what I remember'. (Tomasz, aged 20, focus group, Gdansk, April 1998).

With the feature film *Schindler's List*, whereas women tended to remember 'the girl in the red coat' wandering the street in Cracow after the ghetto was destroyed and its people forcibly moved, men remembered particular scenes of shooting or violence: 'the the evil guy, the mean guy w- he was actually shooting, er, people from I guess the balcony as they walked in the camp and I just thought that was horrible and he didn't – seemed like he didn't care at all' (Peter, focus group, aged 29, Washington DC, April 1999). What we see here is how gendered identities articulate for the individual within a process of what Thomas Austin describes as a negotiation between their self-images and the meanings of media texts (Austin, 1999). The young men re-articulate images that require a negotiation between different discourses of masculinity – male violence versus the male as protector.

The young women, in contrast, articulate socially inherited memories of what is considered to be part of the feminine domain in specific contexts: images of children.

When it came to internet sites related to the Holocaust, of those who mentioned it – British and Americans only – there was another gender divide. It was the textual information and interactive communicative possibilities provided by web sites that women recalled, as with this respondent in relation to the Simon Wiesenthal Multi Media Web Site. 'the Wiesenthal Centre do a good job of, er, keeping things updated and they would host, er, speakers on their site where you could type questions to the person and they would reply to you and it would be posted on a bulletin board type format. So they did do a lot of communication and provide information' (Tracey, focus group, University of Maryland, Washington DC, April 1999. One male respondent, in contrast, stressed that for him it was the images that he found useful: 'I found that, um, the Holocaust Museum has an internet site. Er, um, I found them useful in terms, particularly of the, of the visual, er, images that were there, um, the visual images to me were more than a lot of words – bring home, um, the depth of the hurt' (Peter, aged 29, focus group, Washington DC, April 1999).

What we also see from this and the earlier recollections is that for men – images are recollected in relation to the articulation of particular feelings – they 'bring home, um, the depth of the hurt', 'it was really touching'; whereas for women, they recollect those aspects of socially inherited memory that articulates information and connects disparate elements or people.

Feeling facts

In fact how people position themselves in relation to the memory of facts or feelings is important in understanding the ways in which historical memories are integrated, articulated or remain unarticulated in relation to gender and other subjectivities. Aaron Hass has pointed out that while the children of Holocaust survivors believe that they know more about the events than others because they have witnessed the impact of its aftermath on their parents, research shows that they actually possess no more factual knowledge than their America-Jewish peers (Heller, 1982 cited in Hass, 1995:141). Among Jewish men and women in all three countries in my study, there was certainly a strong sense of 'always having known about the Holocaust' and of there never being a time before respondents knew: 'it was always part of me' was a key phrase used by Jewish respondents. Even if there were no survivors within the family, there was, a structure of feeling, and a direct connection with events was within their peers' families as they grew up. Respondents recalled the shock of seeing 'numbers tattooed on their arms from Auschwitz' (Deborah, aged 21, New York, April 1999.) and overhearing survivors' stories in family conversations (Elizabeth, aged 21, New York, April 1999; Jennifer, aged 30, Washington DC, April 1999; Mandy, aged 21 London, November 2000; Andrew, aged 19, London, November 2000).

The corollary to this, however, among young non-Jews in the US and Britain was a sense of shame at having a period in their lives when they did not know about the Holocaust and a feeling of inadequacy concerning their knowledge gained 'just' from books and school, rather than their family or community: 'I am not Jewish. ... I was embarrassed that I did not known more about the Holocaust, and that I did not know sooner ... the Holocaust was never a common topic of conversation in my home as I imagined it was in Jewish homes. I relied only on school and library books. (Shannan, aged 19, focus group, New York April 1999). What is articulated here is a link between an individual's identity, their social memory and its legitimacy: there is a hierarchy of legitimate knowledge about the past related to our identities. Interpersonal memories from those who are Jewish are deemed more valuable by non-Jews than information from school and books. Further, the meaning of memories about the Holocaust is articulated not simply in terms of 'knowing' the facts, but that understanding comes from facts in some way being personally felt. In this respect, the young people in this study negotiated relationships with the past in ways that partially disrupts dominant discourses of masculinity in Western culture in which men are said to show their feelings less than women. Certainly, in three focus groups (Gdansk, Cracow, London) two Polish women and two Anglo-Jewish women cried or became visibly upset while relating or trying to relate personal stories that had been handed down to them as children. But the emphasis given to understanding the facts of what happened through empathy and feeling was equally stressed by men and women. The difference was that men tended to express this aspect of the meaning of memory through writing or depth interviews, where they did not have to articulate it in front of their peers.

When I met Elie Wiesel, that was a great experience. I actually felt his pain of loss while he explained how his family was brutally murdered at the hands of the German Nazis. I felt as if I went back in time and went through the Holocaust myself. He spoke with so much imagery and pain from the heart that I would have understood if he would have broken down and started to cry, it would have been okay. (Todd, aged 16, Written Life History, New York, April, 1999).

However, in the US particularly, young men were more open about articulating feelings in front of their peers as part of their social inheritance. 'Well, the one that I got the most understanding with was with the one he was talking about "Schindler's List", that was – I don't know that made me wanna cry' (Carlos, aged 16, focus group. New York, April. 1999).

While, there was an enduring theme that the Holocaust needed to be understood emotionally, this connection for men was often described as something experienced relationally, through witnessing the women they were with openly showing an emotional response to the atrocities or through providing emotional support. One respondent, who had been on a visit to Poland with other young Jews from America and Britain, said:

I mean actually one of the kids from England he was kind of like my boyfriendish kind of guy on the trip for like the first week and we were each other's support system for a lot of it. We would walk through the camps holding hands together and we just kind of supported each other and we were about to leave Majdanek right after seeing all the ashes – like he was a guy and he didn't want to cry, he wanted to be all manly – but he just broke down and started crying in the parking lot before we left and like we just held each other and we were both bawling. (Zara, aged 20, depth interview, Washington DC, April 1999).

An African-American man who had been posted to Germany with the American Armed Forces in the early 1990s described how for him the most significant memory related to the Holocaust concerned a visit to Dachau concentration camp where he witnessed his mother cry.

I lived in Germany for four years and I visited a lot of the the museums and, er, Dachau concentration camp there, when my mother came to visit I took her there and my first emotional connection with the Holocaust was watching her cry as we walked through it and then before, before all of this, I'd, I'd never had an emotional connection, it was just, OK, I read about it, saw it on TV and i- it happened and was sad, but that was the first time I had an emotional connection with, er, the Holocaust, watching my mother cry, in a concentration camp as we walked through it. (Peter, aged 29, focus group, University of Maryland, Washington DC, April 1999).

It was through witnessing his mother's maternal response to the death of the children in the camps and by later talking with her about it, that he connected to this aspect of the genocide.

Peter: I think it just, it it, helped you understand it better and helped you to really really understand that this, er, it happened and a lot of people died, you know, and just talking to your mother, because you you don't usually talk to your mother about things like that, but when you see that she's crying, it touched her that way, and that you you can actually sit down and talk to her about that, her memories and understanding of it too ...

Interviewer: And did she – wha- what did she tell you, can you remember?

Peter: um, I guess she just mentioned that i-it was just such a such a tragedy that something like that occurred and I think she w- her main thing was the children there were so many children th- that died, um, and I – we walked through the – I guess the area that was the gas chamber – set up as showers so that really was where she j-just l-lost it. I had to actually, I had to carry her through part of the camp and it just really touched her and i-it and, um, I think that's what it was really, the children dying and and the innocence and it showed how the picture of the people who were actually walking. We walked the path that they walked to the, er, to the gas chamber[2] and to the ovens, so, it was really sad. (Peter, aged 29, focus group, University of Maryland, Washington DC, April 1999)

What this demonstrates is how the meaning we make from mediations of the past is configured in relation to the context of reception: who we visit a memorial sites with, who we watch a programme with provide for situated memories rather than simply memories inherited through 'texts' or cultural mediations with fixed narratives of the events. Other people provide us with additional cultural competence by which to integrate memories. In this case – the mother provides an empathetic response to the events that the young man then remembers in relation to the visit itself. These situated socially inherited memories may then change meaning over time and in articulation with our own identities and past and future memories may in turn modify them. Thus the same respondent described how, after witnessing his mother cry at Dachau, he watched films about the Holocaust with more empathy and understood with greater depth the meaning of genocide.

The fixed, the forgotten and the unsaid

Another important feature of the gendering processes involved in the configuration of socially inherited memories concerns how people make gendered identifications with, and remember the gender of, people from history. James Young has analysed the variations in the same historical story remembered and told by different people. He analyses, in particular, the story of a dancer in the gas chamber in Auschwitz who distracted the SS men sufficiently to grab a pistol and shoot them. The differences in the story, according to Young, 'bespeak the multiplicity of meanings' for both the victim and for 'rememberers afterward' (Young, 1988:40–5). What Young does not explore, though, is that despite the variations there is an underlying gendered consistency to the tales, just as there is within respondents' historical memories in this study. No tale depicts 'her' as 'him', or SS men as SS women. Yet, respondents in my study would change, 'forget', or be confused about other aspects of protagonists' identities in remembering stories of atrocities. A young man from Gdansk, for example, 'forgets' the ethnicity of the man in a particular story, but he does not confuse the man for a woman:

Tomasz: I I I I also remember I, I reminded myself, another, er, another, er, story from *Nalkowska*, it was also horrible, er, about, er, erm ... *about Polish people, I- I- I w- I don't remember or Jewish people it doesn't matter* just strong man from the, er, con- concentration camp, yes
Interviewer: Mmm. Yes.?

Tomasz: er, which were employed by Germans who had to to
               move the bodies to bury them and, er, ... and it wa- it
               was horrible, er, for them em, as if they were against,
               er, their ac-, their friends and their families because
               they because they h- they had to work for for th- for
               the Germans. (Tomasz, aged 20, depth interview,
               Gdansk, April 1998, *my emphasis*).

Tomasz says *it doesn't matter* – Jewish or Polish, 'just a strong man'. If
Tomasz were Jewish perhaps it would matter. But, it is significant that
to him what he wants to remember is the fact of the protagonist being
'just a strong man'.

It is arguable from a feminist post-structuralist perspective that
subjectivity is non-unitary, that it produced in and through 'the
intesections of a multitude of social discourses and practices which
position the individual subject in heterogeneous, overlapping and
competing ways' (Ang and Hermes, 1999:119). It is also the case that
people may identify, as Jan Montefiore (1994) has suggested in relation
to poetry, in wandering and mulitple ways in terms of their gender.
But this does not necessarily therefore mean that people remember in
wandering and multiple ways the gender of people from history. In
fact, the gendered consistency concerning the identity of protagonists
in young people's articulations of the past suggests we make sense of
historical memories in Western late capitalist cultures within broader
social discourses of gender which are far less flexible and thus more
memorable than other aspects of identities. Within our socially
inherited memories, gender is the more stable element in narrative,
providing a common anchor for meaning in which other elements
may be more readily changed or reworked to articulate or resonate
with the rememberer's own identity.

Subsequently, it seems that of the detailed atrocity stories that young
men and women articulated either orally or in written form, these
included the common trope of established gender boundaries being
broken, reversed, or in some way the event challenged dominant
gender definitions of the time then or now. A 20-year-old woman from
West Pomarania, Poland, wrote that she learnt from a range of literary
books 'how War is the worst thing that can happen to a man ...
turning him into an animal to survive.' (Ewa, aged 20, written life
history, Gdansk, April 1998). At this point the memories are general
and lack detail. She then writes how she clearly recalled from Zofia
Nalkowska's *Medaliony* 'an image of women who eat corpses – really

shocking' (Ewa, aged 20, written life history, Gdansk, April 1998). I would suggest that it was the fact that women in particular (not people in general or men and women) were *eating* the flesh of dead people that remains in the constellation of her memory of atrocity since it reverses dominant gendered norms that define women as those who should feed and nurture their families (not eat them). Another Polish woman from Gdansk recalls a moment from a film that breaks the usual conventions of women's roles as carers and caretakers of the young and vulnerable: 'The character was, was talking about about his life in Auschwitz, about his work, about the new transport, um, about I don't know – what it was – that he was – see now – *a mother was pushing a child away from her*' (Anita, aged 21, focus group, Gdansk, April 1998, *my emphasis*).

The images, stories and moving film images of women in the Holocaust that were re-articulated usually concerned moments where gender definitions were threatened or broken. These usually included moments when women's traditional and accepted roles had been unfulfilled or, because of circumstances, 'neglected'. This is shown in the following story, attached to an image of corpses and Nazi women guards that for the respondent challenged the usual maternal responsibility of women providing nurture and sustenance to other people and to children especially.

Naomi: It was a picture of these skinny dead bodies laying on the ground and a picture of these, having made like the, the Germans come in and 'YOU come in, YOU clean up YOUR own mess' and it was these healthy big fat FAT women picking up these dead bodies and , I'm like, its a shame how these women are healthy. They eating every day. They was some BIG women ...

   Voices in the group: Mmmm./hhmm.

Naomi: You should a seen those skinny little Holocaust victims laying on the floor, dead, you could see the a- the in front of their bones and I'm like, and to see the size difference, I'm like, they don't even look human they were so skinny and these women were SO FAT and I was *cursing wanting*, I was just like – how could you sit up there and just look at that? And I'm like – she all big and and she looking at this person, he's all little and frail, and that's terrible. How could they do that and – oh my goodness he was once this size – what happened to him? How did he get to be this

skinny? That was just that picture that just made me really angry.
(Naomi, aged 16, focus group, New York, April 1999).

Less frequently recalled were stories where women had broken codes and conventions by carrying arms or committing violent acts to defend themselves. Just one person mentioned a detailed story about girls acting in the resistance carrying guns in their baskets, and crossing patrols of German soldiers (Agnieszka, aged 23, depth interview, Crakow. April 1998).

As well as the common trope of remembered stories that broke particularly women's established roles, there was also a subordinate trope of stories that concerned gender-specific experiences of the Holocaust. The same respondent from Cracow described the influence that her teacher, a Jewish survivor of Auschwitz, had in her socially inherited memory of the events. She recalled the physical marks of atrocity and brutal treatment scarring the woman's body (she had been attacked by an SS Guard). Embedded in her articulation of a handed-down story was the stripping of women's femininity and affront to their dignity that she remembered when the women had been shaved, epitomised by her teacher, who 'couldn't recognise her mother or her sister because they were all bald' (Agnieszka, aged 23, written life history, Crakow, April 1998). Later on during the interview, she described an inherited memory from her grandmother who, at the age of 20, had been forced to hide in a barn with her sisters for three days to avoid the German soldiers. The unspoken part of the story was that the women would have been subject to assault and rape if they had been discovered. This muteness and silence was a feature of this aspect of young people's socially inherited memories. Although we know that sexual assault and rape were part of the Nazi genocide (see Chapters 2 and 3), memories of rape were mentioned very infrequently. The following recollection is exceptional. 'My grandmother always talks about the Russian soldiers who used to be very cruel. They raped Polish women. ... The German people are alleged to have been very cruel, but Russian people were even more cruel' (Monika, aged 21, written life history, Gdansk, Poland, April 1999).

Initially, we see in this the respondent's attempt to negotiate her own Polish identity in relation to the memory of the behaviour of the Germans and Russians. But, further on, the memory is developed further to articulate the specific use of rape against Jewish women in the genocide: 'My grandmother always describes with tears in her eyes the moments when crowds of Jews were taken to concentration camps and how they were killed in the streets and how German soldiers, Gestapo, raped Jewish women' (Monika, aged 21, written life history, Gdansk, Poland, April 1999).

One other respondent mentioned rape. She too was Polish. 'I know that Jews and Poles were kept in concentration camps. German soldiers made them work very hard; they raped women; they made experiments on people; they burnt the bodies in big ovens' (Ewa, aged 21, written life history, Polish Catholic, Gdansk, April 1998).

They were both female respondents who described these memories of rape and both were in writing, rather than articulated in interviews or with peers in focus groups. The socially inherited memory of rape as part of the Nazi genocide, I would suggest, is so unspeakable that it cannot be articulated in a mixed group and cannot be spoken aloud. Further, this also suggests that memories of rape have, on the whole, not been inherited as part of dominant discourses about the Holocaust in public memory, but rather have been socially inherited in the whispered personal space of familial relationships between women.

There are also elements of the memory of genocide specific to the experiences of men that were not recalled or articulated at all. These were the specific humiliations felt by men – the shaving of earlocks, for example, or, only rarely – the moment of men's and women's separation, described by survivors such as Wiesel and discussed in Chapter 3, when men suffered the shame of being unable to protect their families. Occasionally, there were references by male respondents to the specific tasks that men had to perform in the extermination process that Claude Lanzmann documents in the documentary film epic, *Shoah* (see Chapter 4). One respondent recalled the horrific roles that strong men were forced to take in cremating and burying the bodies of victims; those whom Levi called the 'Crematoria Ravens' who were themselves killed on a regular basis to ensure that they could not be witnesses.

Tomasz: And; er ... er, there was one story I I think about, er, a car when we when the German in invented, er, a new technique of of killing by, erm, they were putting people into the car, er, closed car, er, and the fumes from the car were put into the special room closed, so a kind of, er ...
Interviewer: Yes ...
Tomasz: gassing, I don't know and and these people were er, er, the cars were going just to the wood where they could

be buried and they were, they were killed by by the way and, er, and those strong men had to bury them ... hmmm.
(Tomasz, aged 20, depth interview, Gdansk, April 1998).

I would suggest that it is because those 'strong men' epitomise an established construction of masculinity as physically able and emotionally strong enough to cope with such an horrific task that this aspect of the Holocaust can be articulated, while those memories that radically contradict or overturn dominant discourses of masculinity are not. The men in this story are 'supermen', their normal roles not broken but extended and expanded to a grotesque caricature of masculinity, while specific atrocities to men that resulted in their emasculation are left mute in the realms of silence.

Only one male respondent acknowledged the additional underlying gendered dimension to the Nazis racist selections. 'On the victims' side, women were more likely to be selected straight away because they had children and because they're not as strong – you know for labour' (Jason, aged 22, American, depth interview, January 2001). But in most cases these differences were not made explicit by either men or women. This description is fairly typical. 'The "left" or the "right" meant either to the gas chambers ("showers") or the work part of the camp. Older people and children were usually gassed first because of their inability to provide work at the camp' (Amanda, aged 21, written life history, New York, April 1999). Women articulated socially in-herited memories of the selections in relation to the impact of the sep-aration of family members, linking this to the importance of their own families that often acted as a refuge and haven in their own lives. Thus, in New York, one young woman who wrote: 'My family comes from the island of Trinidad. I am proud of that', wrote how 'families were separated' (Cindy, aged 16, written life history, April 1999). Likewise, one American woman, born in the Dominican Republic, emphasised in her life-history the horror she felt at the fact that people were split up. 'Families were torn apart. To split families apart is a very wrong thing to do ... Family is a very important thing to have in your life. For comfort and reassurance your family will always be there and to take that away is evil' (Alicja, aged 17, written life history, New York, April 1999). A 20-year-old Jewish-American woman, wrote in her life-history how one of the memories that stayed with her from Elie Wiesel's *Night* was the moment when the men were separated from the women and when Wiesel is 'separated from his mother.' (Elena, aged 20, written life history, New York, April 1999).

Men, in contrast, did not write or talk about the socially inherited memory of separation as a significant trauma. This, I would argue, is because the dominant discourses of femininity in all three countries construct women as more contingent and relational: these women respondents' memories are articulations of instances that are discordant with hegemonic ideas of women's relationships with others as carers and nurturers within the family. At the same time, despite the enormous changes in gender roles of the past thirty years in Western cultures, there is within the construction of the masculinities of these countries the dominant discourse that defines men as the protectors of women and children. Thus, for men especially to remember the moment of separation during a genocidal selection is to recall a failure of this aspect of masculinity which is unspeakably shameful. At the same time, as we saw in Chapter 3, in those moments of separation, women ended up in the line for people to be gassed straight away because they were, more often than not, fulfilling their roles as child bearers and carers, mothers or carers of elderly parents. This, I would suggest, makes this aspect of memory, though enormously painful for women, at least speakable.

The one man in the study who did articulate the moment of separation as important, did so through his visual inherited memory of the remains of people's shoes in the US Holocaust Museum. He described how gradually the museum 'sort of wears away at you' and how, although he was not Jewish and he did not feel initially that he had any connection with events that took place such a ' long time ago', it was a display of people's shoes, muddled up and separated that he remembered. For him they acted as a metonym for the separation and absence of families.

> That's all that's left of them, these shoes, and its kind of like ... its pretty symbolic because each one of them obviously had two and all these shoes are kind of mixed, thrown, they're not really together any more, and that's sort of symbolic of like the family and all these families that have just been separated and all these. Those people will have gone through so much together and they've just been sepa-rated and then been destroyed, and all that's left of them are these shoes that are empty and won't walk again. And that was probably the most powerful thing in all my experience, despite other things. (Shannan, aged 19, focus group, New York, April, 1999).

Identification and identity

Although our subjectivities are multiple and constantly in process, who we identify with and position ourselves in relation to in the events of the Holocaust is also in part related to gender. Men in the study, both heterosexual and gay, clearly identified with men in history whether victims, bystanders, perpetrators or witnesses. One American respondent described how sometimes he would identify with the victim because he was gay and at other times his sexuality meant he identified with the perpetrators since he imagined that he could have become alternatively 'one of the perpetrators – acting the worst kind of Nazi to cover myself' (Jason, American, depth interview, March 2001). When looking at a photograph of a Nazi man shooting a woman with a baby, he identified with the man: 'I remember thinking, what was going through the guy's head; what was going through the guy's head; what must he have been thinking shooting the woman?' (Jason, American, depth interview, March 2001). He described how, whatever the situation, he identified strongly with the men in stories, photographs, films and books: 'I can't remember *ever* identifying with a woman, with the women. All the stories I remember, come to think of it, are of men ... I didn't get Anne Frank. It seemed to me to have more to do with her relationships with people, than with the Holocaust. (Jason, American, depth interview, March 2001).

Male respondents' recollections of heroic acts were generally always stories of men. Polish men, for example, recollected the story of the martyr, Maximillian Kolbe, who went to the gas chamber in place of a man with a family. When asked to imagine the meaning of the Holocaust in terms of those murdered, they imagined it in terms of identifying with millions of men being killed.

> I-I always think how, how-how is it possible, er, w-when you when you think of numbers, about millions of people died, it is just impossible to imagine for me, er, when you think of-of one person and when you kill one person, you kill their whole world I think, and, er, if you talk about his, erm, experiences, er, his memories, his family, his feelings, er, his education, love, and an-and if if you think of millions of people killed it is impossible. (Tomasz, aged 20, depth interview, Gdansk, April 1998).

Women also predominantly recalled stories of men who had done heroic acts but they also recalled some women. Gendered identification with aspects of Holocaust memory, however, should not be thought of as fixed. It is intersected by other social discourses and practices, which shift and change the position of the individual subject. Two dominant competing discourses are those of nationality and religion. Thus one respondent who had been on a *March for the Living* tour in 1998, with young Jews from Britain and the US, visited a number of extermination camps in Poland before flying on to Israel. She described how in Warsaw they had all been asked to point to one of the figures in the sculpture of the Ghetto Uprising. She had identified with a woman victim lying on the floor. In Israel, there is an identical sculpture and she no longer identified with the victim, but with a more active protagonist. She had begun the interview with me by defining herself as 'a 20-year-old Jewish-American woman'. When I asked whether she thought there were any differences in the experiences of men and women in the camps they had visited she did not understand the question. And then she said that the people who were leading the tour group, 'were just trying to focus on Jews in general. Gender wasn't really an issue that was ever discussed and I mean I just felt more of a connection with the people being Jewish people' (Zara, aged 20, depth interview, Washington DC, April 1999). Further on she reflected that the time when gender came up more was when they were in Israel. In Poland, the group felt under threat, and one member was spat at by a young Polish boy on the street. In Israel, she stressed, they 'felt safe', 'when the plane landed we kissed the ground'. She noted that the Israeli communities they visited were sharply divided on gender lines and 'women have their very strict role in society. Women have to dress a certain way and men have to dress a certain way'. When they went to Israel she said the girls in the group began wearing long dresses and felt more religious. (Zara, aged 20, depth interview, Washington DC, April 1999). This suggests how our subjectivities and our subsequent relationships with and articulations of socially inherited memories of the past will shift according to the cultural context and discourses that we are immersed in: these cultural and national contexts can serve to either foreground or background gendered subjectivities. In the US, one respondent is a Jewish-American woman; in Poland, amid a culture embedded with the memory of annihilation, she identifies herself primarily as a Jew; in Israel, she is a woman.

In almost all accounts in all three countries there was little identification with the memory of the Nazis' other victims. As Tina Campt (1999) notes in her study of Afro-Germans' experiences of the

Holocaust, as one group was mentioned this 'masks' the telling of the story of another group, or masks the telling of particular atrocities related to the gender of the victims. It tended to be young people who were themselves marginalised within dominant national discourses and contexts, who articulated some of the complexities of Nazi policy in relation to groups, in addition to the Jews and in terms of gender, as with a 17-year-old New Yorker originally from the Dominican Republic:

> Jews weren't the only ones in concentration camps. The so-called 'unwanted' for example, cripples, blacks and gypsies (who have always be persecuted) were some of the other people that were in concentration camps. The weak ones were killed and those that were able to work survived. The conditions in the camps were terrible. Usually children and women died. (Alicja, aged 17, written life history, New York. April. 1999).

Conclusion

What we see from young people's socially inherited memories of the Holocaust in the US, Britain and Poland is that the processes of memory making and its articulation by individuals is gendered in complicated and heterogeneaous ways in different cultural environments. Interestingly, the key mediators in handing down the past are grandmothers. This interpersonal communication is perceived as more valuable than any other source by both men and women, but especially by young women. The presence of their grandmothers' memories is often articulated in contrast to the absence of memories of grandfathers. This absence, however, is expressed also in terms of an irrevocable loss of identity and history for young Jews in all three national contexts, who have often lost many relatives during the Holocaust. Grandmothers act as memory bridges or links to the stories of reticent grandfathers and provide young people with the cultural competence to negotiate conflicting versions of the past between those handed down at home and those articulated in public spaces. When grandmothers are silent, unable to articulate the past, the family tells alternative stories of luck and success of other family members, which are carefully handed down. The memorial authority of women expressed by respondents in this study is in contrast to the authority accorded men by respondents in a study of the sons and daughters of former Nazis. In addition, while a spectrum of cultural mediations were important, constellations of women's memories formed around the written word, while constellations of men's memories formed around images both still and moving, with moments of violence recalled most often. Men and women both expressed the importance of feeling the facts of the past, but men developed an emotional response through women's support or through witnessing women's responses to the past.

In the retelling of stories and events, while men and women might 'forget' other aspects of a protagonist's identity, such as their nationality or religion, they consistently remember someone's gender. This suggests that discourses of gender in the present and about the past form a less flexible structure and act as a common anchor to meaning in people's socially inherited memories and articulations of history. A common trope in memories of atrocity are those stories that disrupt or overturn established assumptions about gender boundaries and discourses, such as when Nazi-targeted women had to reject children or their maternal role. However, differences in the experiences of women and men victims and survivors form only subordinate tropes in young people's memories, or are muted altogether. Rape as part of genocide may be articulated in written form but remains unspeakable. Likewise, men being forced to passively witness their wives and daughters being raped, and the forced abandonment of women and children to their death in the process of selection, although genocidal facts of many male victims' and survivors' experiences, are not articulated in socially inherited memories of the events. Men identify consistently with men – as perpetrators, victims, bystanders and witnesses. Women identify with both women and men from history. But the prominence individuals give to gender issues in history and to their experiences and identities as women or men shifts according to other competing discourses and locations related to nationalism and religion which accord differing senses of belonging and safety, and foreground or background gender.

In these ways, the historical events of the Holocaust are handed down by families, communities and a spectrum of media texts and cultural mediations to subsequent generations of men and women who, in turn, re-articulate and disarticulate the past for others. In the final chapter, I bring together the insights and arguments of the book to suggest broader theoretical implications for how we should understand the complex relationships between gender, culture and memory. For, what we see in this analysis of socially inherited memories of the Holocaust is that the past we inherit and articulate is gendered in a variety of ways in the manner of its telling, in the stories people are told and in the stories we remember to tell. It is this past, in turn, that makes us who we are and who we will become – men and women – as well as being Jews or non-Jews in London, Warsaw or New York.

7
Conclusions: (Dis) Articulations of Gender, Culture and Memory

'Where does all this history and its telling lead, to what kinds of knowledge, to what ends?'

(James Young, 2000:11)

Salt.
10. (With a grain of salt). with reservations.
    vb. (tr) 12. to preserve or cure.

(Collins Concise Dictionary, 1990, p. 1029)

Giving life

When the young artist, Charlotte Salomon, handed over to a friend more than 700 illustrations of her childhood family experiences during Nazi policies with the words 'Keep this safe: It is my whole life' (Salomon cited in Felstiner, 1997:ix) she was signalling that neither her life nor her memories were safe from annihilation and obliteration. Charlotte died in Auschwitz extermination camp where sources indicate that at selection, two-thirds of women were sent immediately to their deaths (Felstiner, 1997:206). Although Charlotte was murdered, her friend kept her 'whole life' safe and so we at least have Charlotte's legacy.[1] Her account, an extraordinarily original combination of words and pictures in vivid gouache, details the contradictions of her particular experiences, not as a Jew, but as a young German-Jewish woman. What this book has argued is that experiences such as Charlotte's were the rule rather than the exception during the Nazi Holocaust. In historical accounts of the past, in autobiographies, in documentary and feature films, in memorial sites and museums, in accounts that are both individually and socially produced, gendered identities need to be integrated as a major factor in understanding how individuals and socially inherited memories of the events are constructed, mediated and (dis)articulated.

In this final chapter, the heterogeneous reflections on cultural mediations and configurations of socially inherited memories of the Holocaust are woven together to build a picture of how various cultural forms and mediations offer different possibilities for articulations of the genocide in relation to gender. Further, how we think about gender and the socially inherited memory of the Holocaust provides some clues as to how we might begin to reframe ways of thinking about the relationships between gender, culture and memory in order to be able to understand more fully how socially inherited memories in societies work in other contexts. As a media academic, I would argue that there are critical implications for those teaching and learning in the areas of media studies as well as historical studies, as too for those cultural practitioners involved in producing mediations about the Holocaust: the contention is that there is the need to orientate and conceptualise the relationships between gender, culture and memory which in turn have broader implications for the broader established theoretical paradigms of how people are thought to inherit the past.

Integrating gender into Holocaust memory

For media scholars, as well as historians, the Nazi Holocaust is a crucial starting-point for discussions of memory and the social inheritance of the past because it was a central point of European history and the 'war on memory' was at its centre. The memory of the events, how and in what ways people remember them, and how within different nations and cultures the memory of the Holocaust is handed down have also been the subject of much academic debate (Huyssen, 1995; Hartmann, 1994; Friedlander, 1993; Krondorfer, 1995; Langer, 1991; Novick, 1999; Zelizer, 1998). As James Young (1988) argues, it is important to understand the ways in which 'the facts' at the time and since are intertwined with cultural forms and structures (p. 4). Part of those facts, at the time and since, are intertwined with cultural forms and structures that are gendered in various ways. Yet the area of women, gender and the Holocaust is one that has only relatively recently gained the interest of Holocaust scholars, and there is still little work on the significance of gender in Holocaust memory (rather than history) and its mediations. By examining a range of different cultural forms and mediations – including historical texts, autobiography, film, memorial sites and museums – it has been possible to discern some of the contradictory processes involved in how the memory of atrocities are handed down differently within various forms in ways that are gendered. By also including some analysis of how young people of different cultural backgrounds have come to understand the events it was possible to explore the importance of interpersonal communication and the gendered contexts of interpretative communities in the generation and social inheritance of our pasts. From this, we need to work towards integrating gender with studies of Holocaust memory and re-conceptualize approaches to socially inherited memories of the past.

In Chapter 2, it was argued that mainstream Holocaust history has generally neglected gender. In the 1980s, however, research began to focus on women and the Holocaust. The problem to bear in mind with approaches that focus on women (rather than gender) is that they miss the particular experiences that men had because they were men and the changing roles and relationships between men and women. To look at one element without the other is to consider only one link in the chain and will miss the articulation of gendered meanings and experiences embedded within atrocity and genocide. Nevertheless, a critical examination of what and how testimonies and available historical sources document gender issues and the Holocaust provides a crucial epistemological foundation for the consideration of gender in relation to more popular mediations of the past. The remaining difficulty, however, is that there is the need for more feminist historical research that investigates the complex ways in which gender and ethnicity were articulated by Nazi policies and practices in different locales and situations. It is also important that this is integrated, or at least linked, to broader historical understandings of the Holocaust.

An analysis of personal memories of the atrocities within autobiographies demonstrates how the competing and contradictory discourses of gender and ethnicity intervene into the articulation of individual survivor's life-writings as well as their re-articulation or disarticulation within our social inheritance of dominant memories of the Holocaust. The contradictions embedded in the stories handed down to us by Jewish men and women who were victimised by the Nazis are evident in the stories they write concerning their survival and recuperation. Although these gendered contradictions of atrocity and survival are negotiated differently for each survivor (and each of the victims), there are some common gendered experiences and tropes evident in survivors autobiographies. There are also common discourses of atrocity – such as the experiences of extreme hunger, starvation, disease, thirst and overcrowding – that cross gender boundaries. An understanding of the ways in which competing aspects of people's gendered subjectivities and their various contradictions are articulated in personal memories of survivors, which then in turn become part of people's socially inherited memories, enables us to engage with, and have a deeper, receptive understanding of, the complexities of men and women's different and shared experiences.

Films are a key medium in our inheritance of the history and memory of the Holocaust and are recalled by young people as making the events 'more real'. However, films, like any other medium, present us with a re-translation of events, whether they are propaganda films, liberation footage, documentary or feature films, they are not historical documents. Part of this retranslation includes the particular ways in which gender is articulated in relation to production structures and the technologies of the form at the time of filming. Propaganda films made by Nazi perpetrators reproduced a particular discourse of nationalism that was gendered, as well as being racist and antisemitic (Gleber, 1993; Friedman, 1993). But they were also produced from within the particular discursive context of SS film crews and embodied gendered genocidal practices that involved the humiliation by SS film crews of men and women in specific ways. Liberation films were produced within the discursive context of men witnessing the aftermath of the Holocaust from the national positions of armies from US, Britain and the Soviet Union entering the camps. At the time gendered identities were simplified to render dominant the themes of witnessing and atrocity; at other moments, though, we see the rendering of disturbing images in which the gender of victims is represented in ways that disrupt genderless memories of the events. With later documentaries, such as Claude Lanzmann's *Shoah*, although criticized for not equally including women, this visual absence articulates the literal absence of women who were murdered. Although we do not have the nine-hour equivalent of *Shoah* there are documentary films, notably those made by women, that do articulate the presence of women in other ways, such as their participation in the resistance. With feature films, though, the tendency has been in big-budget movies to tell a story of the Holocaust using patriarchal narratives, dominant discourses of masculinity and femininity and conventional gendered stereotypes. Although the latter is still valuable in enabling some aspect of the events to be passed on to the post-Holocaust generation, it is necessary, as media and film scholars, and as historians, to be attentive to the fact that the most popular and influential of these – *Schindler's List* – fails to articulate some of the key horrors of genocide that are the most painful to remember: the stripping and overturning of pre-war established gendered values, identities and roles. This does not mean, however, that there are not other, smaller-budget post-war feature films that do tackle the atrocities in ways that endeavour to show how gender inflected in more complex ways the Nazi past (see Insdorf, 1989:230). A number of West German women film-makers, such as Marianne Rosenbaum and Margarethe von Trotta, have shown how Nazi politics operated from German women's perspective (Linville, 1998). *Peppermint Peace* (*Peppermint Frieden*), for example, tackles memory and the late War years from the viewpoint of an inquisitive young German girl (Dir: Rosenbaum, 1983). *Das Schreckliche Madchen* (*The Nasty Girl*) directed by Michael Verhoeven (1989) offers a very interesting deconstruction, in terms both of content and form, of the German triad of church, children and kitchen in its engagement with gender and memories of a small town's involvement in the Holocaust.

Differing Holocaust memorial sites and museums in the USA, Poland and Britain show significant variations in the ways in which gender is articulated in relation to Holocaust memory and discourses of atrocity. It is not possible to argue that all Holocaust museums and memorial sites present gender in particular ways. How gender is articulated is complicated and varied, even across the same institutional 'medium' of the public museum or memorial site. At Auschwitz-Birkenau, the site of genocidal atrocities, the usual dialogical process involved in remembering breaks down at moments and gender is emptied and buried, its memory visible only in the physical line on a map and in the empty remains of the women's camp. At other memorial sites more distant from the place of suffering and death, gender is articulated in other ways. At the US Holocaust Museum the roles of women are more passive, shallow and underdeveloped in relation to the more active and pronounced voice given to men's roles and experiences. Our identification as visitors is assumed to be flexible except in terms of gender, but gender resonances are then in places of the narrative left mystified or incomplete. Both the Museum of Jewish Heritage and the Imperial War Museum's Holocaust Exhibition through a careful balancing of accounts give more equal voice to men and women as Jewish victims but the Imperial War Museum goes a step further in articulating the memory of the Nazis other victims, as well as women's roles in history as perpetrators and liberators. Overall, though, it is possible to conclude that while the dominant narratives of men tend to confirm and reinforce each other across different national museum contexts, the stories of women tend to be more disjointed and discontinuous. The production of Holocaust memory by state institutions is fraught with literal and symbolic gendered tensions. Within these, however, it is evident that curatorial interventions, even by one individual, that are mindful of the particularities of gender can make a difference to the subsequent construction of the memory of past events. At the same time, visitors may make sense of the memory of the Holocaust within the museum context and articulate aspects of gender or ethnicity which are silenced through their own dialogic intertextuality by bringing other texts (books, films, other museums) and experiences (personal subjectivities, imagination, family stories) to the museum to intervene into the narrative. The memory of the Holocaust in the museum and at the memorial site is thus, as with other cultural forms and mediations, not fully fixed by curators or national perspectives but, in gender terms at least, is evolving and in process.

The processes of interpersonal communication and the articulation of socially inherited memories for young people born since the events are also gendered in complicated ways in different national and cultural environments. Overall, young people's grandmothers played a key role in handing down the past. They were perceived, by granddaughters especially, as more valuable than any other sources. The presence of the memories of mothers and grandmothers, though, was often articulated in contrast to the absence of memories of fathers and grandfathers. This absence was most felt, understandably, in terms of an irrevocable loss of identity and history for the young Jews included in the study many of whom had lost many relatives as a result of the genocide in all three national contexts. Grandmothers, in addition, provided access to the repressed stories of reticent grandfathers. They provided the cultural competence to aid young people's attempts to negotiate differences and contradictions in accounts of the past handed down by the State or school and by family members at home. When grandmothers were silent and unable to articulate the past, the family articulated alternative stories of the luck and success of other family members which were often repeated and told in detail. It should be stressed, however, that the memorial authority of women in the family nexus expressed by respondents in this study is location specific: it is in distinct contrast, for example, to the authority accorded men by respondents in Susan G. Figge's study of the sons and daughters of former Nazis (Figge, 1990:195).

Individual women's memories had a greater tendency to be articulated in relation to the importance of the written word, while men's memories were configured around images both still and moving, often embedded in remembered moments of violence. While men and women both expressed the importance of 'feeling the facts' of the past, some men said that they developed cultural competences such as empathy in relation to memory through women's support or through witnessing women's responses to memorial sites.

Young people reveal that while men and women might 'forget' other aspects of a protagonist's identity in a story about the past, such as their nationality or religion, they consistently remember someone's gender. This suggests that subject positions in relation to gendered discourses in the present and about the past are less flexible than subject positions in relation to discourses of the nation or religion. Gender acts as a common anchor to meaning in our inheritance and articulation of history. Within this, a common trope in young people's socially inherited memories of atrocity are those stories that disrupt or overturn dominant discourses of femininity and masculinity, such as when women in the camps could not fulfil their roles as mothers or nurturers. However, differences in the experiences of women and men, both as victims and survivors and their specific gendered experiences, form only subordinate tropes in young people's articulations of the Holocaust or are muted altogether. Rape as part of Nazi genocide is occasionally articulated in written life-histories but remains largely unspeakable. Men forced to passively witness their wives and daughters being raped, and the forced abandonment of women and children to their death in the process of selection, although genocidal facts of some male victims' and survivors' experiences, are not articulated by young people in their socially inherited narratives of events. Overall, young men identify consistently with other men in history – as perpetrators, victims, bystanders and witnesses. Women, in contrast, identify with women *and* men from history. Yet, gendered identities and processes of identification are continually in process, rather than fixed in relation to other felt subjectivities. The prominence given to gender issues and to gendered identities changes according to other competing discourses of nation and religion within given locales, and the sense of belonging and safety these afford aspects of our identity in terms of religion, nationality or ethnic background.

On the basis of these analyses, I would advocate an approach to inte-grating gender into our understanding of Holocaust history and memory that seeks openly to explore the heterogeneous, intersecting and often contradictory experiences related to gender in relation to the past that become articulated or disarticulated within different cultural forms. Thinking about gender and memory is not based simply on counting representations of men and women, or crudely arguing that women were more oppressed than men during the Holocaust or, for that matter, stressing sole differences of experience. Neither is it about suggesting that there is one conclusion to be had or particular features that one will always find. Rather, it is a matter of approach, of perspective, of giving more depth to what we know. Integrating gender into our thinking about the Holocaust is about trying to understand as deeply as possible the meaning of the horrific experiences that people went through, and why and how the genocide against Europe's Jews and other ethnic and social groups happened. It is about an openness in seeking to understand how and why gendered experiences of atrocity afterwards are at particular times left unarticulated, as well as articulated, in complex ways in order within particular localities to rebuild and maintain post-atrocity social relations and consensus. From this, I would suggest, it is then possible to begin to understand more fully the broader ways in which genocide happens in societies and how individuals and societies are constituted through the inheritance of the past.

Looking back

In the biblical story of Lot and his wife, recounted at the beginning of this book, I contended that in this culturally specific story the petrification of Lot's wife could be read as a warning of what happens within cultures and remembering more broadly if, when warned not to, a woman looks back at past atrocities. However, the story of Lot's wife – of what happens when we look back – when we are told that we should not – could also be read as a figurative process of transformation: Lot's wife turning into a pillar of salt may be read as a metaphor for the transformations that can occur, in people and societies, when we re-articulate the past or articulate aspects that were left mute.

Reflecting on how the Nazi Holocaust is handed down in different cultural mediations demonstrates that, overall, the engendering of these particular socially inherited memories is complex and varies according to form and genre within the historical, national and cultural context of production or situation. Different media, as well as the varieties of genres within these, offer different possibilities for the articulation of gender and atrocity, especially in terms of mediating those aspects which constitute gendered traumas such as rape and sexual abuse, and the shame and particular humiliation that many men experienced in being unable to protect their families from violence, rape and murder.

Life-writing in the form of autobiography, as the production of an individual's memory, seems to be less constrained by dominant discourses of masculinity and femininity. Writing by young people, about their socially inherited memories, also seem to allow for the articulation of memories long repressed or in some way unspeakable, such as rape. With film, what was recorded in writing in allied film crews caption sheets while shooting 'witness' footage of the liberation of camps such as Belsen, was often different from what was then subsequently included in the edited visual images of the film and its narration. But documentary moving images are also, as in the film *Shoah*, able to render visually in ways that writing cannot aspects of a gendered absence relating to the murder of women and children that is a feature of the Nazi Holocaust. With feature films, though, commercial imperatives often call for the ready use of conventional patriarchal narratives and discourses which then fail to articulate particular gendered experiences and the overturning of gendered norms and values that is a feature of genocide and atrocity. This does not mean, however, that subaltern memories are unable to surface in smaller, low-budget films in which women are the directors and producers.

With museums and memorial sites, the danger public institutions run, similarly, is that in 'narrativising' the events in an increasingly established way, particular stories and artefacts – such as a male prisoner's uniform – that marginalise the experiences of women gain hegemony and reproduce hierarchies of gender. However, Holocaust museums are complex collective endeavours, in which many researchers, advisers and curators, usually with the advice of survivors, are often involved over a long period of time. This process can allow for moments of intervention by individuals who can effect important shifts in the ways in which gender and the Holocaust are remembered. All the major museums, including the US Holocaust Museum, the Jewish Memorial Museum and the Holocaust wing at the Imperial War Museum have some elements in their memorialisation of the events that were indicative of the gendered conflicts underlying the creation of 'public' memories of the Holocaust. This emphasises that, as much as we are made by what we socially inherit, we also create new forms of social inheritance. It is an ongoing, dynamic, intertextual process in which people's dialogical – or rather polylogical – identification and non-identification with the past is articulated, disarticulated and re-articulated with and between the individual and the collective.

For a deeper understanding of social memories of atrocity and genocide, in the teaching and learning of the Holocaust, it is thus essential that people are allowed and encouraged to explore the ways in which different media, from historiography to digital media, may articulate or disarticulte in a variety of complex ways aspects of identities that include gender. How gender operates in terms of socially inherited memories of atrocities is not as simple as my introductory interpretation of the story of Lot and his wife might suggest. Women are not simply forgotten and men remembered. The pillar of salt is indicative of how there are certain aspects to witnessing (and experiencing and perpetrating) atrocities that are unspeakable but which remain mutely preserved. The unspoken areas of memory enable survivors and societies to rebuild shattered lives and social structures. In time, articulating and recognising the absences and mute spaces may be transformative – it can perhaps be valuable and 'curative' – though like the application of salt itself this is a delicate balance: in the live wounds of memory, it hurts.

Looking foward

As with all books and all accounts, this book has its own mute spaces, gaps and silences. But, as the feminist scholar Dale Spender once argued:

> All knowledge, every record is by definition partial, and the issue is to acknowledge the partiality, the prejudice – and the politics – to point clearly to the omissions instead of passing them off as the full story. When there can only be incomplete accounts it is not constructive to condemn an account for its inconclusiveness. (Spender, 1985:3–4).

This book concentrates mostly on the Jewish dimension of the Holocaust and the gendering of this dimension of the socially inherited memory of the events. At points, the analysis raises issues relating to other groups targeted by the Nazis, such as the Romany and Sinti. However, there is further work that needs to be done in terms of historical research and subsequent work on the socially inherited memory of a number of areas. This includes more work on gender and the memory of Roma and Sinti genocide, gender and policies against Afro-Germans, and gender and the memory of the experiences of gay men and lesbians. My focus has also been primarily on the stories of victims and survivors; there is work to be done on how gender is articulated in the memory of perpetrators, bystanders, witnesses and resisters in the

Holocaust. The book also does not analyse gender in media texts and cultural mediations such as art, music and photography, and how these articulate memories in important gendered ways that are also part of people's constellations and configurations of Holocaust memory. Neither have I included detailed analysis of digital technologies such as Holocaust web sites and CD Rom materials, since this forms part of a new study published elsewhere.[2] There are also many additional texts, films and museums that could have been included. The making and articulation of the social memories of the Holocaust for young people in countries other than the US, Poland and Britain, such as Germany and Israel, would make additional important studies. This book is intended simply as a beginning, an opening – an initial contribution rather than a 'right answer' – to this field of study and people's understanding of the connections between the areas of gender, culture and memory, and how societies inherit the past.

There are, in addition, connections to be made and work to be done on other experiences and memories of atrocities. How gender is constructed, disarticulated, articulated and re-articulated in the social memories of Rwandan genocide for example, may be at points similar to the rendering of the memory of the Holocaust, but also very different. This is not only because of differences in the manner of the atrocities themselves but also because how the dead are remembered, how social memories are constructed and practiced are different within different cultural and historical contexts. Although, this is something which I develop more fully elsewhere,[3] what I would contend here is that memory, like other core aspects of self and society, such as sexuality (see Foucault, 1979; Weeks, 1985), is best understood as the term for an historical and cultural construct. Evidence showing variable patterns of memory making and memory practices in different societies and at different times (Edmonds, 1999; Nora, 1997; Jonkers, 1995) shows that memory is not necessarily constituted by universal ideas or shared practices. Reinhart Koselleck (1990) has shown in his essays on the subject in *Futures Past* how a tripartite sense of time and our relation to it was developed around the turn of the seventeenth and eighteenth centuries. As Huyssen (1995) notes, 'The way our culture thinks about time is far from natural even though we may experience it as such' (p. 8). Even the language used to express time and memory are specific to a culture, as Oliver Sacks (1991) shows in *Seeing Voices: A Journey into the World of the Deaf* in which a young deaf boy learns a sense of past, present and future through the acquisition of language. The value different societies give to remembering and forgetting; how memory is conceptualized in relation to other beliefs such as fantasy, will vary (Casey, 1987; Colley, 1998; Shrimpton, 1997). Likewise, the kind of memory practices a society or culture uses will vary: although the colonizing Spanish in the sixteenth century initially dismissed Andean memory techniques as mere acts of drunkeness and amnesia, they later realised that Andean social memory was being articulated through the complex relationships between place, people, song, dance, symbols and drinking (Abercrombie, 1999).

Memory in and of itself is not a fixed concept: it is socially constructed. It is the product of and in turn the producer of an historical moment and cultural locale. Like other core beliefs, such as sexuality, it is difficult to think outside of the conceptualisation of memory into which we are inscribed. Western late capitalist cultures seem – as I argued at the start of the book – obsessed with memory and remembering. Its dominant conceptualisation of memory is based on a sequential and teleological view of time underpinned by an either/or logic common to Western philosophical traditions. Thus memory is distinct from fantasy and is conceived of in relation to another aspect of the past – history. This view of memory, like many other Cartesian and post-Enlightment ways of thinking, is largely bi-polar and conceived of in hierarchical dichotomous opposition to forgetting. Western culture and societies police elements that blur these boundaries, that arise from the interstices. We teach our children time present, time past, time future. Forgetfulness and forgetting trouble us. Yet even within Western societies there are other memorial practices and ideas which have points of liminality or intersection with this hegemonic view of memory. For example, the art of memory valued by the Ancient Greeks and developed in medieval times is present in modern-day books claiming to teach us how to improve our memories (Buzan, 1999:66).

Likewise, there are points of liminality between Sigmund Freud's pre-psychoanalytic theory of abreaction in which he declared that the individual's compulsion to repeat painful experiences comes from our inability to recall the prototype, and earlier ideas within Buddism, in which 'knowledge of former abodes' is a component path to enlightenment (Lopez, 1993). Similarly, the much older Buddist term *smrti* (mindfulness) bears strong resemblances to the sense of 'holding in mind' used within psychodynamic psychoanalysis (Wayman, 1993:133–47).

These variations and intersecting forms and practices of memory are also evident in the differing relationships to the past within the various groups targeted by the Nazis. Naming the dead in Europe and America may be a longstanding dominant idea of what is right as memorial practice, as evidenced by war memorials and the recent response to the attack on the World Trade Centre on 11 September 2001 (Simpson, 2001). But, if in a culture the name of the dead should not be mentioned in case they return to haunt the living – as Patrick Jasper Lee (2000) argues in relation to Romany 'gypsies' – then this different conceptualisation of how one should remember the dead will in turn influence and intersect with how *The Porrajmos* (The Devouring) – the Nazi murder of Romany people – is (not) talked of and (not) represented by other cultures.

Finally, I have never had to go to one of my friends in the dead of night to push this or any other manuscript into their hands, fearful for my life and seeking urgently for a record of my life to be remembered in my place. I am very fortunate: this book, unlike Charlotte Salomon's, is not 'my whole life'. But it is the result of and rests on many other people's lives, research and media practices, and the subject of the book itself arises because of the deaths and suffering of many millions of people during recent European history. I would, as a result, contend that the legacy and lessons of the Holocaust, as well as other horrific aspects of the past, are something that we all struggle with either knowingly or unknowingly: as Stanley Cohen (2001) in *States of Denial* argues, there are many ways of knowing about atrocities. One Holocaust survivor, asked if she can ever forget what happened to her, said 'it is like ripples on water. They start off big and get smaller.' (video installation, Imperial War Museum). We are all influenced in different ways by these ripples, as well as the ripples from other genocides and mass murders. Shortly before she died in July 2000, one of my grandmothers, talking to me about her memories of the Second World War and the Nazis hatred of 'gypsies', quietly said, 'If they'd made it here, you wouldn't exist.' Her memory, of her 'gypsy' grandmother, meant that she believed that she would have been subject to Nazi policies of sterilization and murder. This handed-down memory I interpret as a recognition of the fragility of citizenship and the rights that go with it, requiring ongoing vigilance. This book argues that we should not ignore the fact that memories of 'they' and 'you' and hence 'me' are in important ways gendered. But also, I would stress that they, you and me should not be thought of as over there somewhere in history, in another country, in another place, with other people, but, in terms of ongoing racism, 'ethnic cleansing' and geno-cide, they are also in the here and now, wherever and whoever you

188 of the Holocaust

and me are. As Eva Hoffman (1998) in her exploration of people's memories of former Shetl life in a small town in Eastern Europe writes: 'The task is not only to remember, but to remember strenuously – to explore, decode and deepen the terrains of memory. Moreover, what is at stake is not only the past but the present' (p. 14).

Since 1945, within the definition of the Genocide Convention of 1948 (Article II), many further genocides have taken place around the world, including those in Cambodia, East Timor, Rwanda and Burundi, Sierra Leone and the former Yugoslavia.[4] The War on their memory continues.[5] With each attempt to remember, forget or reconstruct the past, we create ourselves and different futures. However, reconciling men and women to the heterogeneous and multivalent ways in which gender is an integral but complicated part of what happened in the Holocaust, and how this is passed down to us, cannot be redemptive as James Young (2000:11) warns. It cannot 'cure' shattered lives. It cannot restore the missing murdered of Europe's heart and all that has been lost with them. A book can never make amends, nor is this book meant to. In the spirit of *tikkun* (repair or mending),[6] though, it is my hope that this will enhance the processes of trying to understand the meaning and significance of the incremental steps that lead to genocide, the deaths of victims, the experiences of survivors and our own inheritance of these memories, in ways that may more deeply inform and guide.

Notes

Notes to Chapter 1

1. The art of memory valued by the Ancient Greeks and developed in medieval times is still present in modern day books claiming to teach people how to improve their memories. Hence, Tony Buzan in *Use Your Memory* (1999) argues that by using a series of images and systems people can artificially enhance their memories. He combines this idea with contemporary ideas in brain science and New Age ideas on how thought and imagination can result in material changes. The Roman Room System, as he names it:

    > is particularly amenable to the application of the left and right cortical skills, and to the Memory Principles ... if you begin to imagine yourself, in possession of certain items that exist in your imaginary room, both your memory and creative intelligence will begin to work paraconsciously on ways in which you can actually acquire such objects, increasing the probability that you will eventually do so.' (Buzan, 1999:66).

2. Part of this erasure of Jewish memory began in 1936 with a law in Germany banning stonemasons from carving Jewish gravestones (Young, 1988:189).
3. In the material relating to the trial of the commander of Helmbrechts, Alois Dorr, a number of former prisoners describe how one Jewish women was forced to stand in the snow with her hair shorn, because she had in her possession a photograph. (See S. K. Dorr, Vol. 4, p. 607, cited in Goldhagen (1997), note 54, p. 584).
4. For example, survivor Gena Turgel (1995) describes in *I light a Candle* how the Nazis forced people to participate in the erasure of their crimes. 'It was the tradition for relatives to participate in the Nazi's ritual of death, and the day after my sister and her "husband" were shot, we had to carry the wood for the bodies to be burned, my mother and sister Hela and I together. As always, the Nazis wanted to destroy every trace of evidence from their crimes. (p. 62).
5. Research on gender and memory in cyberspace is forming part of my new study at South Bank University on digital heritage. For a publication that discusses some of the preliminary results of this work see: Anna Reading, 'Clicking on Hitler: The Virtual Holocaust@Home' (323–39) in Zelizer, B. (ed), *Visual Culture and the Holocaust*, Rutgers University Press, 2001.
6. For general historical research on the Romany see Bauer, (1994); Hancock (1996); Kenrick and Puxon (1972); Lewy (2000); Milton, 1997 and Ramati, 1986. For literature on the Nazi persecution of gay men see Heger, 1994; Lautmann (1998); Rector (1981), Plant (1988). On the persecution of lesbians see Elman (1999). For a perspective on the persecution of Slavs see Lukas (1997); Wytwcky (1980). Donald Niewyk and Frabcis Nicosia's (2000) *The Columbia Guide to the Holocaust* provides a short up-to-date bibliography relating to historical research on the Nazi's other victims.

Notes to Chapter 2

1. In the American Civil War, there were 5213 cases of nostalgia reported among white troops in the North in the first year. Thought to be in some way infectious, 'in some camps, soldiers were punished for singing or whistling tunes that reminded them of home' (Colley, 1998:3). Not until the nineteenth century did nostalgia as a clinical entity begin to disappear from diagnoses, although it remained a familiar theme in Victorian culture and writing (Colley, 1998:2–3).

Notes to Chapter 3

1. One account of a perpetrator that I do not look at in this book but which was mentioned by young people in Poland is *Commandant of Auschwitz* by Rudolf Hoess. This is an autobiography first published in a Polish translation in 1951 under the title *Wspomnienia* (Warsaw: Wydanictwo Prawnicze). The German text was published in 1958 as *Kommandant in Auschwitz* by Deatsche verlags-Anstalt. Although a version of the book was published in English by Wiedenfeld and Nicolson in 1959, it went out of print and was not republished with the full text until 2000 by Phoenix Press. The account was written by Hoess in prison in Cracow, Poland, in 1947, on the suggestion of the Polish criminologist Dr Stanislaw Batawie. Hoess was executed following trial in April 1947. An analysis of gender and atrocity in this text forms part of a further separate paper (Reading, forthcoming).
2. Judith Zur, in her work on the memories of violence among Mayan Indian War Widows who experienced La Violencia (1978–85) in which villages were bombed and people murdered by death squads, has shown how 'Intolerable truths may be rejected and less painful versions, constructed. Pertinent detail (in terms of absolute truth) may be omitted, either consciously or as the result of memory fragmentation)' Judith Zur in 'Reconstructing the Self through Memories of Violence among Mayan Indian War Widows', (In Ronit Lentin (ed) (1997) *Gender and Catastrophe*. London and New York: Zed Books., p. 63.
3. See, for example, Cynthia Crane's (2000) Divided Lives *The Untold Stories of Jewish–Christian Women in Nazi Germany.*, New York: St Martin's Press.

Notes to Chapter 4

1. The English word 'usher' has its roots in the words 'ostiarius' (door-keeper), 'ostium' (door) and 'os' (mouth/bone). See T. F. Hoad (1993) *English Etymology*, Oxford University Press.
2. See, for example, Thomas A. Abercrombie's (1999) fascinating study of memory, *Pathways of memory and Power: Ethnography and History Among Andean People,* Madison, Wisconsin, University of Wisconsin Press.
3. Special thanks go to Jenny Owen and Barbie Zelizer for their comments on earlier versions of this chapter.
4. See also Nora Levin (1973), *The Holocaust: The Destruction of European Jewry 1933–1945*, New York: Schocken Books, p. 231.

5. An earlier film of eight minutes duration, made in 1942, was discovered in a cupboard in the Czech Republic in the 1990s. Since named the 'The First Theresienstadt Film', its provenance is explored in Karel Magry's 'The First Theresienstadt Film, 1942', *Historical Journal of Film, Radio and Television,* vol. 19 no. 3. 1999. A copy of the film is held in the Imperial War Museum's Film Archive, London, UK.

6. A copy of the British Army shot *Memory of the Camps* (F3080) is held by the Imperial War Museum's Film Archive, London, UK. There is also a VHS version, ME0057. The archive also has copies of the original secret caption sheets by film crews, as well as an archive of oral histories of the British men that shot the film going into the concentration camps in Germany.

7. See, for example, the comments of the following survivors: 'My mother didn't even give us a piece of bread, nothing. We just had that egg' (Nitzan, 1998:117). 'The Nazis took the child away from me ... my child would be now forty-four years old. She was four years old when they took her from my arms' (Small, 1998:88–9).

8. For a German documentary on the memory of women at Ravensbruck see Loretta Walz (Dir) (1995) *Erinneren An Ravensbruck*; For a film about 'gypsies' and the Holocaust, see *Forgotten Holocaust* (George Case Dir, 1989).

9. Post-production was also wrought with gender and age-related anxieties: The laboratory processing the atrocity films was so concerned about the impact of the footage that, according to Elizabeth Sussex (1984), although originally 'They had young girls working on the coding or numbering of the film ... they took them off' (p. 93).

10. This is unlike the post-war analogy established in Israeli culture between strong masculinity and Jews (see Dworkin, 2000:102).

Notes to Chapter 5

1. Many thanks to Joan Ringelheim, Director of Oral History, US Holocaust Museum for her comments on an earlier version of this chapter.

2. According to the *Encyclopedia of the Holocaust* (1990 Macmillan, New York, volume 1), edited by Israel Gutman in March 1942 the women's section established at the camp in Auschwitz 1 was moved on 16 August to Birkenau (p. 117).

3. The *Chronicle of the Lodz Ghetto* shows that there were more women present than men. And more men were dying from the conditions (Dobroszycki, 1984).

4. Other examples of Holocaust museums' stated objectives in relation to citizenship and democracy include the Sydney Jewish Museum of the Holocaust and Australian Jewish History which states: 'The Museum challenges visitors' perceptions of democracy, morality, social justice and human rights'. (see www.join.org.au/ sydimus/about/htm). The Holocaust Memorial Centre, Michigan has as one of its stated objectives 'To help future generations understand and direct their lives to the maintenance of an open, free society'. (see http://holocaustcenter.org).

5. Such national discourse, as a number of writers have noted, forgets the other aspect of America's past with its roots in the slave trade.

6. The Imperial War Museum itself has a much longer history, however: it was first established in 1917 to document the history of the First World War and the contributions made by people in Britain and its Empire. It has had various homes in London, but was established on its current site in what used to be the Bethlem Royal Hospital on Lambeth Road, London, in 1936. At the outbreak of the Second World War its remit was extended to include documentation of the conflict, and after 1953 this remit was extended further to include all world conflicts in which British citizens or Commonwealth peoples were a part. It is now Britain's 'national museum of twentieth century conflict' (Imperial War Museum, 2001: www.iwm.org.uk:) seeking to 'provide for and to encourage, the study and understanding of the history of modern war and war-time experience' (Crawford, 2001: www.iwm.org.uk). It has six sites in the UK, with one of the largest holdings on war-related materials, including 158,000 books and documents and six million photographs, as well as approximately four million metres of cinefilm and 32,000 hours of sound recordings (Imperial War Museum, 2001: www.iwm.org.uk:). As well as being Britain's main museum of conflict, it is also a memorial to those who 'served the country and the Commonwealth' (Shenfield, 2000:3).

7. The Imperial War Museum, although in the heart of the Britain's capital, is not situated symbolically near the seat of justice or democracy as are the US Holocaust Museum and Museum of Jewish Heritage. However, it is situated in an area of London that suffered great losses during the bombardments of the Second World War which is evidenced in the architectural gaps and disjunctures in the Victorian and Georgian architecture replaced with post-war road plans and tower blocks. In this sense, the architecture of the museum itself is a surviving memorial remnant from before the Second World War.

Notes to Chapter 6

1. Respondents are referred to by first name pseudonyms, their stated age, place and date of interview. Other self-identified aspects of identity are also included.

2. The focus in the chapter is on how gender impacts on memory and thus how the respondent describes the memory of his visit to Dachau Concentration Camp and his mother's response to the mass murder that was the Holocaust. However, it is important to note the historical debates that are raised by the respondent's recollection of walking the path to the gas chamber at Dachau. There was a gas chamber that was technically capable of gassing human beings in the vicinity of the camp itself but there have been longstanding debates about the extent to which it was used for homicidal purposes. Information provided by the museum website states that this particular gas chamber was never used.(see www.kz-gedenkstaette-dachau.de). Some historians argue that the large gas chamber in Dachau was built for homicidal purposes and was used at an 'experimental' level. Four other smaller gas chambers at Dachau are described as fumigation chambers (see for example Eugene Kogon et al (1993) *Nazi Mass Murder: A Documentary History of the Use of Poison Gas*. New Haven: Yale University Press, 203–204 and document posted at www.nizkor.org/

hweb/camps/dachau). What is agreed is that systematic gassing was carried out further afield under the guise of invalid transports from the camp to Hartheim Castle near Linz. 3,166 people were murdered using carbon monoxide gas. Sources are agreed that thousands of people were killed at the camp itself as a result of summary executions, torture, medical experiments, starvation, disease and frostbite.

Notes to Chapter 7

1. See Mary Lowenstal Felstiner's account in *To Paint her Life: Charlotte Salomon and the Nazi Era.* University of California Press, Berkeley, Los Angeles, London 1997. The Joods Historisch Museum (Jewish Historical Museum) in Amsterdam hold the Charlotte Salomon collection – 700 paintings and words for her work *Life? Or Theater?*
2. Reflections on the articulation of gender and memory in digital technologies is a new research project following on from this book. An early version of some of the research can be found in 'Clicking on Hitler: the Virtual Holocaust @ home' (323–39) in Barbie Zelizer (ed) (2001) *Visual Culture and the Holocaust.* New Brunswick, New Jersey. Rutgers University Press.
3. A broader theorisation of the relationships between gender, culture and memory is the subject of a forthcoming essay in the journal *Media, Culture and Society.*
4. For a useful overview of post-war genocide see S. D. Stein's website (www. ess.uwe.ac.uk/genocide/genderf.htm). Under the *Genocide Convention 1948*, genocide means any of the following acts committed with intent to destroy, in whole or in part, a national, ethnical, racial or religious group, as such: a) Killing members of the group; b) Causing serious bodily or mental harm to members of the group; c) Deliberately inflicting on the group conditions of life calculated to bring about its physical destruction in whole or in part; d) Imposing measures intended to prevent births within the group; e) Forcibly transferring children of the group to another group. See S. D. Stein. Genocide in E. Cashmore (ed) (1996) *Dictionary of Race and Ethnic Relations. Fourth Edition.* London: Routledge.
5. The women of Srebrenica, for example, who are the survivors of the genocide after the fall of Srebrenica in the former Yugoslavia in which 7079 men disappeared, continue to fight for justice. See www.gendercide.org/ case_srebrenica.html. In the writing of this book, Jeffrey, a survivor of the massacres in Rwanda, told me his story of survival while every member of his family were murdered. He said that in the three years in which he had been in the UK he had told his story to no one, except to someone in the Home Office, because no one in Britain, once they knew he was Rwandan, had ever asked or been prepared to listen to him.
6. For an essay that discusses the interlinking of *tikkun atzmi* (mending of the self) and *tikkun olam* (mending of the world) in feminist holocaust scholarship see Susan E. Nowak. 'In a World Shorn of Color: Toward a feminist Theology of Holocaust Testimonies' (33–45) in Esther Fuchs (1999) *Women and the Holocaust: Narrative and Representation. Studies in the Shoah*, vol. xxii Lanham, New York, Oxford: University Press of America.

Bibliography

Primary and Secondary Printed Sources

Abercrombie, Thomas, A. (1999) *Pathways of Memory and Power: Ethnography and History Among an Andean People*. Madison, Wisconsin: University of Wisconsin Press.

Akhmatova, Anna (1984) 'Lots Wife' (p. 191) Trans from the Russian by Richard Wilbur, in Cosman, Carol, Keefe, Joan, and Weaver, Kathleen (eds) *The Penguin Book of Women Poets*. London: Penguin.

Alster, L. (1994) 'Spielberg's Ark,' *Times Educational Supplement*, No. 4052, February 25, B. 13.

Altshuler, Linda A. and Cohn, Anna R. (1983) 'The Precious Legacy' pp. 24–38 in Altshuler, David (ed.) *The Precious Legacy: Judaic Treasures from the Czechoslovak State Collections*. New York: Summit Books

Anderson, Linda (1997) *Women and Autobiography in the 20th Century: Remembered Futures*. London: Prentice-Hall.

Ang, Ien with Joke, Hermes (1996) 'Gender and/in Media Consumption' (pp. 109–29), in *Living Room Wars: Rethinking Media Audiences for a Postmodern World*, London: Routledge.

Arpadi, Charlotte (1991) 'Memoirs'. Unpublished papers in the US Holocaust Museum Archives, RG 02 121, Box 17.

Augustine, St (1996) 'From Confessions' pp. 5–8, in McKonkey, J. (ed.) *The Anatomy of Memory: An Anthology*. New York and Oxford: Oxford University Press.

Austin, Thomas (1999) '"Desperate to see it": Straight Men watching *Basic Instinct*' (pp. 147–62) in Maltby, R. and Stokes, M. *Identifying Hollywood's Audiences: Cultural Identity and the Movies*. London: BFI Publishing.

Bacon, Gershon (1998) 'The Missing 52 Percent: Research on Jewish Women in Interwar Poland and Its Implications for Holocaust Studies' (pp. 55–67), Dalia Ofer and Lenore J. Weitzman (eds) *Women in the Holocaust* . New Haven and London: Yale University Press.

Bardgett, Suzanne (2000a) Untitled draft paper for *News of Museums History*.

Bardgett, Suzanne (2000b) Director the Holocaust Exhibition, Imperial War Museum, London, UK. Personal communication. (interview), 24 February.

Barkai, A. (1989) *From Boycott to Annihilation: The Economic Struggle of German Jews, 1933–1943*, Hanover, P.A: University Press of New England.

Barnhurst, Kevin (1998) 'Young Citizens, Power and Media', *Media Culture and Society*, vol. 20: 201–18.

Barthes, Roland (1972) *Mythologies*, London: Jonathan Cape.

Bauer, Yehuda (1994) 'Gypsies' (pp. 441–55), in Yisrael Gutman and Michael Berenbaum (eds), *Anatomy of the Auschwitz Death Camp*, Bloomington: Indiana University Press.

Bauman, Zygmunt (1989) *Modernity and the Holocaust*, Oxford: Polity.

Baumel, Judith Tydor (1998) *Double Jeopardy: Gender and the Holocaust.* London: Portland, Vallentine Mitchell.

Bausinger, Hermann (1990) *Folk culture in a world of Technology.* Bloomington: Indiana University Press.

Beasley, Faith (1990) *Revising Memory: Women's Fiction and Memoirs in 17th century France,* New Brunswick: Rutgers University Press.

Becker, Lutz (2001) 'Introduction to Der Fuhrer Schenkt Den Juden Eine Stadt: Film as Propaganda', *The Holocaust, Genocide and the Moving Images: Film and Television Representations since 1933,* Imperial War Museum, 23–27 April 2001.

Bell, Susan Croag and Yalom, Marilyn (eds) (1990) *Revealing Lives: Autobiography, Biography and Gender,* Albany: State University of New York Press.

Berenbaum, Michael and Roth, John (1989) *Holocaust: Religious and Philosophical Reflections,* New York: Paragon House.

Berenbaum, Michel (ed) (1990) *Mosaic of Victims: Non-Jews Persecuted and Murdered by the Nazis,* New York: New York University Press.

Bhandare, Shaila (1993) *Memory in Indian Epistemology and Status,* Delhi, India: Sri Satguru Publications.

Bielenberg, C. (1984) *The Past is Myself.* London: Corgi.

Blumer, Herbert (1933) *Movies and Conduct.* New York: Macmillan – now Palgrave Macmillan.

Bober, Robert (1998) *What News of the War?* London: Hamish Hamilton.

Bock, Gisella (1993) 'Racism and Sexism in Nazi Germany: Motherhood, Compulsory Sterlization and the State' (pp. 161–86) in Carol Rittner and John K. Roth, *Different Voices: Women and the Holocaust,* New York: Paragon.

Boguslawska-Swiebocka, Renata and Swiebocka, Teresa (1995) 'Auschwitz in Documentary Photographs' (pp. 34–45), in Swiebocka, Teresa *Auschwitz: A History in Photographs,* Warsaw: Kziazka and Wiedza.

Boltanski, Luc (1999) *Distant Suffering: Morality, Media and Politics,* Cambridge: Cambridge University Press.

Bondy, Ruth (1998) 'Women in Theresienstadt and the Family Camp at Birkenau' (pp. 310–26) in Dalia Ofer and Lenore J. Weitzman (eds) *Women in the Holocaust,* New Haven and London: Yale University Press.

Boyarin, Jonathan (ed) (1994) *Remapping Memory: The Politics of Time space.* Minneapolis: University of Minnesota Press.

Boyars, Christine (1994) *The City of Collective Memory: Its Historical Imagery and Architectural Entertainments,* Massachusetts: MIT.

Braxton, Joanne, M. (1989) *Black Women Writing Autobiography: A Tradition, Within a Tradition,.* Philadelphia: Temple University Press.

Bridenthal, R., Grossman, A. and Kaplan, M. (eds) (1984) *When Biology Becomes Destiny.* New York: Monthly Review Press.

Broad, P., (1972) 'Reminiscences', in *KL Auschwitz Seen by the SS: Rudolf Hoss, Pery Broad, Johann Paul Kremer,* Oswiecim: Auschwitz-Birkenau State Museum.

Broughton, Trev Lynn (1999) *Men of Letters, Writing Lives: Masculinity and Literary Auto/Biography in the Late-Victorian Period.* London: Routledge.

Browstein, Lauren (1992) 'The Politics and Aesthetics of Memorialization: the Holocaust Memorial at Treblinka, Poland', unpublished MA thesis. University of Virginia, US Holocaust Museum Archives, RG24.019.

Bruzzi, Stella (2000) *New Documentary: A Critical Introduction,* London and New York: Routledge.

Buckingham, David (1993) 'Boys talk: television and the policing of masculinity', in Buckingham, D. (ed) *Reading Audiences: Young People and the Media*. Manchester: Manchester University Press.

Buzan, Tony (1999) *Use Your Memory*, London: BBC Books.

Camft, Tina (1999) *Towards a Social Technology of Memory: Reading Afro-German Narratives of the Third Reich*, unpublished paper at Frontiers of Memory Conference, September, 17–19 Institute of Education, London.

Casey, E. (1987) *Remembering: A Phenomenological Study*, Bloomington: Indiana University Press.

Chanfrault-Duchet and Marie-Francoise (2000) 'Textualisation of the self and gender identity in the Life Story' (pp. 61–75) Tess Cosslett, Celia Lury and Penny Summerfield (eds) *Feminism and Autobiography: Texts, Theories, Methods*, London and New York: Routledge.

Charman, Terri (2001) 'The Eternal Jew: Film as Propaganda', *The Holocaust, Genocide and the Moving Image: Film and Television Representations Since 1933*, Imperial War Museum, 23–7 April.

Cohen, Stanley (2001) *States of Denial: Knowing About Atrocities and Suffering*, London: Polity.

Colley, Ann C. (1998) *Nostalgia and Recollection in Victorian Culture*, Basingstoke: Macmillan.

Commentary and Shot List., A70. 515/1-5/ Imperial War Museum (IWM) Document File: Concentration Camp Film, Imperial War Museum Film Archive, London.

Connerton, Paul (1989) *How Societies Remember*. Cambridge: Cambridge University Press.

Corner, John (1996) *The Art of Record: A Critical Introduction to Documentary*, Manchester: Manchester University Press.

Cosman, Carol, Keeje, Joan and Kathleen Weaver (1978) *The Penguin Book of Women Poets* Harmondsworth: Penguin.

Cosslett, Tess, Lury, Celia, and Summerfield, Penny (eds) (2000) *Feminism and Autobiography: Texts, Theories*, London and New York: Routledge.

Crane, Cynthia (2000) *Divided Lives: the Untold Stories of Jewish–Christian Women in Nazi Germany*, New York: St Martins Press.

Crawford, Robert (2000) 'Foreword' (p. 3) in Paulsson, G. Steve, *The Holocaust: The Holocaust Exhibition at the Imperial War Museum*, London: Imperial War Museum.

Crownshaw, Richard (1999) 'Ethnic Identity and Cultural Heritage: Belsen In the Museum' (pp. 295–303) in Stokes, J . and Reading, A., *The Media in Britain*, Basingstoke: Palgrave Macmillan.

Czech, Danuta (1990) *Auschwitz Chronicle 1939–1945: From the Archives of the Auschwitz Memorial and The German Federal Archives*, New York: Henry Holt and Company.

Davidowicz, Lucy S. (1975) *The War Against the Jews,* New York: Holt, Rinehart and, Winston.

Davies, J. (1994) 'Moving Pictures', *Times Educational Supplement*, No, 4081, 16 September, A.24.

Davin, Anna (1972) 'Women and History', in Wandor, M. (ed) *The Body Politic*, London: Stage 1.

Day, Ingeborg (1980) *Ghost Waltz*, New York: Viking.

De Silva, Cara (ed) (1996) *In Memory's Kitchen: A Legacy From the Women of Terezin*. Northvale, NJ: Jason Aronson.

Delage, Christian (2001) Introduction to Night and Fog (1955): Holocaust and Documentary in Film and TV, *The Holocaust, Genocide and the Moving Image: Film and Television Representations Since 1933*, Imperial War Museum, 23–7 April.

Dobryszycki, Lucjan (1984) *Chronicles of the Lodz Ghetto 1941–44*, New Haven and London: Yale University Press.

Doneson, Judith E. (1978) 'The Jew as a Female Figure in Holocaust Film', *Shoah: A Review of Holocaust Studies and Commemorations*, vol. 1 no.1, 1978, 12.

Doneson, Judith E. (1987) *The Holocaust in American Film*, New York, Jerusalem: The Jewish Publication Society.

Dworkin, Andrea (2000) *Scapegoat: the Jews, Israel and Women's Liberation*, London: Virago.

Edmonds, Mark (1999) *Ancestral Geographies of the Neolithic: Landscape, Monuments and Memory*, London: Routledge.

Ehrlich, Zenka (2001) Der Fuhrer Schenkt Den Juden Eine Stadt: Film as Propaganda. *The Holocaust , Genocide and the Moving Image; Film and Television Representations Since 1933*, Imperial War Museum, 23–7 April, London.

Eibeshitz, Jehoshua and Eilenberg-Eibeshitz, Anna (1994) *Women in the Holocaust* 2 vol, Brooklyn: Remember Books.

Eisenbach, A. (1957) 'Dokumenty i materialy III' pp. 35–50, in T. Bernstein, A. Eisenbach and A. Rutkowski (eds) Eksterminacja Zydow na Ziemiach Polskich W Okresie Okupacji Hitlerowskiej: Zbior Dokumentow (*The Extermination of the Jews on Polish Territory During Nazi Occupation: A Collection of Documents*), Warsaw: Zydowskie Instytut Historyczny.

Eley G. and Grossman, A. (1997) 'Watching Schindler's List', *New German Criticism* 71, 41–62.

Elman, Amy (1999) 'Lesbians and the Holocaust' (pp. 9–18) in Fuchs, Ester (ed.) *Women and the Holocaust: Narrative and Representation. Studies in the Shoah*, vol. XXII, Lanham, New York and Oxford: University Press of America.

Elvidge, K. J. (1945) 'Letter to a Friend', 29 May 1945, File 89/10/1, Imperial War Museum Archives.

Epstein, Helen (1988) *Children of the Holocaust: Conversations with Sons and Daughters of Survivors*, London: Penguin.

Feig, Konnilyn G. (1983) *Hitler's Death Camps: the Sanity of Madness*, New York: Holmes and Meier.

Fein, Helen (1987) 'Introduction', in Fein, Helen (ed.), *The Persistent Question: Sociological Perspectives and Social Contexts of Modern Antisemitism*, Berlin and New York: Walter de Gruyter.

Felstiner, M. L. (1997) *To Paint her Life: Charlotte Salomon in the Nazi Era*, Berkley: University of California Press.

Figge, Susan G. (1990) 'Father Books: Memoirs of the Children of Fascist Fathers', (pp. 193–201). in Susan G. Bell and Marilyn Yalom, *Revealing Lives: Autobiography, Biography and Gender*, Albany: State University of NY Press.

Flinkter, Moshe (1971) *Young Moshe's Diary: The Spiritual Torment of a Jewish Boy in Nazi Europe*, Jerusalem: Yad Vashem.

198 *Bibliography*

Fogelman, Eva (1988) 'Therapeutic Alternatives of Holocaust Survivors and Second Generation' in Braham, R. L. (ed.) *The Psychological Pespectives of the Holocaust and of its Aftermath*. New York: Columbia University Press.

Foucault, Michel (1979) *A History of Sexuality. Vol. 1. Trans. Robert Hurley*.

Foucault, Michel (1980) *Power/Knowledge: Selected Interviews and Other Writings, 1972–1977*, New York: Pantheon.

Frank, Otto H. and Pressler, Mirjam (1997) *Anne Frank: The Diary of A Young Girl*, The Definitive Edition, London: Penguin.

Frankl, Viktor (1984) (first published 1946) *Man's Search for Meaning*, New York: Washington Square Books.

Friedlander, Saul (1993) *Memory, History and the Extermination of the Jews of Europe*, Bloomington: Indiana University Press.

Friedman, Ina (ed) (1990) *The Other Victims; First Person Stories of Non-Jews Persecuted by the Nazis*, Bosto: Houghton Mifflin.

Friedman, Regine Mihal (1993) 'Male Gaze and Female Reaction: Veit Harlan's Jude Suss (1940), (pp. 117–33) in Frieden, Sandra, McCormick, Richard. W, Petersen, Vibeke R, Voegelsang and Laurie Melissa (eds) *Gender and German Cinema: Feminist Interventions. Volume II. German Film History/German History on Film*, Oxford: Berg.

Fuchs, Esther (1999) 'Introduction' (pp. ix–xv) in Fuchs, Ester (ed) *Women and the Holocaust: Narrative and Representation. Studies in the Shoah*, Vol XXII, Lanham, New York and Oxford: University Press of America.

Fukujama, Francis (1992) *The End of History and the last Man*. London: Hamilton.

Galinski, Antoni (1983) 'Nazi Camp for Gypsies in Lodz', *The Main Commission for Investigation of Nazi Crimes in Poland*, International Scientific Session on Nazi Genocide in Poland and Europe 1939–1945, Warsaw, April 14–17.

Gauch, Sigfrid (1979) Vaterspuren Eine Erzählung. (*Father Tracks*), Konigstein/Ts Athenaous.

Gethin, Rupert (1993) ' The Matikas: Memorization, Mindfulness and the List' (pp. 149–72) in Gyatso, Janet (ed) *In the Mirror of Memory: Reflections on Mindfulness and Remembrance in Indian and Tibetan Buddhism*, Delhi-India: Sri Satguru Publications.

Gilbert, Martin (1987) *The Holocaust: The Jewish Tragedy*. London: HarperCollins.

Gilbert, Martin (1996) *The Boys: Triumph Over Adversity: The Story of 732 Young Concentration Camp Survivors*, London: Phoenix.

Gilbert, Martin (1997) *Holocaust Journey: Travelling in Search of the Past*. London: Phoenix.

Gitelman, Zvi (ed) (1997) *Bitter Legacy: Confronting the Holocaust in the USSR*, Bloomington: Indiana University Press.

Gleber, Anke (1993) '"Only Man Must Be and Remain a Judge, Soldier and Ruler of the State": Female as Void in Nazi Film', (pp. 105–16), in Frieden, Sandra; McCormick, Richard W, Petersen, Vibeke R, Voegelsang, Laurie Melissa (eds) *Gender and German Cinema: Feminist Interventions. Volume II. German Film History/German History on Film*, Oxford: Berg.

Goldenberg, M. (1996) 'Lessons Learned from Gentle Heroism: Women's Holocaust Narratives', *Annals of the American Academy of Political and Social Science*, 548, (Nov.) 87–92.

Goldhagen, Daniel Jonah (1997) *Hitler's Willing Executioners: Ordinary Germans and the Holocaust*, London: Abacus.

Gonin, M. W. Lieutenant Colonel (1945) Report on the liberation of Bergen-Belsen Concentration Camp *Imperial War Museum Archives, File, 85/38/.*

Gottesfeld Heller, Fanya (1993) *Strange and Unexpected Love: A Teenage Girl's Memoirs*, Hoboken, New Jersey: KTAV Publishing.

Gottesfeld Heller, Fanya (2000) *Women and the Holocaust Conference*, Museum of Jewish Heritage, New York, 9 March.

Gourevitch, Philip (1999) 'Nightmare on 15th Street', *Guardian*, 4 December 1999, review, 1–3.

Grant, Linda (1998) *Remind Me Who I am, Again*, London: Granta.

Gurewitsch, Brana (ed) *Mothers, Sisters, Resisters: Oral Histories of Women Who Survived the Holocaust*, Tuscaloosa and London: University of Alabama Press.

Gutman, Israel (1990) *Encyclopedia of the Holocaust Volume One*. New York: Macmillan – now Palgrave Macmillan.

Haaken, Janice (1998) *Pillar of Salt: Gender, Memory and the Perils of Looking Back*. New Brunswick, New Jersey and London: Rutgers University Press.

Habermas, Jürgen (1987) *Eine Art Schadeusabwicthlung*. Frankfurt am Main: Suhr Kamp.

Hadlow, Janice (2001) 'Holocaust and Documentary in Film and TV: ZDF Holocaust Series', paper presented at The Holocaust, Genocide and the Moving Image: Film and Television Representations Since 1933, Conference, Imperial War Museum, April 2–27, London.

Halbwachs, Maurice (1980) *The Collective Memory*, New York: Harper and Row.

Halbwachs, Maurice (1992) *On Collective Memory*, Chicago: University of Chicago Press.

Hall, Stuart (1987) 'Minimal Selves', in ICA Documents 6. *Identity, the Real Me: Post Modernism and the Question of Identity*, London: ICA. 446.

Hancock, Ian (1996) 'Responses to the Parraimos: the Romani Holocaust' (pp. 39–64), in Alan Rosenbaum (ed), *Is the Holocaust Unique? Perspectives on Comparative Genocide*. Boulder, Colorado: Westview Press.

Hanks, Patrick (1989) *The Collins Concise Dictionary of The English Language*, 2nd Edition. London: Collins.

Hanley, Lynne (1991) *Writing War: Fiction, Gender and Memory*, Amherst: University of Massachusettes Press.

Hartmann, Geoffrey H. (ed) (1994) *Holocaust Remembrance: the Shapes of Memory*, Oxford: Basil Blackwell.

Hass, Aaron (1990) *In the Shadow of the Holocaust: The Second Generation*, Cambridge: Cambridge University Press.

Hass, Aaron (1995) *The Aftermath: Living with the Holocaust*, Cambridge: Cambridge University Press.

Heger, Heinz (1994) *The Men with the Pink Triangle: The True Life and Death Story of Homosexuals in the Nazi Death Camps*, Boston: Alyson Publications.

Hein, Nate (2000) 'Impossible Journey: A Holocaust Guidebook Toward Understanding the Incomprehensible', a senior thesis submitted to Friends World Program of Long Island University (European Centre) in partial fulfilment of the requirement of a degree.

Heinemann, M. E. (1986) *Women Writers and the Holocaust*, Westport, CT: Greenwood.

Herf, Jeffrey (1997) *Divided Memory: the Nazi Past in the Two Germanys*, Cambridge, Mass: Harvard University Press.

Herman, Judith Lewis (1992) *Trauma and Recovery: From Domestic Abuse to Political Terror*, London: Pandora.

Hilberg, Raul (1985) *The Destruction of the European Jews*. 3 vols New York.: Holmes and Meier.

Hilberg, Raul (1992) *Perpetrators, Victims and Bystanders: The Jewish Catastrophe, 1933–1945*, London: Lime Tree.

Hirsch, Herbert (1995) *Genocide and the Politics of Memory: Studying Death to Preserve Life*, Chapel Hill: University of North Carolina Press.

Hobson, Dorothy (1982) *Crossroads: The Drama of a Soap Opera*, London: Methuen.

Hoess, Rudolf (2000) *Commandant of Auschwitz*, Introduced by Primo Levi, London: Phoenix Press.

Hoffman, Eva (1998) *Shtetl: The Life and Death of a Small Town and the World of Polish Jews*, London: Secker and Walburg.

Hooper-Greenhill, Eileen (2000) *Museums and the Interpretation of Visual Culture*, London: Routledge.

Hoppner, R. H. (1971) 'Letter from SS Sturmbannfuhrer Rolf Heinz Hoppner to SS Sturmbannfuhrer Adolf Eichman, Posen, July 16 1941' (pp. 87–8), in R. Hilberg (ed) *Documents of Destruction: Germany and Jewry, 1933–1945*, Chicago IL: Quadrangle Books.

Horowitz, Sarah R (1994) 'Memory and Testimony in Women Survivors of Nazi Genocide' (pp. 258–82), in Baskin, J. (ed) *Women of the Word: Jewish Women and Jewish Writing*, Detroit, MI: Wayne State University Press.

Horowitz, Sarah R. (1997) *Voicing the Void: Muteness and Memory in Holocaust Fiction*, Albany: State University of New York Press.

Horowitz, Sarah R. (1998) 'Women in Holocaust Literature: Engendering Trauma Memory', (pp. 364–78) in Ofer, Dalia, and Weitzman, Lenore J (eds) *Women in the Holocaust*, New Haven, CT and London: Yale University Press.

Horowitz, Sarah R. (2000) 'Engendering Holocaust Memories', *Women and the Holocaust Conference*, Museum of Jewish Heritage, New York, 9 March .

Hughes, Alex (1999) *Heterographies: Sexual Difference in French Autobiography*, New York: New York University Press.

Huttenbach, Henry R. (1998) 'The Cult of Anne Frank: Returning to Basics' (pp. 79–86), in Carol Rottner (ed) *Anne Frank in the World; Essays and Reflections*, Amonk, New York: M. E. Sharpe.

Huyssen, Andreas (1995) *Twilight Memories: Marking Time in a Culture of Amnesia*, London: Routledge.

Hyman, Paula. E. (1995) *Gender and Assimilation in Modern Jewish History: The Roles and Representations of Women*, Seattle: University of Washington Press.

Hyman, Paula. E. (1998) 'Gender and Jewish Family in Modern Europe' (pp. 25–34), in Ofer, Dalia and Weitzman, Leonore, J. (eds) *Women in the Holocaust*, New Haven and London: Yale University Press.

Insdorf, Annette (1989) *Indelible Shadows: Film and The Holocaust*, Cambridge, New York: Cambridge University Press.

Jonkers, Gerdien (1995) *The Topography of Remembrance: The Dead, Tradition and Collective Memory in Mesopotamia*, Leiden: New York: Koln: E. J. Brill.

Kaplan, Marion A. (1979) The Jewish Feminist Movement in Germany: The Campaigns of the Jüdischer Frayenbund, 1904–1938, Westport, Connecticut: Greenwood.

Kaplan, Marion A. (1998) *Between Dignity and Despair: Jewish Life in Nazi Germany*, New York and London: Oxford University Press.

Kaplan, Marion A. (2000) 'Jewish Women and Writing about the Holocaust', *Women and the Holocaust Conference*, Museum of Jewish Heritage, New York, 9 March.

Karay, Felicja (1998) 'Women in the Forced Labour Camps' (pp. 285–309), in Dalia Ofer and Lenore. J. Weitzman (eds) *Women and the Holocaust*, New Haven and London: Yale University Press.

Karpf, Anne (1996) *The War After: Living With the Holocaust*, London: Minerva.

Kenrick, Donald and Puxon, Grattan (1972) *The Destiny of Europe's Gypsies*, New York: Basic Books.

Kenrick, Donald and Puxon, Grattan (1995) *Gypsies Under the Swastika*, Hatfield, Hertfordshire: University of Hertfordshire Press.

King, Nicola (1996) 'Autobiography as Cultural Memory: Three Case Studies' (pp. 50–62), *Cultural Memory*, no 30, winter, *New Formations: A Journal of Culture/Theory/Politics*,

Kingston, Hong, Maxine (1981) *The Women Warrior: Memoirs of a Girlhood Among Ghosts*, London: Picador.

Klibanski, Bronka (1998) 'In the Ghetto and in the Resistance' (pp. 175–186), in Ofer, Dalia and Weitzman, Leonore, J. (eds) *Women in the Holocaust*, New Haven and London: Yale University Press.

Koontz, Claudia (1984) 'The Competition for Women's Lebensraum', in Renate Bridenthal, Atina Grossmann and Marion Kaplan (eds) *When Biology Became Destiny: Women in Weimar and Nazi Germany*, New York: Monthly Review Press.

Koontz, Claudia (1987) *Mothers in the Fatherland: Women, the Family and Nazi Politics*, New York: St Martin's Press.

Kornreich Gelissen, Rena with H. Dune Macadam (1997) *Rena's Promise: The Story of Two Sisters in Auschwitz, London:* Orion.

Koselleck, Reinhart (1990) *Futures Past*, Cambridge: MIT Press.

Kramarae, Cheris and Treichler, Paula A. (1985) *A Feminist Dictionary*, London: Pandora Press.

Krondorfer, Bjorn (1995) *Remembrance and Reconciliation*, New Haven, Conn: Yale University Press.

Kuhn, Annette (1995) *Family Secrets: Acts of Memory and Imagination*, London: Verso.

Kuhn, Annette (1999) 'Space, Place and Cinema', Frontiers of Memory Conference, Institute of Education, London, 17–19 September.

Kushner, Tony (1994) *The Holocaust and the Liberal Imagination: A Social and Cultural History*, Oxford: Blackwell.

Kushner, Tony (1997) 'Introduction' (pp. 1–16), in Cesarani, David., Richmond, C. and Reilly, J. (eds) *Belsen in History and Memory*, Ilford: Frank Cass.

LaCapra, Dominick (1998) *History and Memory After Auschwitz*, Ithaca, NY: Cornell University Press.

Lacey, Kate (1996) *Feminine Frequencies: Gender, German Radio and the Public Sphere, 1923–1945*, Michigan: University of Michigan.

Laclau, E. and Mouffe, C. (1985) *Hegemony and Socialist Strategy*, London: Verso.
Lakoff, George and Johnson, Mark (1980) *Metaphors We Live By*, Chicago: University of Chicago.
Lang, Berel (1999) *The Future of the Holocaust: Between History and Memory*, Ithaca, NY, London: Cornell University Press..
Langer L. Lawrence (1991) *Holocaust Testimonies: The Ruins of Memory*, New Haven and London: Yale University Press.
Langer, L, Lawrence (ed) (1995) *Art From the Ashes: A Holocaust Anthology*, New York, Oxford: Oxford University Press.
Langer, L. Lawrence (1995) *Admitting the Holocaust*, Oxford: Oxford University Press.
Langer, L. Lawrence (1998) 'Gendered Suffering? Women in Holocaust Testimonies' (pp. 351–63), in Ofer, Dalia and Weitzman, Leonore, J. (eds) *Women in the Holocaust*.
Lanzmann, Claude (1985a) *Shoah: An Oral History of the Holocaust: The Complete Text of the Film*, New York: Pantheon Books.
Lanzmann, Claude (1985b) 'The Being of Nothingness: An Interview with Claude Lanzmann', reproduced in Kevin Macdonald and Mark Cousins (eds) (1996) *Imagining Reality: The Faber Book of Documentary*, London: Faber and Faber 322–5.
Laska, Vera (ed) (1983) *Women in the Resistance and in the Holocaust: Voices of Eyewitnesses*, Westport, CT and London: Greenwood.
Lautmann, Rudiger (1998) 'The Pink Triangle: Homosexuals as "Enemies of the State"' (pp. 345–57), in Michael Berenbaum and Abraham Peck (eds) *The Holocaust and History: The Known, the Unknown, the Disputed, and the Re-examined*, Bloomington, Indiana University Press.
Le Goff, Jacques (1992) *History and Memory*, New York: Columbia University Press.
Le Goff, Jacques (1992), *History and Memory*, New York and Oxford: University of Columbia Press.
Lee, Patrick Jasper (2000) *We Borrow the Earth: An Intimate Portrait of the Gypsy Shamanic Tradition and Culture*, London: Thorsons.
Lentin, Ronit (2000) *Israel and the Daughters of the Shoah: Reoccupying the Territories of Silence*, New York: Oxford, Berghahn Books.
Levi, Primo (1988) *The Drowned and the Saved*, London: Abacus.
Levi, Primo (2000) *If This is a Man. The Truce, London:* Abacus.
Levi, Trude (2001) 'The Holocaust in Feature Film: Survivors' Right to Reply', *The Holocaust, Genocide and the Moving Image: Film and Television Representations Since 1933*, Imperial War Museum, London, April 23–7.
Levin, Nora (1973) *The Holocaust: The Destruction of European Jewry 1933–1945*, New York: Schocken.
Lewy, Guenter (2000) *The Nazi Persecution of the Gypsies*, New York: Oxford University Press.
Leydesdorff, S, Passerini, Luisa, and Thompson, Paul (eds) (1996) 'Gender and Memory', *International Yearbook of Oral History and Life Stories*, vol. 4, June 1996.
Liebmann, David (1999) Personal communication (*interview*) 12 April, Assistant Director of Education, *Museum of Jewish Heritage*, New York.
Linenthal, Edward T. (1995) *Preserving Memory: The Struggle to Create America's Holocaust Museum*. London: Penguin

Linville, Susan E. (1998) *Feminism, Film, Fascism: Women's Auto-Biographical Film in Postwar Germany*, Austin: University of Texas.

Lipsitz, G. (1990) *Time Passages: Collective Memory and American Popular Culture*, Minneapolis: University of Minnesota Press.

Lipstadt, Deborah (1994) *Denying the Holocaust: The Growing Assault on Truth and Memory*, London: Penguin.

London: Allen Lane.

Lopez, Donald S. (1993) 'Memories of Buddha', in Gyatso, Janet (ed) *In the Mirror of Memory: Reflections on Mindfulness and Remembrance in Indian and Tibetan Buddhism*, Delhi-India: Sri Satguru Publications.

Lukas, Richard (1997) *Forgotten Holocaust: The Poles Under German Occupation, 1939–45*, New York: Hippocrene.

Lury, Celia (1998) *Prosthetic Culture: Photography, Memory and Identity*, London: Routledge.

Mah, Adeline Yen (1997) *Falling Leaves: The True Story of an Unwanted Chinese Daughter*, London: Penguin.

Maier, Charles (1980) *The Unmasterable Past: History, Holocaust and German National Identity*, Cambridge, Mass: Harvard University Press.

Mais, Yitzchak (2000) 'Introduction' Women and the Holocaust Conference. Museum of Jewish Heritage, March 9th, 2000, New York.

Manchel, F. (1995) 'A Reel Witness: Steven Spielberg's Representation of the Holocaust in Schindler's List', *Journal of Modern History*, vol. 67 no. 1, 83–101.

Manchel, F. (1998) 'Mishegoss: Schindler's List: Holocaust Representation and Film History', *Historical Journal of Film, Radio and Television*, vol. 18 no. 3, 431–7.

Marcus, P and Rosenberg, A (1988) 'A. Philosophical Critique of the "Survivor Syndrome" and Some Implications for Treatment', in Randolph L. Braham (ed) *The Psychological Perspectives of the Holocaust and its Aftermath*, New York: Columbia University Press.

Marcus, Paul and Rosenberg, Alan (eds) (1989) *Healing Their Wounds: Psychotherapy with Holocaust Survivors and their Families*, New York: Praeger.

Martin, Elaine, (ed.) (1992) *Gender, Patriarchy and Facism in the Third Reich: The Response of Women Writers.* Detroit: Wayne State University Press.

Masson, Jeffrey M. (1984) *The Assault on Truth: Freud's Suppression of the Seduction Theory*, London and Boston: Faber and Faber.

Mayaram, Shail (1997) *Resisting Regimes: Myth, Memory and the Shaping of Muslim Identity*, Delhi: Oxford University Press.

McConkey, James (1996) *The Anatomy of Memory*, Oxford: Oxford University Press.

McRobbie, Angela (1991) *Feminism and Youth Culture: From* Jackie *to* Just Seventeen, London: Macmillan Education.

Mead, Margaret (1964) *Continuities in Cultural Evolution*, New Haven and London: Yale University Press.

Michaels, Anne (1997) *Fugitive Pieces*, London: Bloomsbury.

Miller, Marjorie (1994) 'Breaking the Silence: Schindler's List Forces German's To Look At Their History', *Los Angeles Times* v, 113, 7 March, F1. col. 2.

Milton, Sybil (1991) *In Fitting Memory, The Art and Politics of Holocaust Memorials*, Detroit: Wayne State University Press.

Milton, Sybil (1997) 'Holocaust: the Gypsies (pp. 171–207), in Samuel Totten et al. (eds)' *Century of Genocide: Eyewitness Accounts and Critical Views*, New York: Garland.

Montefiore, Jan (1994) *Feminism and Poetry: Language, Experience and Identity in Women's Writing*, London: Pandora.

Museum of Jewish Heritage: A Living Memorial to the Holocaust (undated) *Fact sheet*. New York: Museum of Jewish Heritage.

Muszyncy, Lech and Muszyncy Danuta (1995) *Cementarz Zydowski W Lodzi*, Lodz: Bibliophiles/Lodz City Council.

Myers, Oren and Zandberg, Eyal (2000) 'The Soundtrack of Memory: Ashes and Dust and the Commemoration of the Holocaust in Israeli Popular Culture', paper submitted for publication with *Media, Culture and Society* (Sage).

Nagorski, A. (1993) 'Spielberg's Risk: the Director takes a chance with a Holocaust Drama shot in Black and White', *Newsweek*, vol. 121 no. 21, May 24, 60–2.

Neuman, Shirley (1991) *Autobiography and Questions of Gender*, London Frank Cass Publishers.

Niewyk, Donald and Nicosia, Francis (2000) *The Columbia Guide to the Holocaust*, New York: Columbia University Press.

Nitzan, Margie (1998) 'Oral Testimony' (pp. 115–27), in Brana Gurewitsch (ed) *Mothers, Sisters and Resisters: Oral Histories of Women who Survived the Holocaust*, Tuscaloosa and London: University of Alabama Press.

Niven, W. J. 'The Reception of Steven Spielberg's Schindler's List in the German Media', *Journal of European Studies*, vol. 25 no. 98, 165–90.

Nora, Pierre (1992) *Les Lieux de Memoire*, vols 1–3, Paris: Gallimard.

Nora, Pierre (1997) *Realms of Memory: The Construction of the French Past, Vol, I, Conflicts and Divisions*, trans. Arthur Goldhammer, New York: Columbia University Press.

Novick, Peter (1999) *The Holocaust and Collective Memory: The American Experience*, Bloomsbury, London.

Nowak Susan E. (1999) 'In a World Shorn of Color: Toward a feminist Theology of Holocaust Testimonies' (pp. 33–45), in Esther Fuchs, *Women and the Holocaust: Narrative and Representation, Studies in the Shoah*, vol. xxii, Lanham, New York and Oxford: University Press of America.

Ofer, Dalia and Weitzman, Leonore, J. (eds) (1998) *Women in the Holocaust*, New Haven and London: Yale University Press.

Okin, Susan, M. (1980) *Women in Western Political Thought*, London: Virago.

Oldfield, P (1987) 'German Women in the Resistance to Hitler', in Reynolds, S. (ed) *Women, State and Revolution: Essays on Gender and Power in Europe since 1789*, Amherst: University of Massachusetts Press.

Parkinson, J. M. (1945) Imperial War Museum, file 93/27/1, Letter, 27 May, pp. 1–3.

Pascal, J (1998) 'Patriarchal Attitudes', *Jewish Quarterly*, Winter 1998/9, no. 172, pp. 72–4.

Paulsson, G. Steve (2000) *The Holocaust: The Holocaust Exhibition at the Imperial War Museum*, London: Imperial War Museum.

Pines, D. (1993) 'The Impact of the Holocaust on the Second Generation', in D. Pines (ed) *A Woman's Unconcious Use of Her Body*, London: Virago.

Piotrowski, P. (1998) *Poland's Holocaust: Ethnic Strife, Collaboration with Occupying Forces and Genocide in the Second Republic, 1918–1947*, Jefferson, NC and London: McFarland.

Plant, Richard (1988) *The Pink Triangle: The Nazi War Against Homosexuals*, New York: Henry Holt.

Portelli, Alexandro (1999) 'Fact and Memory', *Frontiers of Memory Conference*, Institute of Education, London, 17–19 September.

Porter, Gaby (1996) 'Seeing through Solidity: A feminist perspective on museums' (pp. 105–26), in Sharon Macdonald and Gordon Fyfe (eds) *Theorizing Museums*, Oxford: Blackwell.

Powers, Charles T. (1997) *In the Memory of the Forest*, London: Anchor.

Poznanski, Renee (1998) 'Women in the French–Jewish Underground: Shield-Bearers of the Resistance?' (pp. 234–252) in Ofer, Dalia and Weitzman, Lenore, J. *Women and the Holocaust*, London: Yale University Press.

Proces Hossa (The Trial of Hoss) *Archives of the Auschwitz State Museum*, XX34.

Propp, Vladimir (1928) *Morphology of the Folktale*, trans 1958. Lawrence Scott, Bloomington: Indiana University Press.

Radway, Janice (1987) *Reading the Romance*, London: Verso.

Ramati, Alexander (1986) *And the Violins Stopped Playing; The Story of the Gypsy Holocaust*, New York: Franklyn Watts.

Reading, Anna (1992) *Polish Women, Solidarity and Feminism*, Basingstoke: Macmillan – now Palgrave Macmillan.

Reading, Anna (1996) 'Socially Inherited Memory, Gender and the Public Sphere: The Case of Poland', unpublished Phd thesis, University of Westminster, London, UK.

Reading, Anna (1999) 'Scarlet Lips in Belsen: Culture, Gender and Ethnicity in the Policies of the Holocaust', *Media Culture and Society*, vol.21 no. 4, July, 481–502.

Reading, Anna (1999) 'Selling Sexuality in the Lesbian and Gay Press' (pp. 265–72), in Stokes, Jane and Reading Anna (eds) *The Media in Britain: Current Debates and Developments*, Basingstoke: Macmillan.

Reading, Anna (2001) 'Clicking on Hitler: the Virtual Holocaust @ home' (323–39) in Zelizer, Barbie (ed) *Visual Culture and the Holocaust*, New Brunswick, New Jersey: Rutgers University Press.

Rector, Frank (1981) *The Nazi Extermination of Homosexuals*, New York: Stein and Day.

Reisz, Mathew (1997) 'The Odour of Sanctity: A New Look at Anne Frank's Diary', *Jewish Quarterly*, summer, no.166, pp. 41–3.

Rich, F. (1994) 'Schindler's Dissed', *New York Times*, vol. 143, sec. 4, 6 February E. 17 (N.), E. 17 (L.), column 5.

Rigler, Hannah Sara (1998) 'Interview with Hannah Sara Rigler by Joni Sue Blinderman' (pp. 145–61), in Gurewitsch, Brana (ed) *Mothers, Sisters, Resisters; Oral Histories of Women Who Survived the Holocaust*, Tuscloosa, Alabama: The University of Alabama Press.

Ringelblum, E. (1992) *Last Writings. Volume 2*, Jerusalem: Yad Vashem.

Ringelheim, Joan (1993) 'Women and the Holocaust: A Reconsideration of Research' (pp. 374–408), in Rittner, Carol and Roth, John K. *Women and the Holocaust: Different Voices*, New York: St Martin's Press.

Ringelheim, Joan (1998) 'The Split Between Gender and the Holocaust' (pp. 340–50), in Ofer, Dalia and Weitzman, Lenore, J. *Women and the Holocaust*, London: Yale University Press.

Ringelheim, Joan (1999) Director, Department of Oral History, US Holocaust Museum, Washingston DC, *personal communication*, (interview), 6 April, Washington DC.

Ringelheim, Joan (2001) Director, Department of Oral History, US Holocaust Museum, Washingston DC, *personal communication*, (e-mail), 9 June.

Rittner, Carol and Roth, John K. (eds) (1993) *Different Voices: Women and the Holocaust*, New York: Paragon.

Roach, Joseph (1996) *Cities of the Dead: Circum-Atlantic Performance*. New York, NY, Chichester: Columbia University Press.

Rose, Stephen (1996) 'The Making of Memory' (pp. 55–9), in James Mckonkey *The Anatomy of Memory: An Anthology*, Oxford: Oxford University Press.

Rosenweig, R. and Thelen, D. (1999) Extract from 'The Presence of the Past: Popular Uses of History in American Life', *Humanities: When the Stones Speak: Communicating Across the Ages*, Special Issue, January/February, vol. 20 no. 1, 15–16. Also posted at www.chnm.gmu.edu/survey.

Roth, John and Berenbaum, Michael (1989) *Holocaust: Religions and Philosophical Implications*, New York: Paragon House.

Rousso, Henry (1991) *The Vichy Syndrome: History and Memory in France since 1944*, London: Harvard University Press.

Rowbotham, Sheila (1975) *Hidden From History: Three Hundred Years of Women's Oppression and the Fight Against It*, Harmondsworth: Pelican Books.

Rudman, J. (1945) 'Letter from Belsen', *Imperial War Museum Archives*, 14.5.45. 94/51/1.

Rupp, L. J. (1978) *Mobilizing Women for the War: German and American Propaganda 1939–45*, Princeton, NJ, Princeton University Press.

Sacks, Oliver (1990) *Seeing Voices: A Journey Into the World of the Deaf*, London: Picador.

Salomon, Charlotte (1998) *Life? Or Theatre?*, 'Introduction' by Judith C.E. Belinfante, Christine Fischer-Defoy, Ad Petersen, Norman Rosenthal, trans by Leila Vennewitz, Waanders Publishers, Zwolle, Royal Academy of Arts, London.

Samuel, Ralphael (1994) *Theatres of Memory: Volume I*, London: Verso.

Schlink, Bernhard (1999) *The Reader*, London: Phoenix.

Schur, M. (1972) *Freud: Living and Dying*, New York: International Universities Press.

Schwarcz, Vera (1998) *Bridge across Broken Time: Chinese and Jewish Cultural Memory*, New Haven and London: Yale University Press.

Schwartz, A. E. (1994) 'Laughter in the movie house', *Washington Post* vol. 117, March 16, A 19, col. 6, 19.

Secret Caption Sheets (1945) Document File: Concentration Camp Film, Belsen Concentration Camp, Imperial War Museum Film Archive, A700/300 –700/312 p. 31.

Secret Caption Sheets (1945) Document File: Concentration Camp Film, Sandbostel Camp, 14 May, Imperial War Museum Film Archive, 2716 A700/334/1.

Shandler, Jeffrey (1999) *While America Watches: Televising the Holocaust*, Oxford: Oxford University Press.

Shenfield, Barbara (2000) 'Message From the Chairman' *Despatches: The Magazine of the Friends of the Imperial War Museum*, December, p. 3.

Shrimpton, Gordon S. (1997) *History and Memory in Ancient Greece*, Montreal, Kingston and London: Mcgill-Queens University Press.

Simpson, David (2001) 'Naming the Dead' (pp. 3–7), *London Review of Books*, vol. 23, no. 22, November.

Sklar, Robert (2000) 'The Holocaust in Contemporary Cinema' (pp. 11– 20), *Dimensions*, vol. 14, no. 2.

Small, Brandla (1998) Oral Testimony (pp. 86–94), in Brana Gurewitsch (ed) *Mothers, Sisters, Resisters: Oral Histories of Women who Survived the Holocaust*.

Smith, Michael (2001) 'Panel Discussion on Documentary Film', *The Holocaust, Genocide and the Moving Image: Film and Television Representations Since 1933*, Imperial War Museum, 23–27, April, London: UK.

Smolen, Kazimierz (1995a) 'Auschwitz: The Nazi Murder Camp' (pp. 13–32), in Swiebocka, Teresa (ed) *Auschwitz: A History in Photographs*. English translation by Johnathan Webber and Connie Wilsack, Warsaw: Ksiazka I Wiedza.

Smolen, Kazimierz (1995b) 'Auschwitz Today: The Auschwitz-Birkenau State Museum' (pp. 259–80), in Swiebocka, Teresa (ed) *Auschwitz: A History in Photographs*, English translation by Johnathan Webber and Connie Wilsack, Warsaw: Ksiazka I Wiedza.

Sokolowska, M. (1977) 'Women's Experience Under Socialism', in Zollinger-Giele, J. and Chapman-Smock, A. (eds), *Women's Roles and Status in Eight Countries*, New York: John Wiley and Sons.

Sorlin, Pierre (2001) 'How to look at an "Historical" Film' (pp. 25–49), in Marcia Landy *The Historical Film: History and Memory in the Media*, New Brunswick, New Jersey: Rutgers University Press.

Sparks, Colin with Reading, Anna (1998) *Communism, Capitalism and the Mass Media*, London: Sage Publications.

Spender, Dale (1985) *For the Record: The Making and Meaning of Feminist Knowledge*, London: The Women's Press.

Spolar, C. (1994) 'The Kids Who Laughed until It Hurt', *Washington Post*, vol. 117, 10 March, C. 1, col. 1.

Sprengnether, M. (1995) 'Mourning Freud' (pp. 142–65), in Elliot, A. and Frosh, S. (eds) *Psychoanalysis in Contexts: Paths Between Theory and Modern Culture*, London: Routledge.

Steinberg, Joe (1995) 'Sendler's List: The Valor of the Righteaous Gentile', *Jewish Currents*, January, pp. 24–26.

Steiner, George (1971) *In Bluebeards Castle: Some Notes Towards the Redefinition of Culture*, New Haven: Yale University Press.

Steinlauf, Michael (1997) *Bondage to the Dead. Poland and the Memory of the Holocaust*, Syracuse, NY: Syracuse University Press.

Stokes, Jane and Reading, Anna (eds) (1999) *The Media in Britain*, Basingstoke: Macmillan – now Palgrave Macmillan.

Stokes, Melvyn and Maltby, Richard (eds) (1999) *Identifying Hollywood Audiences: Cultural Identity and the Movies*, London: BFI Publishing.

Sussex, Elizabeth (1984) 'The Fate of F3080', *Sight and Sound*, Spring. (pp. 92–7).

Swiebocka, Teresa (1995) *Auschwitz: A History in Photographs*, Warsaw: Kziazka and Wiedza.

Swindels, Julia (1985) *Victorian Writing and Working Women*, Oxford: Oxford University Press.

Taylor, R. (1979) *Film Propaganda in Soviet Russia and Nazi Germany*, London: Croom Helm.

Tec, Nechama (1999) 'Reflections on Resistance', *Women and the Holocaust Conference*, Museum of Jewish Heritage, 9 March 2000.

Tegal, Susan (2001) 'Jud Suss: Film as Propaganda', *The Holocaust, Genocide and the Moving Image: Film and Television Representations Since 1933*, Imperial War Museum, 23–7 April.

Thornham, Sue (2000) *Feminist Theory and Cultural Studies: Stories of Unsettled Relations*, London: Arnold.

Till, Karen Elizabeth (1996) *The Place and Politics of Memory: a Geo-ethnography of Museums and Memorials in Berlin*, unpublished thesis, University of Wisconsin-Madison, United States Holocaust Museum Archives, UMI.963518.

Turgel, Gena (1995) *I Light a Candle*, London: Valletine Mitchell.

Tyrnauer, Gabrielle (1989) *Gypsies and the Holocaust: A Bibliography and Introductory Essay*, no. 2, Montreal Institute for Genocide Studies.

Unger, Michael (1998) 'The Status and Plight of Women in the Lodz Ghetto' (pp. 123–42) in Dalia Ofer and Lenore, J. Weitzman, *Women in the Holocaust*, New Haven and London: Yale University Press.

United States Holocaust Memorial Museum (1999) *The Holocaust: A Historical Summary*, Washington DC: United States Holocaust Memorial Museum.

United States Holocaust Memorial Museum (1999) *Visitors Guide*, Washington DC: United States Holocaust Museum.

Urry, John (1996) 'How Societies Remember the Past' (pp. 45–68), in Macdonald, Sharon and Fyfe, Gordon (eds) *Theorizing Museums*, London: Blackwell.

Van Houts, Elizabeth (1999) *Memory and Gender in Medieval Europe 900–1200*, Basingstoke: Macmillan Press – now Palgrave Macmillan.

Van Zoonen, Liesbet (1991) 'Feminist Perspectives on the Media', in J. Curran and M. Gurevitch (eds) *Mass Media and Society*, London and New York.: Edward Arnold.

Van Zoonen, Liesbet (1994) *Feminist Media Studies*, London: Sage.

Waldman, Diane and Walker, Janet (eds) (1999) *Feminism and Documentary*, London, Minneapolis: University of Minnesota Press.

Walker, J. (1999) 'Film, Video and the Vicissitudes of Historical Memory', paper presented at Frontiers of Memory Conference, Institute of Education, London, 17–19, September.

Wallace, Mike (1996) *Mickey Mouse History and Other Essays on American Memory*, Temple University Press.

Warren, Mary Anne (1985) *Gendercide*, London: Rowman and Allanheld.

Warszawski, Ruth Marlene (1996) *The Role of Archives in Remembering the Holocaust*, unpublished Phd, Columbia University, US Holocaust Museum Archives, UMI 9706919.

Wayman, Alex (1993) 'Buddist Terms for Recollection and Other Types of Memory' (pp. 133–47), in Gyatso, Janet (ed) *In the Mirror of Memory: Reflections on Mindfulness and Remembrance in Indian and Tibetan Buddhism*, Delhi, India: Sri Satguru Publications.

Webber, Jonathan (1995) 'Personal Reflections on Auschwitz Today' (pp. 282–291), in Swiebocka, Teresa (1995) *Auschwitz: A History in Photographs*, Warsaw: Kziazka and Wiedza.

Wechsberg, Joseph (1966) *Blue Trout and Black Truffles*, New York: Knopp.

Weeks, Jeffrey (1985) *Sexuality and its Discontents: Meanings, Myths and Modern Sexualities*, London: Routledge and Kegan Paul.

Weinberg, Jeshajahu and Elieli, Rina (1995) *The Holocaust Museum, in Washington*, New York: Rizzoli.

Weitzman, Lenore J. (1998) 'Living on the Aryan Side in Poland' (pp. 187–222), Dalia Ofer and Lenore J. Weitzman (eds) *Women in the Holocaust*, New Haven and London: Yale University Press.

Weitzman, Lenore. J and Ofer, Dalia (1998) 'Introduction: the Role of Gender in the Holocaust' (pp. 1–18), in Dalia Ofer and Lenore, J. Weitzman. *Women in the Holocaust*. New Haven and London: Yale University Press.

White, Hayden (1987) *The Content of the Form: Narative Discourse and Historical Representation*, Baltimore: Johns Hopkins Press.

Wiesel, Elie (1982) *Night*, London. New York: Bantum Books.

Wiesel, Elie (1983) 'Does the Holocaust Lie Beyond the Reach of Art?' *New York Times*, Arts and Leisure, 17 April, p. 1, 15.

Wiesel, Elie (1989) 'Foreword' (pp. xi–xii), in A. Indsdorf *Indelible Shadows: Film and The Holocaust*, Cambridge and New York: Cambridge University Press.

Wood, Nancy (1999) *Vectors of Memory; Legacies of Trauma in Postwar Europe*, Oxford: Berg.

Wyschogrod, Edith (1998) *An Ethics of Remembering: History, Heterology and the Nameless Others*, Chicago: University of Chicago Press.

Wytwcky, Bohdan (1980) *The Other Holocaust*, Washington DC: Novak.

Yad Vashem Archives 03/3475, Estate of Vanda Zoltan, covering the rescue of Carl Lutz in Hungary.

Yahil, Leni (1990) *The Holocaust: The Fate of European Jewry, 1932–1945*, trans by Ina Friedman and Haya Galai, New York: Oxford University Press.

Yates, Frances A. (1999) *The Art of Memory*, London: Routledge and Kegan Paul.

Yonkers, Gerdien (1995) *The Topography of Remembrance: The Dead, Tradition and Collective Memory in Mesopotamia*, Leiden: E. J. Brill.

Young, James E. (1988) *Writing and Rewriting the Holocaust: Narrative and the Consequences of Interpretation*, Bloomington and Indianopolis: Indiana University Press.

Young, James E. (1993) *The Texture of Meaning: Holocaust Memorials and Meaning*, New Haven and London: Yale University Press.

Young, James E. (2000) *At Memory's Edge: After-Images of the Holocaust in Contemporary Art and Architecture*, New Haven and London: Yale University Press.

Zaglada Zydow Krakowskich (1996) "Gestum", Kracow: Agencja Reklamowo-Wydawnicza.

Zelizer, Barbie (1992) *Covering the Body: The Kennedy Assassination, the Media, and the Shaping of Collective Memory*, Chicago: University of Chicago Press.

Zelizer, Barbie (1998) *Remembering to Forget: Holocaust Memory Through the Camera's Eye*, Chicago and London: University of Chicago Press.

Zur, Judith (1997) 'Reconstructing the Self through Memories of Violence among Mayan Indian War Widows (pp. 64–76), Ronit Lentin (ed) *Gender and Catastrophe*, London and New York: Zed Books

Electronic Sources

Bandy, Alex (2000) 'The Forgotten Holocaust', *The Patrin Web Journal*. http:www.geocities.com/Paris/5121/forgotten.htm. (23.12.00).

Charlottle Salomon Exhibition (1999) Jewish Historical Museum, Netherlands, www.jhm.nl (11.1.99).

Crawford, Robert (2001) *Home Page: Imperial War Museum, Lambeth*, www.iwm.org.uk.lambeth/corpinfo.htm (5.1.01).

Foxman, Abraham H. 'Film Fable Scores in Telling Holocaust Story', November 1998, www.adl.org/opinion/film-fable.html (29.9.1999).

Imperial War Museum (2001) 'History and Role of the Imperial War Museum', www.iwm.org.uk/corphist.htm (4.1.01).

Loshitsky, Y. (1999) Schindler's List Review. www.geocities.com/ Hollywood/Studio/5066/Moviereview P.S/Schindler's List html. (15.11.99).

Miller, Shirley A. (1998) 'The Road to Porrajmos: the gypsy Holocaust', *The Patrin Web Journal*, http: www. geocities.com/Paris/5121/road-to-porrajmos.htm. (23.12.00).

Mukherjee, Neel (2000) 'Different approaches to death, funerals and mourning', review of Arthur J. Magida and Stuart M. Matlins (1999) *How to be a Perfect Stranger*, Kelowna, Canada: Northstone Publishing. www.globalideasbank.org/ w2go/WTG-12.HTML. (23.12.00).

Stein, S. D. 'Genocide' from E. Cashmore (ed) (1996) Dictionary of Race and Ethnic Relations. 4th edn, London, Routledge, www.ess.uwe.ac.uk/genocide. (15.7.01).

Tanner, Harold (2000) 'The Roma Persecution' *The Patrin Web Journal*, http:www.geocities.com/Paris/5121/forgotten.htm. (23.12.00).

www.gendercide.org. (15.7.01).

Yad, Vashem (2001) 'July 23: Red Cross Mission Visits Theriesienstadt', www.yad_vashem.org.uk. (10.4.2001)

Filmography: Features and Documentaries

Chronicle of the Liberation of Auschwitz (1945) Poland. (Soviet Army Production: Cameramen: N. Bykow, K. Kutub-Zade, A. Pawlow and A. Woroncow).

Comme Si E'Etait Hier (As If It Were Yesterday) (1980) Belgium. Directed by Myriam Abramowicz and Ester Hoftenberg.

Genocide (1975) GB (Thames TV for World at ar series). Directed by Michael Darlow.

Holocaust (1978) USA (NBC-TV). Directed by Marvin Chomsky. Script by Gerald Green.

Judgement at Nuremberg (1961) USA. Directed by Stanley Kramer. Scripted by Abby Mann.

Kitty: Return to Auschwitz (1980) GB (Yorkshire Television). Directed by Peter Morley.

Les Violons du Bal (1973) France. Directed and scripted by Michael Drach.

Life is Beautiful (1999) (La Vita E Bella) Italy. Director and scriptwriter, Roberto Benini.

Memory of the Camps. (1945) GB British Army Film and Photographic Unit. Executive Director, Alfred Hitchcock. Executive Producer, Sidney Bernstein.

Nuit et Brouillard (Night and Fog) (1955) France. Directed by Alain Renais. Script by Jean Cayrol.

Peppermint Peace (Peppermint Frieden) Germany. Directed and scripted by Marianne S.W. Rosenbaum.

Schindler's List (1994) USA. Directed by Stephen Spielberg.

Shoah (1986) France. Directed by Claude Lanzmann.

Sisters (1979) Germany. Directed by Margarethe Von Trotta.

Sophie's Choice (1982) USA. Directed and scripted by Alan Pakula, from the novel by William Styron.

The Diary of Anne Frank (1959) USA. Directed by George Stevens. Scriptwriter: Frances Goodrich and Albert Hackett.

The Eternal Jew (Der Ewige Jude) (1940) Germany. Directed by Fritz Hippler.

The Garden of the Finzi-Continis (1970) Italy. Directed by Vittorio de Sica. Scripted by Cesare Zavattini.

The Last Stop (Ostatni Etap) (1948) Poland. Directed by Wanda Jakubowska. Scripted by Gerda Schneider and Wanda Jakubowska.

The Nasty Girl (Das Schreckliche Madchen) (1989) Germany. Directed by Michael Verhoeven.

The Pawnbroker (1965) USA. Directed by Sidney Lumet. Scripted by Morton Fine and David Friedkin.

The Wall (1982) USA (CBS-TV) Directed by Robert Markowitz. Script by Millard Lampell, from the novel by John Hersey.

Triumph of the Will (1935) Germany. Directed by Leni Riefenstahl.

Index